Restricting Handguns
The Liberal Skeptics Speak Out

"Can I get it back when the cops go on strike?"

Restricting Handguns

The Liberal Skeptics Speak Out

Edited by

DON B. KATES, JR.

Foreword by
FRANK CHURCH

NORTH RIVER PRESS, INC.

Manufactured in the United States of America

Library of Congress Cataloging in Publication Data
    Main entry under title:

Restricting handguns.

    1. Firearms — Law and legislation — United States —
Addresses, essays, lectures.   2.   Firearms — Addresses,
essays, lectures.   I.   Kates, Don B., 1941-
KF3941.A75R47   344'.73'0533   79-12043
ISBN 0-88427-033-5
ISBN 0-88427-034-3 pbk.

First printing: April, 1979
Second printing: October, 1979

ACKNOWLEDGEMENTS

The author gratefully acknowledges permission to reprint from the following sources:

The *New York Law Forum*, for permission to reprint portions of Mark Benenson's article "A Controlled Look at Gun Controls," which originally appeared in Vol. 14 thereof.

The Second Amendment Foundation, for permission to reprint portions of David T. Hardy's monograph *No Case for Stricter Firearms Control: A Rebuttal to the Report of the General Accounting Office.*

The *Chicago-Kent Law Review*, for permission to reprint portions of an article by David T. Hardy and John Stompoly entitled "Of Arms and the Law," which appeared in Vol. 51 of the *Law Review*. This material, revised and supplemented, is the discussion of the Second Amendment herein.

The *Civil Liberties Review* for permission to reprint portions of my debate with Rep. Robert Drinan that appeared in Vol. 3, Nos. 2 and 3 (June/July and August/September, 1976), Copyright © 1976 by the American Civil Liberties Union.

The frontispiece cartoon is by Bill Mauldin. © Copyright 1978 Chicago Sun-Times. Reprinted courtesy Chicago Sun-Times and Bill Mauldin.

DEDICATION

To B.K.P., J.E.B., and K.M.O. (in order of appearance), this book is affectionately dedicated.

SUMMARY OF CONTENTS

FOREWORD *by Frank Church*   xi

INTRODUCTION   1

SECTION I: Toward a History of Handgun Prohibition in the United States   7

Don B. Kates, Jr.

Historical misconceptions based on inappropriate projections of present attitudes towards firearms and restrictions into the past; attitudes of the Founding Fathers; ownership of revolvers comparatively rare in the West; earliest weapons restrictions universal in the West by 1850, while Northeastern states like New Jersey had none (beyond the prohibition of dueling) until well into the 20th Century; era of severe restriction of handgun ownership, 1870-1934 — beginning in the South and involving primarily Southern, Midwestern, and Western states; New York's comparatively late Sullivan Law (1911) is an exception in the Northeast, but is emulated by Arkansas, North Carolina, Missouri, Michigan, Hawaii, and Oregon; purpose of these laws is to disarm blacks, the laboring poor, and the foreign-born in order to prevent social unrest; banning handguns becomes a "liberal" cause only with the failure of the previous liberal panacea for violent crime, prohibition of liquor; state and federal efforts at handgun prohibition increasingly fail since 1934 because public support has dwindled steadily, and continues to do so.

SECTION II: Comparative Cross-Cultural Statistics   31

Colin Greenwood and Joseph Magaddino

Superintendent Greenwood discusses homicide, robbery, and firearms accidents in Great Britain and comparatively in the United States, Switzerland, Mexico, and Jamaica in light of the firearms legislation and availability of different kinds of firearms in each of those countries. Professor Magaddino provides detailed figures on the ownership of various kinds of firearms in the United States and discusses firearm suicides and accidents. He also discusses his econometric comparison of state gun laws to criminal violence statistics in the United States, concluding that handgun prohibition appears to have no effect in reducing violent crime.

SECTION III: Critiquing the Case for Handgun Prohibition

   Mark K. Benenson and David T. Hardy   69

Selections from the writings of two acknowledged authorities in the area of criminal laws regulating firearms. They find the arguments offered to support handgun bans to be based upon juggling of statistics, comparisons between demographically non-comparable areas, nonsequiturs, and basic misconceptions about the nature of homicide and other violent crimes. Particular attention is given to statistics offered by federal agencies championing firearms prohibition.

SECTION IV: The Effect of Handgun Prohibitions in Reducing Violent Crime

   Handgun Prohibition and Homicide: A Plausible Theory Meets the Intractible Facts

   Mark Benenson and Don B. Kates, Jr.   91

Utilizing every possible combination of comparisons, the handgun-banning states are found to have equivalent or higher levels of violent crime than the handgun-allowing states, despite the fact that the banning states are demographically less crime-prone. This result is validated by a federally funded University of Wisconsin study in which every known demographic variable was neutralized. Examination of the attempts to explain away the results of such studies suggest instead that handgun prohibitions are inherently unenforcable, at least against the tiny number of disturbed individuals who commit homicidal assaults. This is confirmed by evidence from Great Britain and Canada where national handgun prohibitions have failed to disarm such people. Assuming that a handgun ban could somehow be effective against them, the "best case" result would be only a marginal decrease in homicides, for assault would be carried out with knives and clubs which are almost as lethal as handguns; however, especially in domestic homicide the result might be to increase homicide four-fold since assaults would be carried out with shotguns and rifles which are far more lethal. There is no evidence that ownership of firearms causes ordinary citizens to be more violent. The "proliferation of handguns" for self-defense is indeed evidence of a sick society; but the cure (if any) lies not in inhibiting self-defense, but in long-term change in the cultural and social factors that produce violent people, so that the rest of the people need no longer fear for their lives.

Handgun Availability and the Social Harms of Robbery: Recent Data and Some Projections

David T. Hardy and Don B. Kates, Jr.   118

Because gun-armed robbers rarely meet resistance, they are statistically far less likely than other armed robbers to injure their victims. If it were possible to take all guns away from robbers, they would focus their attacks (as otherwise-armed robbers do now) upon the elderly, the handicapped, and other individuals, rather upon commercial targets; they would then have to commit more robberies to maintain the same income since such "softer" targets are less renumerative. A hypothetically effective ban of handguns would increase the use in robbery of sawed-off long guns which are far more lethal. But, in fact, handgun bans are not enforcable against hardened criminals, and, to the extent that over a fifty-year period, the banning of legal manufacture reduced handguns in circulation, illegal manufacture would replace it. In one day Vietnamese and Pakistani peasants can produce functional copies of presently available handguns using tools considerably less sophisticated than millions of American households presently contain.

SECTION V: Self-Defense, Handgun Ownership, and the Independence of Women In a Violent, Sexist Society

Carol Ruth Silver and Don B. Kates, Jr.   139

Discussion of self-defense with a focus on women and handguns. The calculus of benefits from handgun prohibition is skewed, since national statistics on gun crimes are collected yearly and widely published, while data on seld-defense are not; what limited data are available suggests that self-defense may save fifteen times as many lives as handgun crimes take; known possession of a handgun by a potential victim is a substantial deterrent to crime and probably forestalls the commission of substantial numbers of violent assaults. Unlike burglary and household robbery, rape and violent assaults against women can be deterred and repulsed by handgun possession. As to the morality of women's armed self-defense, the law presumes that women can and will defend themselves, and there are no police resources available to protect women who have been threatened or attacked by former husbands and boyfriends. Horrible as it is to contemplate shooting someone, musings about "better solutions" are of little use to a woman who is being beaten or strangled to death. Handgun access is particularly vital to underprivileged and minority women (and men) living in areas where the police have given up on crime control.

SECTION VI: Constitutional and Civil Liberties Implications of Handgun Prohibition

The Second Amendment as a Restraint on State and Federal Firearm Restrictions

David T. Hardy   171

Historical purpose of the Second Amendment to protect the individual right to own firearms against infringement by the federal government; application of the Second Amendment against the states by the Fourteenth Amendment; the deterrent effect, even today, of an armed populace upon military or other leaders who might contemplate establishing a dictatorship against the American people.

The Necessity of Access to Firearms by Dissenters and Minorities Whom Government is Unwilling or Unable to Protect

John Salter and Don B. Kates, Jr.   185

Examples from the modern civil rights movement (of which Professor Salter was a leader) and elsewhere.

The Potentiality for Civil Liberties Violations in the Enforcement of Handgun Prohibition

David T. Hardy and Kenneth L. Chotiner   194

Any attempt to enforce a handgun prohibition would entail massive violation of the constitutional prohibition against unreasonable search and seizure; proposals for data banking of extensive records as to the one-half of all American households possessing a firearm (or the one-quarter that possess a handgun) threaten the right of privacy.

BIOGRAPHIES OF CONTRIBUTORS   217

NOTES   221

FOREWORD

I have always opposed all forms of federal gun control in my more than twenty years in the United States Senate. Gun controls are an anathema to the people I represent. Being born and bred in Idaho, that is a fact I know well. Just last November, Idahoans voted overwhelmingly to approve by referendum an initiative banning gun controls in our state. They are fully aware that federal, and even state and local gun controls, which have been tried are proven failures.

Restricting Handguns — The Liberal Skeptics Speak Out makes a powerful case against the control of firearms. Author Don Kates, with certified credentials as a civil rights activist and anti-poverty lawyer, shocked the liberal establishment when his condemnation of controls appeared in the *Washington Post*. Jaws dropped throughout the Nation's Capitol when his article was published in the Sunday *Post's* "Outlook Section."

Now Professor Kates has compiled this collection of his own writings and those of other nationally prominent liberals. His book puts the lie to the notion that "support for gun control is the litmus-test of liberalism." His contributors include officials from the American Civil Liberties Union and Amnesty International, and activists from the women's movement, the civil rights movement, the Indian Movement, the anti-poverty movement — in short, liberals from familiar fronts.

Many will ask, "How can this be?" But after reading the book, the questioners are more likely to ask themselves about the validity of their own views.

Liberal readers may be surprised to learn that the earliest

restrictions on ownership of firearms were directed against blacks, not criminals. Later these state and local statutes were expanded to encompass foreign immigrants passing by the Statue of Liberty. Modern liberal thought cherishes civil rights, little knowing that advocacy of gun controls rests on a plank of prejudice from the past.

As Professor Kates correctly asserts, the political climate of the 1930s was the Springtime for Federal gun controls. Prohibition had produced a wave of gangsterism. Its reign of terror was brought home to every American by constant radio and newspaper accounts, but most graphically by the film fantasies of Babyface Nelson and Ma Barker. The weekly outing to the movies usually turned out to be an extended exposure to gangland violence and mayhem.

Anyone in Congress in those years was under heavy pressure to approve federal bans on "gats and tommy-guns." That the federal firearms laws of the period actually showed some restraint was a triumph of prudence over passion.

One might have thought that the Second Amendment to the Constitution, which addresses the right of the people to keep and bear arms, would have stood as an impenetrable barrier to federal gun control laws. But this did not prove true either then, nor afterwards. In its sole case since the 1930s in which the Second Amendment was considered, the Supreme Court resorted to an old evasion action: it emphasized the founding fathers' fear of standing armies — the necessity of a "well-regulated militia" — to subordinate the people's basic guarantee against any federal taking of firearms.

Bolstered by the Court's refusal to invoke the Second Amendment, and unmindful of the history of gun control based on bygone bigotry, liberal advocates demanded more stringent federal restrictions in the dark days following Dallas. The awful assassinations of the Kennedy brothers and Martin Luther King, Jr., along with their resultant riots — black riots — kindled their determination. That tide crested in 1968, producing a flood of ill-considered regulations, like ammunition registration, which the Justice Department itself now admits proved useless in the fight against crime.

Some ten years later, I believe the tide is turning. With a large vote of thanks to Professor Kates, liberal skepticism over gun control is coming out of the closet. In recent years, the controllers have been unable to make any further headway in Congress. In fact, last year the House and Senate joined to reject decisively the Firearms Bureau's backdoor design for federal registration, even to the point of striking back at the Bureau by reducing its appropriation. Gunowners, so long on the defensive in Congress, may soon have the opportunity to swing the pendulum back in their direction.

Activists for minority rights, women's rights, rights for the poor — all human rights — are coming to understand that gun controls work against their interest. In the inner cities, where the police cannot offer adequate protection, the people will provide their own. They will keep handguns at home for self-defense, regardless of the prohibitions that relatively safe and smug inhabitants of the surrounding suburbs would impose upon them. This is the truth of it, as everyone will learn who reads *Restricting Handguns — The Liberal Skeptics Speak Out.*

FRANK CHURCH
United States Senate

March 1979

INTRODUCTION

I ask myself how rationally I might respond if the government enacted some comparable prohibition against something to which I was passionately attached — Handel's *Water
Music*, say . . . and, with this modest exercise, begin for the
first time to suspect that there may be rational reasons why I
have never met a gun nut was not cracked on the subject. . . .
I've also been wondering how I got so far into the anti-gun
bag. . . . Beyond the hysteria of the pro-gun people, the
major influence on my feeling has been the time I put in on
police beats or otherwise reporting on violence. It does not
take long in such settings to see a lot of killing and maiming
and to note that guns are involved in most of it.

I developed out of such experience, I suspect, strong
feeling that felt like strong thinking. I came to see guns as
bad, and not just a little bit bad. Hating them was a way of
dealing with feelings that too many corpses stirred up. . . . As
it happens, I still disapprove of guns. I still don't want them
in my house. . . . But there are limits to the contempt with
which I can try to jam my view down other people's
throats.

> — Patrick Owens, a *Newsday* columnist, in a 1978
> article entitled "Rediscovering the Right to Bear
> Arms."

When I originally agreed to prepare this book for Bill Cowan of
North River Press, my idea was just to gather together the best
already published materials reflecting liberal skepticism about

"gun control." As I began looking, however, it became clear that important areas were not covered by presently available materials. To fill the gaps I either had to cajole the authors into expanding their original articles or to get them, or others, to write new ones — or to do it myself. As a result, while two of the articles presented here have appeared elsewhere, nine are either entirely new or greatly revised from earlier publication.

In my naive enthusiasm I came perilously near overstepping the space limitations Bill and I had agreed upon. To remain within them, I found it necessary to omit one already published piece that I would have been delighted to print. Even worse, I suddenly had to "de-commission" an article which, no more than ten days before, I had cajoled a colleague to start writing at considerable cost to his own academic endeavors. Lack of space inevitably raised problems as to footnotes. Some of the authors — and I count myself as a chief offender — tend toward extremely locquacious footnotes, while others are commendably brief. Distended footnotes are pedantic and graceless enough in a journal article. They are senseless if space is at a premium, particularly in a book format where the footnotes are crammed into the nether end, making it impossible for readers to devote much time to them and still retain the thread of the textual narrative. So I have ruthlessly cut both the extent and the number of footnotes; in some articles I have gone so far as to dispense with footnotes altogether, substituting general references instead.

Defining the Topic

It has been said that "support for gun control is the litmus-test of liberalism." Yet this book presents a series of anti-"gun control" essays by people who fall easily within the vague general parameters of liberalism: an ACLU official; a former American chairman of Amnesty International; several who were deeply involved in the civil rights movement; two lawyers who formerly provided legal services for the poor; two people who are presently involved in the women's movement; and one who is involved in the Indian movement.

Before considering why such people might oppose "gun control," it is pertinent to point out that that term rarely appears in these pages. People who treat the area of firearms legislation seriously eschew it because it is so amorphous as to be virtually meaningless. It does not even necessarily connote *restriction* of firearms ownership. The Swiss government engages in "gun control" when it requires every man of military age to keep a machine gun (i.e. a fully automatic assault rifle) in his house. So does the Israeli government when it enrolls virtually the entire adult population (male and female) in the military reserves, issues vast numbers of submachine guns and assult rifles to be kept in civilian premises, and requires every reserve officer and noncom to carry one whenever even temporarily in uniform, including when going to and from civilian employment in major cities.

Handgun Permit (Prohibition) Laws

Even used in its more common meaning of firearms restrictions, "gun control" is highly ambiguous. It can refer to prohibition of civilian handgun ownership (Sullivan-type laws) or just to registration requirements which do not deprive people of weapons per se but only force them to report their ownership to the government, or to minimal and sensible steps like banning firearms possession by persons with violent crime records. None of the authors represented here opposes this last very narrow and specific prohibition. Our opposition is concentrated on proposals like the broad general prohibition of handguns advocated by such organizations as the U.S. Conference of Mayors, the National Coalition to Ban Handguns, etc. This would be accomplished through federal legislation (roughly comparable to the systems existing in Britain and Canada) under which handgun possession would be forbidden except for the military, the police, and those civilians accorded special permission by the FBI or some other police agency authorized to issue permits. Such legislation is referred to throughout this book as a national Sullivan Law (because New York's Sullivan Law preceded the British and Canadian systems) or simply as "handgun prohibition." It is not literally prohibition because a privileged few civilians would have permits. But its sponsors contemplate that a national Sullivan Law would be administered as or more harshly than it is in New York City where virtually every application is automatically denied. The intention is to render illegal well more than 99% of the 50 million civilian handguns and confiscate them to the extent possible. (Sullivan-type discretionary licensing must be distinguished from the less common "mandatory licensing" system [Illinois, Connecticut] under which the police have no discretion. They must issue the permit to any adult applicant unless he is disqualified by reason of felony conviction, mental commitment or some other ascertainable reason. This is the equivalent of the "check-out" system in many other states, under which the store will not release the gun to the buyer for a few days, while the police check to make sure that his record is clean.)

In addition to opposing Sullivan-type legislation, the authors represented in this book necessarily also oppose national handgun registration. It is no longer seriously argued that the enormous cost of compiling and maintaining national registration records will have any commensurate crime-reductive value. Its only real purpose is to identify present owners so that their handguns can be confiscated when a national Sullivan Law is enacted.

It would be superfluous for this Introduction to explore in depth the reasons which variously motivate the authors represented here to oppose a Sullivan Law or any other form of general handgun prohibition. One point is so frequently misunderstood that it does deserve emphasis, however. It is by no means necessarily the position of all those represented here that handguns are good things, that people ought to own them, that they are useful for self-defense, or deterring crime, or anything else. There is every difference between not liking something — or even thinking it evil — and thinking it should be proscribed by government. For instance, I can and do oppose banning liquor and pot, even though I do not indulge in them, advise others not to do so and consider liquor, at least, a positive evil. A sophisticated analysis of the criminalization decision takes into account not only the harms alleged to result from possession of things like liquor, pot, or guns, but the capacity of the criminal law to reduce those harms and the costs of trying to do so. Unfortunately most of the "gun control" debate never gets beyond the abstract merits of guns — a subject on which those who view them with undifferentiated loathing are no more rational than those who love them. The position of all too many who would ban guns is indistinguishable from Archie Bunker's views on legalizing pot and homosexuality: "I don't like it and I don't like those who do — so it ought to be illegal."

Beyond the weighing of costs against benefits, there is something even more fundamental. The ultimate issue in the handgun debate is this: Even if banning handguns turned out to be, on balance, an effective method for reducing crime, would it be a morally acceptable method, a just method? Millions of citizens will defy a handgun ban, because, whether rightly or wrongly, they believe they have a constitutional right and an urgent necessity to have handguns to defend their families. To break such defiance will require, at a minimum, severe punishment of hundreds of thousands of respectable, otherwise law-abiding citizens, many of them minority and underprivileged people living in the high-crime areas of our nation. I find it unacceptable for a society that cannot protect its people to punish them for keeping or acquiring what they believe to be the necessary means of protecting themselves and their families.

Consider a typical case reported by a New York City newspaper: A small middle-aged black cab driver with a crippled arm (whom I shall call Jimmy Washington) was preparing dinner in his Harlem tenement. A junkie broke in and began beating Mr. Washington over the head with a lead pipe, demanding money with each blow. Having already been mugged twice that month, Mr. Washington didn't have any money. But the junkie didn't give him time to mention that fact — and anyway he didn't seem inclined to stop beating the cabbie's head in for any explanation less convincing than actual cash. So Mr. Washington grabbed a "Saturday Night Special" and shot the junkie dead. In about twenty minutes the police arrived, arrested Mr. Washington, took him to the emergency ward, and then booked him into the police hospital for an extended stay — because, of course, Mr. Washington did not have a permit for the gun. Living in a Harlem tenement and working in the worst areas of the city, do not qualify as reasons for a gun permit, not even if, like Mr. Washington, an applicant has no criminal record. New York City permits are issued only to the very wealthy, the politically powerful, and the socially elite. Permits are also issued to: private guard services employed by the very wealthy, the banks, and the great corporations; to ward heelers and political influence peddlers; and (on payment of a suitable sum) to reputable "soldiers" of the Mafia — but not to the likes of Jimmy Washington.

But we should not be distracted even by important issues like equal administration or the self-defense utility of handguns. The fundamental question is: Do we want to send Jimmy Washington and hundreds of thousands of others like him to jail? After all, sending people to jail is what making it a crime to own a handgun is all about.

The leaders of the movement for a national Sullivan Law are proposing a *mandatory* minimum one-year sentence for anyone found with a handgun — not for misusing it, just for having it. They realize that nothing less drastic will suffice for a serious attempt to enforce national confiscation. As the author of this proposal frankly explained it, "we have to terrify the people," to make them more frightened of the law than of not having the handgun they believe is vital to their survival. I cannot accept "terrify[ing] the people" as a legitimate tactic in a democratic society — particularly not when the source of the problem is the government's failure or inability to protect the people in the first place.

Even if I believed that sending Jimmy Washington to jail would eventually reduce crime, I would find it no more acceptable than arming the police with the Gestapo-like powers that sometimes are also promoted as a way to reduce crime. Doubtless some more "tough-minded" readers will disagree. They will feel that if banning handguns would sharply reduce crime this would justify the imprisonment of any number of Jimmy Washingtons. But at the very least the example of Jimmy Washington should establish where the burden of proof lies. It is up to the advocates of handgun prohibition to prove that there is a sufficient crime-reductive effect to justify jailing Jimmy Washington. The burden of proof should lie upon the proponents of a national Sullivan Law in any event. In a free country, it is up to those who want to restrict the liberty of the people to show that the benefits which are likely to accrue outweigh the likely costs. But that burden of proof is particularly heavy when the liberty in question is so deeply valued by a large part of the population that it can be abrogated only by severely punishing many.

As you read each of the following essays, I hope you will ask yourself whether the argument for handgun prohibition is sufficiently strong and convincing to justify the costs it will impose on the Jimmy Washingtons of our nation.

SECTION I: Toward a History of Handgun Prohibition in the United States

DON B. KATES, JR.

Introduction

Though the debate on handgun prohibition bristles with historical assumptions, there has been no specialized inquiry into the development of such legislation in the United States, nor would it be possible to cover in detail so extensive a topic in the limited space available here. I have chosen therefore to focus on two major, and a number of attendant minor, misconceptions which appear to be shared alike by proponents and opponents of handgun prohibition — though, of course, their attitudes toward these historical assumptions are deeply colored by their views on the general issue.

The first of these misconceptions is that unfettered handgun ownership was the pattern of the raw Western frontier, while legal restrictions on handgun ownership developed initially in the Northeast and thence moved West and South in direct relationship to the growth of urbanization. The second misconception is that the movement for handgun probhition had its origins in Eastern, liberal, labor-oriented social philosophy and had as its purpose the control of criminal, rather than political, activity. (Reactions to these misconceptions generally vary according to whether the assessor views himself as liberal or conservative, the East as civilized or "sissified," and the Western tradition as one of brutal *machismo* or of an independent, self-reliant yeomanry.) Corollary to these misconceptions is the assumption that handgun prohibitions are more likely to characterize our urban and densely populated states and that popular support for them has increased in linear progression as urbanization and population density have increased across the country. Finally, it is assumed that handgun prohibition enjoys majority support, which is frustrated by the machinations of a "gun lobby" composed of well-heeled lobbyists for "the arms merchants."

In part these two misconceptions represent our relative ignorance of nineteenth century urban America, and the romanticized myth of the Old West perpetrated by cinematic and other fictional accounts. But the single most important factor is a projection into a past in which it did not exist of a fundamental division in present attitudes of the American people, of which the "gun control" controversy is symptomatic. B. Bruce-Briggs, a historian and social policy analyst who approaches this controversy as a neutral, has described that division in a brilliant essay aptly entitled "The Great American Gun War" [*The Public Interest*, Fall, 1976]:

> [The handgun prohibition controversy] represents a sort of low grade war between two alternative views of what America is and ought to be. On the one side are those who take bourgeois Europe as a model of a civilized society: a society just, equitable and democratic; but well ordered, with the lines of responsibility and authority clearly drawn, and with decisions made rationally and correctly by intelligent men for the entire nation. To such people, hunting is atavistic, personal violence is shameful, and uncontrolled gun ownership is a blot upon civilization.
>
> On the other side is a group of people who do not tend to be especially articulate or literate, and whose world view is rarely expressed in print. Their model is that of the independent frontiersman who takes care of himself and his family with no interference from the state. They are "conservative" in the sense that they cling to America's unique pre-modern tradition — a non-feudal society with a sort of medieval liberty writ large for every man. To these people, "sociological" is an epithet. Life is tough and competitive. Manhood means responsibility and caring for your own.

The position the first of the groups described by Bruce-Briggs believes its views to have occupied in American history is vividly expressed in a postcard I received a few weeks ago from an eminent law professor. He wrote about a *Harper's* article in which I argued that banning handguns was both futile and dangerous. He shared my concern that a handgun ban could only be enforced through repugnant police activities, but was appalled at what he took to be my advocacy "of an armed society." Presumably because his postcard bore a picture of the library at Monticello, he asked rhetorically, "What would Thomas Jefferson have thought?"

Before answering that question, it is useful to emphasize a distinction which my eminent colleague overlooked in reading my article. It is possible for me to oppose firearms restrictions without wholeheartedly endorsing the idea of an armed society — just as I can and do oppose anti-homosexual laws without advocating that people become homosexuals. Many criminologists and criminal law specialists oppose handgun restrictions as involving great financial, constitutional, and human costs in enforcement and no commensurate gain in reducing crime. Yet these same people do not own handguns, are not target shooters or sportsmen, and often disapprove of gun ownership for self-defense.

Laying aside for the moment Jefferson's views on firearms ownership, his attitude toward firearms restriction was entirely negative. Among the foremost guarantees in a model state constitution he penned in 1776 was "no free man shall be debarred the use of arms within his own land." But inquiry into Jefferson's reasons reveals that he and the rest of the Founding Fathers were guilty of the charge my eminent colleague leveled against me — they believed in, and advocated, "an armed people." In *The Federalist*, No. 46, Madison congratulates his countrymen on "the advantage of being armed, which the Americans possess over the people of almost every other nation"; he dismisses with contempt the despotisms of Europe that "are afraid to trust the people with arms." In No. 29, Hamilton asserts that all that is necessary to guarantee liberty "to the people at large" is that they be allowed to be "properly armed and equipped. . . ." Despite the enormous political gulf between these men and Patrick Henry at this time, the latter voiced the same sentiments: "The great object is that every man be armed . . . everyone who is able may have a gun."

Much of the Founding Fathers' advocacy of firearms ownership was based upon a belief that ultimately a free people must be able to defend their liberties physically. But they considered firearms not only politically expedient for the people, but personally desirable as well. The foremost advocate of this view was Thomas Jefferson, who wrote his fifteen-year-old nephew:

> A strong body makes the mind strong. As to the species of exercises, I advise the gun. While this gives a moderate exercise to the body, it gives boldness, enterprise and independence to the mind. Games played with the ball, and others of that nature, are too violent for the body and stamp no character on the mind. Let your gun therefore be the constant companion of your walks.

Jefferson was not only the greatest intellect of his generation in the United States, but also an ardent outdoorsman and naturalist, a superb horseman, a talented amateur gunsmith, and the keeper of a veritable armory of handguns and long guns at Monticello. What, indeed, would Thomas Jefferson have thought of modern notions that "hunting is atavistic . . . and uncontrolled gun ownership is a blot upon civilization"?

When the idea of drastically restricting handgun ownership first surfaced in the United States, it was based upon philosophical concepts far removed from those of Jefferson or the rest of the Founding Fathers. But before ownership restrictions came restrictions of carrying and use of firearms, particularly of handguns. These began to surface even before Jefferson's death in 1826 — but on the frontier, not in the more settled areas of the country.

Handguns and Handgun Laws on the Western Frontier

The myth of the Old West portrays it as a violent land where everyone carried a revolver. In fact, violence was not endemic to the West, its inhabitants rarely went armed, and when they did so it was rarely with a revolver. For most of the nineteenth century Western revolver ownership was largely confined to outlaws, the military, the police, and company security personnel. Practicalities and economics dictated the rifle and (to a lesser extent) the shotgun as the weapons of Western expansion. On the practical level, the Western settler needed a weapon first of all for hunting, and secondly for defense against Indians. The highly inaccurate and extremely short range black-powder handgun of the period was appropriate for neither use. To the settler who could afford a firearm — and many could not, after buying agricultural implements, livestock, seed, wagon, etc., for the trek West — the first choice was a rifle. If the family were lucky enough to be able to afford two firearms, it would be two rifles or rifle and shotgun. Excepting Indian attack, the Western settler had little to fear from other humans. Assuming the rare instance in which he did anticipate the kind of "shootout" portrayed in fiction, he would carry his shotgun or rifle and most likely have it all over any opponent so foolish as to appear with only a revolver.

For the Western settler, the revolver was a luxury and, until the late 1860s, an extraordinarily expensive one at that. When Samuel Colt's revolutionary weapon first appeared in 1835, it sold for $35.00, a then enormous sum representing many weeks' wages even for a regularly salaried clerk or skilled workman. As a result the Colt factory closed within six years; when business revived through military procurement orders during the Mexican War, Colt had to fill them by manufacturing guns at the Pratt and Whitney plant.

The handgun did not become financially accessible to most Americans until the end of the Civil War brought the sale of large stocks of military surplus weapons. Even then, the military surplus sale of enormous numbers of Henry and Spencer repeating rifles at comparable prices was a more attractive buy for the Western settler. Thus handguns did not begin to flood into the West in overwhelming numbers until the late 1860s with the appearance of numerous extremely cheap off-brands which, for obvious reasons, were generically termed "suicide specials." Even then, and certainly in the years preceding 1875, handguns were more widely distributed in the East than the West. By the 1870s the practice of Eastern manufacturers of men's ready-to-wear trousers was to sew a holster into the right hip pocket of every pair made, to allow the concealed gun-carrying which was still legal in the East.

As the Western frontier was the area in which handguns were most likely to be associated exclusively with criminals, it was the area in which the first restrictions on their use developed. The earliest of these banned the carrying of concealed weapons and applied to knives and other weapons as well as handguns. These laws appeared in the then frontier states of Kentucky (1813), Indiana (1819), and Arkansas and Georgia (1837). The only even arguably "Eastern" state to adopt such legislation was Virginia (1838), which at that time had its own western frontier (now West

Virginia). By 1850 every Western state barred the carrying of concealed weapons. In contrast, none of the Northeastern states adopted even that mild a restriction until nearly the turn of the twentieth century. Until 1924, for instance, the only gun law in New Jersey was the prohibition of dueling.

Development of Handgun Ownership Restrictions in the Post-Civil War South

The former slave states were the first to move beyond restricting handgun use to restricting handgun ownership. To understand why, it is necessary to consider the social upheaval resulting from the abolition of slavery. As I have said in another context ["Attitudes Towards Slavery in the New Republic," 53 *Journal of Negro History* 33, 37]:

> Slavery was not just an economic institution; it was a social, and by exclusion, a political one as well. By constitutional, statutory, decisional, administrative and customary law the position of the slave was fixed. He could not possess arms or liquor, make contracts, own land or personalty, travel freely, give testimony or learn to read or write, act independently as a religious leader, compete in the free labor market — above all, he had no political rights. The prohibition of arms, liquor and travel was enforced by a more or less well organized system of special and general searches and night patrols of the *posse comitatus.* Justice to the slave was, within the law or within its enforcement, summarily meted out by masters, possemen and judicial officials alike. As Mr. Chief Justice Taney succinctly expressed it [in the Dred Scott case, the slave had] "no rights which the white man was bound to respect."

Immediately after emancipation destroyed this ornate system of social and political control, the Southern legislatures restored it by enacting the Black Codes. These fixed the black population in serfdom, denying all political rights, excluding them from virtually any chance at economic or social advancement — and, of course, forbidding them to own arms. The indignant Congress of 1866 reacted with a Civil Rights Act, and then the Fourteenth Amendment.

Denied legal avenues for social control, the South substituted illegal methods: a system of massive private terrorism acquiesced in by the public authorities. Having accomplished its objectives by 1876, this campaign of beatings, arson, murder, etc. trailed off into the minimum amounts of intermittent violence necessary to maintain the social and economic status quo. Though a majority in many parts of the South after the Civil War, the blacks were highly vulnerable to such terrorism. Their organization and communications were poor, and above all, they possessed few firearms, and those mostly obsolete. Except for those who had served in the Union Army, blacks had virtually no experience with guns, for ante bellum laws made their possession by even free Southern blacks a highly penal offense. Few blacks had been able to afford revolvers or modern repeating rifles even in the military surplus sale period immediately after the war, much less when the prices returned to normal. Though in theory the Army was available to protect the blacks, it could not be everywhere at once. And when the Southern delegations returned to Congress they reduced it to a maximum of 25,000 enlisted men, many of whom were diverted West by the Indian wars. Though the withdrawal of the Army as part of the Electoral Compromise of 1876 has been pictured as a betrayal of black aspirations, it was actually more a formal surrender to a victory already won by violence-enforced white supremacy.

Meaningful black access to self-defense weapons occurred only in the mid-1870's when the cheap off-brand revolvers began to be sold in the South in large numbers. The Klan recognized in the mere existence of these a threat to its previous virtual monopoly of violence, although by this time the blacks were generally crushed and quiescent. Moreover, in ensuing years those who ruled the South found that there were challengers other than the blacks against whom the forces of social control might have to be exerted. Agrarian agitators arose to inform poor whites that they were trading their political and economic group identity for a fraudulent racial solidarity with a false imperative of preserving white supremacy. For a while men like Tom Watson even dared suggest that poor whites had more in common with poor blacks than with wealthy planters, produce dealers, railroad magnates, merchants, and manufacturers. In the cities of the South similar views were being expressed by other agitators as the laboring poor began to organize for better wages and working conditions.

Though the reactions of Southern legislatures to the threats of racial and economic change differed in detail, they evinced a common purpose. Those who might menace the status quo must be denied access to arms, while the monopoly of those who would preserve it (if necessary by violence and terror) must be assured. The very next session of the legislature (1870) after white supremacists had regained control of Tennessee set the earliest pattern of legal restrictions. This was a ban on selling all but "the Army and Navy model" handgun, i.e. the most expensive one, which was beyond the means of most blacks and laboring people. Klansmen were not inconvenienced, having long since acquired their guns (many of them surplus Army and Navy weapons), nor were the company goons, professional strike-breakers, etc., whose weapons were supplied by their corporate employers. By 1881 white supremacists were in power in the neighboring state of Arkansas and had enacted a virtually identical "Saturday Night Special" law with virtually identical effect.

Instead of formal legislation, Mississippi, Florida, and the rest of the Deep South states simply continued (in effect) to enforce the pre-emancipation statutes forbidding blacks to possess arms, the Fourteenth Amendment notwithstanding. When blacks appeared with arms these were confiscated, though often the more kind-hearted sheriffs tolerated the possession of obsolete hunting weapons by blacks who were known not to be trouble-makers. No such indulgence was shown as to revolvers, however. Though the sale of these to blacks could not be prohibited per se, it was understood that retailers would report to local authorities whenever blacks (or a white agitator) purchased pistols or ammunition. The sheriff would then arrest them and confiscate their pistols which would be either destroyed or turned over to the local Klavern. In short order, blacks, and whites unpopular with local authorities, learned that pistol purchases were a waste of hard-earned cash, and dangerous to boot.

Mississippi formalized this custom by enacting the first registration law for retailers in 1906. It required them to maintain records of all pistol and pistol ammunition sales, making these available for inspection on demand. This was part of a trend toward formalizing firearms restrictions, which the Southern states exhibited toward the end of the century, perhaps because of the increasing concern about handgun ownership by certain groups of whites (See discussion in the next section). Alabama in 1893 and Texas in 1907 imposed extremely heavy business and/or transaction taxes on handgun sales in order to resurrect the economic barriers to ownership. Simpler yet was the approach South Carolina adopted in 1902, banning all pistol sales except to sheriffs and their special deputies — i.e., company goons and the KKK.

But in 1911 sophisticated, cosmopolitan New York State rendered obsolete all previous concepts in handgun ownership restriction with the introduction of the flexible, surgically clean Sullivan Law. Of proven success in dealing with political dissidents in Central European countries, this system made handgun ownership illegal for anyone without a police permit. New York City police thereby acquired official authority to implement the disfavor with which they had long looked at possession of handguns by the city's Italian population.

The Sullivan Law established the pattern for police permit requirements which were adopted in the succeeding twenty-three years in Arkansas, Hawaii, Michigan, Missouri, New Jersey, North Carolina, and Oregon. These enactments represented the fruits of a nationwide handgun prohibition campaign by conservative business interests in the early part of the century. Across the land, legislators in conservative states were importuned by business lobbyists bearing glowing endorsements of the Sullivan Law concept from such (then) arch-conservative institutions as the *New York Times* and the American Bar Association. Among the most importunate were national and local businessmen's associations which emphasized the increasing incidence of armed robbery.

Handgun Restrictions and "The Immigration Problem"

The great importance armed robbery seems to have played in this early campaign indicates yet another dimension of the handgun prohibition movement — its relationship to hatred and fear of the foreign-born. Armed robbery was associated in the public mind with foreign immigrants, not just because they were considered naturally lazy and inclined to violent acquisitiveness, but because armed robbery was a recognized tactic of the "foreign-born anarchist." In America from at least the turn of the century, and in Europe from the 1870s on, revolutionaries used bank and commercial robberies as a means of gathering funds to finance their underground activities. The businessmen's associations could point out that Sacco and Vanzetti were originally apprehended for violation of Massachusetts' new handgun law, and that they were executed for murder committed in the course of several armed robberies of which they were convicted. Symptomatic of the concerns underlying the businessmen's campaign for Sullivan-type legislation is the fact that even the states that rejected that concept substituted, instead, a flat ban of the ownership of firearms, or at least handguns, by aliens.

It is no coincidence that the period 1870-1934, which saw far more states enacting far more drastic handgun restrictions than ever after, was also the most xenophobic period of American history. Though hatred of foreigners was nothing new, it reached its apogee in this era, as the stream of immigration was darkened by Southern and Eastern European peoples, and the Know Nothings gave way to the Immigration Restriction League and the American Protective Association. However, it must be recognized that such feelings were not the province of the ignorant and the foolish alone. Xenophobia was powerfully supported by the learning and social science of the day, and in ways that lent credence to the desirability of denying handguns to the foreign-born. Well before the turn of the century, an early social psychologist emerged from Ellis Island to announce that most of the foreign-born he had tested there (in English) were feeble-minded. It followed that such people should not be allowed to have handguns, particularly since contemporary criminologists believed that violent acquisitiveness was an inherited characteristic associated with mental retardation.

Many deemed this correlation between feeble-mindedness, violence, and Eastern or Southern European ancestry confirmed by the high incidence of crime among the new immigrants. Most of these had settled in or around the urban areas of the East. Employment opportunities were often scarce there for people with only an agricultural background and mediocre English skills, and in an era characterized by rampant xenophobia and by repeated economic slumps, panics, and depressions. Under these circumstances it is scarcely surprising that some of the new immigrants followed their adopted country's fine old tradition of violent crime. In fact, like all ghettoized minorities, their depredations were largely confined to their own people and their own neighborhoods. But the average newspaper reader of the period would be unlikely to pick that fact out of the constant diet of stories and exposés of robberies committed by Italian, Jewish, or other immigrant gangs, and of helpless, innocent young white women kidnapped into vile slavery.

The attitude of contemporary newspapers and many of their readers is well illustrated by the argument that Professor Kennett gives in repudiating a charge sometimes made against the Sullivan Law. It is not true, he says, that this law was a cynical political ploy by which corrupt politicians hoped to disarm the gangs of their rivals for office while keeping their own gangs armed. Rather, the Sullivan Law was a sincerely motivated answer to crime — within the framework of contemporary views of the nature of crime:

> [There] was the clear inference that the new measure would strike hardest at the foreign-born element who were seemingly responsible for most of the violence in the city. It had long been held that pistols were found "chiefly in the pockets of ignorant and quarrelsome immigrants of law-breaking propensities" [quoted from a newspaper editorial]. The Italian population seemed particularly addicted to criminality (the [New York] *Tribune's* annual index frequently crosslisted the entries "crime" and "Italians"). As early as 1903 the authorities had begun to cancel pistol permits in the Italian sections of the city. This was followed by a state law of 1905 which made it illegal for aliens to possess firearms "in any public place." This provision was retained in the Sullivan Law.

Beyond the issue of apolitical crime was that of the ideological fitness of these immigrants to have handguns. Almost all of them were known to be Jews, Catholics, or anarchists. Of the three, Jews were least suspect ideologically, being considered no more than usurious Christ-killers and perhaps congenitally criminal as well. But the influx of a vast mass of Catholic immigrants was necessarily a source of disquiet in a nation with an aggressively Protestant libertarian tradition, and particularly to generations raised on Macaulay's *History of England* and Lea's *History of the*

Inquisition. The hierarchical form of their Church was regarded as predisposing the immigrants against democracy and republican institutions, and toward the despotic governments of the lands from whence they came. As they were considered ignorant, prejudiced, superstitious — and utterly submissive to religious authority — it was easy to imagine them being led by the nose into any adventure their priests might choose for them.

But if the deeds of "Bloody Mary," Guy Fawkes, and James II gave ancient warning of the dangers of Catholicism, the evil done by "foreign-born anarchists" was a clear and present menace headlined daily in reports from here and abroad. "Anarchists" had assassinated Czar Alexander II (1881), the Austrian Empress Elizabeth (1898), Italian King Humbert (1900), Spanish Premier Canalejas (1912), and our own President McKinley (1901). Mc Kinley's assassin, the foreign-born Leon Czolgosz, did indeed describe himself as an anarchist, but with a fine impartiality the newspapers of the time also bestowed that epithet on people who would more accurately have been classified as communists, socialists, syndicalists, Wobblies, or even peaceful trade unionists. The term anarchist, with the now almost redundant prefix "foreign-born," became synonymous with any radical or otherwise highly divergent political view; it was occasionally even applied to the assassin of President Garfield (1881) and the attempted assassin of former President Roosevelt (1912), though neither of them were foreign-born or even remotely an anarchist.

Similarly "anarchist" or "radical" was widely applied to any labor organization or agitation, it being reflexively assumed that such groups were largely composed of, and led by, foreigners of alien political persuasions. When Canada adopted its handgun permit law in 1919, the debate was replete with references to the recently crushed general strike. This was (erroneously) believed to have been engineered and led by foreigners, and the law's sponsors reviewed at length the absurdity of allowing handgun ownership to those who "bring their bad habits, notions, and vicious practices into this country."

Simiarly, highly publicized incidents involving blacks, foreign-born radicals, or labor agitators seem to have provided the immediate occasion — if not the sole motivation — for most of the American handgun ownership restrictions adopted in the 1901-34 period. The 1934 Hawaii and 1913 Oregon statutes were responses to the concern felt about labor-organizing by "foreign-born radicals" in the port of Honolulu and Oregon lumber mills respectively. The South Carolina law appears to have been an immediate response to the assassination of President McKinley some months before. It barred only the purchase of pistols weighing less than three pounds and having a barrel less than twenty inches long. Any pistol exceeding those specifications (and none existed, then or now) clearly could not have been concealed in a bandaged arm as Czolgosz's pocket pistol was. Though in the long run New York's Sullivan Law was aimed at every kind of crime to which the foreign-born were believed inclined, its immediate motivation seems to have been anarchists and radicals. It was enacted in the backlash from the London siege of the Houndsditch anarchists and an attempted assassination of New York's mayor by a crazed working-man, which recalled the McKinley assassination.

The Michigan version of the Sullivan Law was hurriedly enacted in the aftermath of a famous trial in which Clarence Darrow defended a black civil rights leader. (Dr. Ossian Sweet, who had moved into an all-white neighborhood, was accused of murder for shooting one of a mob that attacked his house while Detroit police looked on.) The Missouri permit law was enacted in the aftermath of a famous and bloody St. Louis race riot.

The Arkansas, Michigan, Missouri, and North Carolina laws were expressive of one of the lowest periods of race relations in modern American history. A younger generation of blacks — led by soldiers returning from World War I familiar with guns and willing to fight for the equal treatment they had received in other lands — had to be painfully reintroduced to the forces of social control. Once again in the 1910s and 1920s did the Klan become a major force in the South. Once again the public authorities stood by while murders, beatings, and lynchings were openly perpetrated. Once again the handgun legislation of Alabama, Arkansas, Mississippi, Missouri, Tennessee, and Texas deprived the victims of the means of self-defense, cloaking the specially deputized Klansmen in the safety of their monopoly of arms.

But the resurgent Klan of these years was not limited to the South geographically, nor was its concern with blacks alone. The Klan was a force in southern New Jersey and Illinois, in Indiana, Michigan, and Oregon. All of these enacted either handgun permit laws or laws barring alien handgun possession in the years

1913-34. A few years after the Oregon gun law, Klan support helped pass a law banning parochial schools in that state. The Klan opposed not only blacks, but Catholics, Jews, labor radicals, and the foreign-born in general, and these too often fell victim to lynch mobs or other, more clandestine, attacks.

It bears emphasis that such activities were not the sole province of the Klan. The businessman's Sullivan Law campaign occured during the years of a concerted effort by employers and employers' associations to destroy the emergent labor unions through a systematic campaign of drastic wage decreases, lockouts, imported strikebreakers, and surveillance, harrassment, black-listing, and physical attack upon trade unionists — all carried out with the acquiescence or active support of local authorities. One of the most blatant incidents occured in Bixbee, Arizona, where 221 supposed labor radicals were rounded up by a posse and forcibly deported from the state. A 1901 Arizona law barred the carrying of handguns within city limits and provided for the temporary confiscation of strangers' weapons, to be returned when they left town. Needless to say, the carrying ban was not applied to the members of the posse, and the provision for returning confiscated guns was omitted as to the deportees.

A Caveat on Geography and Fear of Immigration

Though my discussion of this topic is already long, it is necessary to address an issue that may occur to some readers. Since the states that adopted drastic handgun ownership restrictions in the era 1870-1934 were remote from Ellis Island, how can it reasonably be thought that they felt themselves threatened by the dangers of immigration? The answer is simply that the phenomenon in question was hysteria, not a rational reaction. In every effort of workers in these and adjoining states to organize, to demand better wages and working conditions, was seen the lurking specter of "anarchism," and in every outbreak of "anarchism" was supposed to be the influence of the foreign-born.

I encountered such nativist hysteria in a somewhat different context when, as a lawyer for California Rural Legal Assistance, I brought a lawsuit to void California's English literacy requirement for voting as applied to our clients who were literate in Spanish. I found that this requirement had been introduced into the California legislature in 1891 by a representative of the American Protective Association. Its purpose was not to disenfranchise the Chinese (this had been accomplished by the Constitution of 1879) nor blacks — though the author praised literacy requirements in Mississippi and other Southern states. Rather, his declared purpose was "to protect the purity of the ballot box from the corrupting influences of the disturbing elements from abroad." He seems to have expected these "ignorant classes, who are coming here from Europe, [which is] unloading the refuse of the world upon our shores," to be translated immediately to California from Ellis Island. For he predicted that, unless his measure were enacted, "it will soon come to pass that this element will direct in our politics and our institutions will be overthrown." Motivated at least in part by the same hysterical fears, legislatures (including California) also enacted drastic handgun ownership restrictions in general or against aliens in particular.

In summary, however irrationally, Americans (and Canadians) in the era 1870-1934 felt themselves threatened by a number of forces they associated with the handgun: blacks who wouldn't keep their place; radicals, labor agitators, assassins, robbers, and, by a process of further association, the foreign-born. Reminded of Madison's contempt for "governments [which] are afraid to trust the people with arms," many late nineteenth- and early twentieth-century Americans would have responded that policies that were safe and sound in a population of fine Anglo-Saxon stock were foolish and irresponsible when that population became infected with the feeble-minded, the congenitally criminal, partisans of divisive alien philosophies, and others unable to understand and revere republican institutions. The association in the public mind of the handgun with blacks and the foreign-born criminal, anarchist or labor agitator was at least one major impetus behind the handgun ownership restrictions adopted in this country and Canada during the period 1870-1934. The spirit in which such permit laws were enacted and administered is well expressed by the following from a 1918 New Hampshire case upholding that state's ban of alien firearms ownership, which a 1924 California court repeated in upholding California's similar statute as to handguns:

> Native citizens are justly presumed to be imbued with a natural allegiance to their government which unnaturalized

foreigners do not possess. The former inherit a knowledge and reverence for our institutions, while the latter as a class do not understand our customs or laws, or enter into the spirit of our social organization.

Handgun Prohibitions and "Liberal" Thought Since the 1920s

Though many bases for the handgun restrictions in the era 1870-1934 would deeply offend present liberal sensibilities, they were not necessarily repugnant to those considered liberal then. While generally supportive of white laboring people, American liberalism had by the 1890s largely abandoned the Negro and was ambivalent toward the foreign-born. Liberals were themselves deeply concerned about crime and would not have opposed handgun prohibition in principle. If they opposed it at all, it was only because it diverted attention from their own pet solution to violence, the prohibition of alcohol. Loath as we modern liberals are to admit it, Prohibition was the *cause celebre* of four generations of American liberals, the brightest and the best, the most progressive and humane, political figures of their times. Susan B. Anthony started out as a Prohibition speaker. Others who saw in Demon Rum the cause of domestic and acquaintance homicide (as well as robbery and innumerable other social ills) included such luminaries of American liberalism as William Lloyd Garrison, Henry Ward Beecher, Theodore Parker, Frederick Douglass, Jane Addams, William Jennings Bryan, and at least in their youth, Eleanor Roosevelt and Hugo Black. Before dismissing their views as absurd, remember that liquor is a factor in more homicides than are handguns, by about 64 to 50 percent; as Professor Donald Lunde has noted, "Persons with a urine alcohol level of .20-.29 percent (about twice the level required for conviction of drunk driving) make up the largest group of persons arrested for violent crimes."

It was only after the failure of Prohibition became manifest that many of the people who had supported it found in handgun prohibition a similar promise of cutting through the complex social, cultural, and institutional factors that produce violent crime. The addition of this veteran core of social reformers to the already very influential forces calling for handgun prohibition seemed to make a national Sullivan Law a real possibility in the heady early New Deal days of expanding federal power. President

Roosevelt was known to be strongly sympathetic. As Governor of New York, he had vetoed a repeal of the Sullivan Law. The likelihood that handgun prohibition might divert attention from Prohibition was to F.D.R. not a disadvantage, but a major attraction. Whatever its substantive merits, as a political issue in the Democratic party Prohibition was highly divisive. During the preceding two presidential campaigns (1924 and 1928) it had been one of several factors that threatened to dissolve the party into its component sectional and ideological parts. The evident primacy of the national economic emergency enabled F.D.R. to dump Prohibition in 1932, as even the most die-hard Prohibitionists were far too liberal to support Herbert Hoover. (Indeed, as Harvard historian Frank Freidel notes in his analysis of the election, "the nine-point recovery program [adopted in the 1932 convention of the Prohibition party was] practically identical to that later adopted by." F.D.R.)

The commonality of goals and underlying assumptions between handgun and liquor prohibition gave F.D.R. hope that the former could be substituted for the latter in the hearts and minds of Prohibitionist Democrats. Since drinkers numbered in the many millions, but handgun owners less than ten million, the adverse effect on the party of this new prohibition crusade was likely to be considerably less. Thus, even as F.D.R. campaigned on his promise to repeal the Eighteenth Amendment, he was proposing strict federal regulation of handgun ownership. Soon after Prohibition repeal had become a reality, his Attorney General presented Congress with a proposal for national handgun registration along with a host of other firearms restrictions. (The fact that yet another foreign-born assassin had attempted to kill F.D.R. — and had killed the Mayor of Chicago who was with the President — was thought likely to spur sentiment for this proposal.)

But two factors on which the Administration had not counted resulted in a defeat so decisive that drastic handgun ownership restrictions were not to be again seriously considered by Congress for over thirty years. The first of these factors was that F.D.R. was not alone in perceiving the similarity of goals and assumptions underlying the two prohibitions. So also did a lot of other Americans who had become thoroughly disenchanted with the Great Experiment. Americans had grown both skeptical of the likelihood that trying to ban widely popular commodities could stop crime and profoundly weary of the enormous police intrusions which such attempts necessarily entailed. Illustrative of how deep and widespread was the disenchantement is the opposition to a federal gun law voiced by a congressman whose state had earlier pioneered both liquor and handgun prohibitions: "I tell you that right now in the State of Arkansas there are more federal agents camped on its soil, nosing into the private affairs of individuals, than we have state, county, township, and municipal officers." And a *Saturday Evening Post* editorial offered the pertinent question: "If the federal government cannot prevent the landing of shiploads of rum, how can it stop the criminal from getting the most easily concealed and most vital tool of his trade?"

Another factor which combined with, and helped mightily to stimulate, such sentiments was the strong representations made by gun owners through such groups as the new United States Revolver Association and the older National Rifle Association. The growing threat of state, and now national, confiscation had induced great numbers of handgun owners (and long-gun owners who were afraid their weapons would be next) to join these organizations. By 1930 the N.R.A. had swelled from a tiny, elite organization concerned with arranging, organizing, and providing standards for marksmanship contests to a mass organization forcefully representing its members' fears for their rights and property. Faced with thousands of letters from little people they had never heard of, or from, before on any other issue, the Congress rapidly backed away from handgun prohibition — even while vehemently denouncing the NRA for organizing the letter-writing campaign.

"The Gun Lobby" and the Defeat of Handgun Prohibitions

Thus was born the so-called gun lobby which is often credited (or blamed) for the failure of both federal and state legislatures to enact onerous restrictions on handgun ownership. The concept of the "gun lobby" is used by advocates of handgun prohibition as the concept of "the liquor lobby" was used by partisans of Prohibition to explain their many defeats before the eventual enactment of the Eighteenth Amendment and the Volstead Act. But both the comparison and the term "lobby" are highly misleading, for they call up pictures of a powerful industry blocking legislation through insidious pressures or corrupt influence. However true this may have been of nineteenth-century liquor interests, the firearms industry has never been a major force in American business, nor has it opposed legislative regulation of its products.

As to its economic importance, an expert finds that "in no census year has small arms production exceeded .03 percent of total industry." Moreover, to the limited extent of its lobbying power, the domestic small arms industry has actually supported federal firearms restrictions. The federal Gun Control Act of 1968, which banned mail-order gun sales and imports of military surplus firearms, was something domestic manufacturers had been impotently urging for decades. Professor Kennett notes: "in their feelings about 'cheap mail-order guns' the major small arms companies antedated Senator Thomas Dodd by a half century."

Though the 1968 Act unquestionably made acquiring firearms more costly, the effect was not that the number of people buying guns was reduced (as the Act's sponsors may have hoped), but rather that the people had to buy their guns more expensively from domestic manufacturers (as the manufacturers had hoped). The fact is that when social conditions convince people that they need a firearm to protect themselves and their families, they are going to get one, no matter what the cost. Indeed, it is sometimes argued that the Act's sponsors knew this and intended only to restrict access to firearms by minorities and the poor: "The Gun Control Act of 1968 was passed not to control guns but to control blacks," claims liberal journalist Robert Sherrill — an advocate of gun laws. Similarly, B. Bruce-Briggs notes in his *Public Interest* article: "It is difficult to escape the conclusion that the 'Saturday Night Special' is emphasized because it is cheap and is being sold to a particular class of people. The name is sufficient evidence — the reference is to 'niggertown Saturday night.' "

In 1968, Smith and Wesson and six other major firearms manufacturers went on to endorse a national system of Sullivan Law-type mandatory licensing for handgun owners. Because Smith and Wesson has continued to push this (which is also the program of the subsequently organized National Coalition to Ban Handguns and National Council to Control Handguns) it is suffering a nation-wide boycott organized by outraged gun owners. (S&W has little to fear from such a boycott, for its back orders from domestic and foreign police and other government agencies far exceed its annual handgun production.)

While the pejorative implications of "lobby" do not really apply to either side in the handgun prohibition controversy, the *proponents* come closer to it, while the opponents qualify only as a "people's lobby." Compare their sources of funding and respective means of influencing legislation: A few years ago a liberal millionaire who had himself heavily invested in the military arms industry loaned a new national handgun prohibition organization the money to finance a nationwide mail solicitation for funds. It collapsed when the responsive contributions barely exceeded the amount of the loan. In contrast, although the National Rifle Association does not itself lobby, and so could technically be qualified to receive tax-exempt contributions, it has never attempted to qualify. While it would doubtless not turn down a millionaire's contributions, its enormous funding comes almost exclusively from membership dues and contributions of $50.00 or less. The same is true of other organizations that do lobby, like the Citizen's Committee for the Right to Keep and Bear Arms, Gun Owners of America, the Firearms Lobby of America, and the NRA's own separate lobbying organization. In terms of influence upon legislative bodies, the forte of the handgun prohibition movement (like the liquor prohibition movement before it) is the articulate support given by many of the most humane, good-hearted, and progressive leaders in public and academic life. In contrast, the forte of the gun organizations, demonstrated time after time from 1934 to the present, is the marshaling of overwhelming numbers of individual citizens. These are often not particularly articulate people, and individually they are completely without influence. But in the aggregate they are a force to be reckoned with. Illustrative is a 1978 controversy in which Congress prevented the Carter Administration from imposing regulations on the firearms industry that the gun organizations had denounced as tantamount to national gun registration. Informed citizens should have been aware of the issue, for it was heavily and repeatedly publicized in the media during months of regulatory agency and Congressional hearings. In addition, the antigun organizations circulated repeated pleas for public support:

> This is our first opportunity in some time to let the Carter Administration know that the *majority* of the public wants

reasonable gun control [National Coalition to Ban Handguns; emphasis in original]. The majority of Americans want stronger handgun control, but they must be heard. Write a letter or postcard. Urge friends *and* family to do the same . . . [National Council to Control Handguns].

The final tally of responsive mail was nearly 283,000 letters and over 62,000 postcards — 7,800 supporting the proposed regulations and 337,000 opposing them.

This is typical of public response whenever handgun restrictions are considered by any branch of federal or state government. Even the most ardently antigun legislators admit to being daunted by the fact that constituent response is always overwhelmingly hostile, sometimes by more than a 50-1 ratio. For liberals to dismiss such responses as "the gun lobby" is not only misleading, but hypocritical to boot. Such phenomena we correctly describe as "democracy in action" when letters from NAACP or Sierra Club members pour in on legislation they oppose.

Public Opinion on Handgun Prohibition

The inability of the anti-gun organizations to marshall the majoritarian support they claim prompts deeper examination of those claims. They turn out to be based upon answers to questions in a series of polls that are so vaguely worded as to make the answers unintelligible. How can we assign meaning to inquiries like "should the laws covering the sale of handguns be made more strict?" [Gallup, 1975] without knowing how strict the respondent thought the laws were already? The only poll ever to explore that found that 79 percent of the public could not even identify three out of five of the simplest federal gun-sale restrictions. Predictably, the less restrictions the respondent knew about, the more likely he was to think "stricter" laws were needed. A recent poll in Missouri (a state with exceptionally stringent gun laws) was published with the headline "Voters Back Gun Control." Upon examination, the answers showed a majority did not support licensing procedures similar to those which (though they apparently didn't know it) have existed in Missouri for 65 years.

Even when the polls try to solicit opinion as to a specific kind of restriction, inadequate wording often renders the question meaningless. Thus the frequent question whether a "license" or "permit" should be required for handgun ownership may be interpreted by a New Yorker in light of the Sullivan Law (i.e., virtual handgun prohibition) but by an Illinois resident in light of that state's automatic licensure for anyone free of criminal convictions. Other respondents may interpret it as implying some kind of proficiency testing, as in drivers licensing. The pollsters are ill-equipped either to formulate questions or interpret results because they are themselves lamentably ignorant of current law or proposed changes. Thus the commentary to a recent poll release finds its authors confusing handgun licensure (in any of its forms) with handgun registration. Similarly, Gallup releases contain gross mischaracterizations of state gun laws.

Handgun prohibition appears to enjoy only minority support — and that steadily dwindling — according to the results of the few polls that have directly asked whether respondents want to "outlaw handguns except for police use" [Gallup, September 4, 1959; June 5, 1975]. In the 1959 Gallup poll 59 percent of respondents favored outlawing handguns, with 35 percent opposed and the rest expressing no opinion. But by 1975 sentiment had reversed, the same question elicited a 55 percent negative response with 41 percent supporting. Harris' 1975 question as to a "law that banned the ownership of all handguns by private citizens" found 57 percent opposed and 37 percent favoring. Three years later the minority supporting handgun restrictions had dwindled still more, according to a Cambridge Reports (Patrick Caddell) national poll commissioned by one of the anti-gun organizations. Even as to the less drastic measure of leaving presently owned guns but banning "the future manufacture and sale of all handguns," 23 percent strongly favored this and 9 percent somewhat favored it (total 32 percent), while 36 percent were strongly opposed and 22 percent somewhat so (total 58 percent).

The mistaken impression that the public supports handgun prohibition has been powerfully aided by the strong personal support which Gallup, Harris, etc. give such legislation. The partisanship of Gallup releases is epitomized by one that began by describing three recent tragedies with guns and then continued: "the public today shows itself willing to adopt stricter firearms legislation which might possibly have averted [these incidents]." (A pro-gun fanatic could, of course, have picked out three incidents of people defending themselves with handguns and proceeded to the effect that these people would be dead today if legislation now favored by the public, etc., etc.) Although Gallup releases headline even a one-percentage-point increase over several years in public *support* for "gun control," Gallup has never mentioned the complete reversal in sentiment on banning handguns between 1959 and 1975. Indeed, in the 1975 release, even the question and results on handgun prohibition are buried in the back; the release is headlined: "Public Overwhelmingly Favors Registration of All Firearms." Similarly, the 1975 Harris Poll, in which fewer people yet supported handgun prohibition, is headlined "Strong Support For Gun Control."

Greater yet was the opposition to handgun prohibition revealed by the 1975 Decision Making Information poll, one of two really extensive polls ever done of public attitudes on the gun issue. (The DMI and the 1978 Cambridge Report poll, both privately commissioned — though by opposite sides — involved many times more questions than the Gallup, etc., which are limited to three or four.) In the DMI poll, 39 percent of the respondents were strongly opposed to handgun prohibition and 31 percent inclined to opposition (total 70 percent) while 15 percent strongly endorsed it and 10 percent were inclined to (25 percent).

Handgun prohibition advocates dismissed the DMI poll because it had been commissioned by the NRA, even though it was independently conducted with scrupulous neutrality by a prestigious private polling organization. But the accuracy of the DMI results, as opposed to that of Gallup and Harris, seemed demonstrated when handgun prohibitionists put it to a public referendum in Massachusetts, a state they selected as electorally the most liberal in the nation. Though Gallup and Harris had said that a majority of Easterners and urbanites support banning handguns, the Massachusetts initiative lost by slightly more than 70 percent. It carried not one major city, not even Cambridge.

The trend in state legislation is itself strong evidence of a steady, long-term decrease in public support for handgun prohibition. In the first thirty-four years of the twentieth century nine states enacted laws either banning handgun sales completely or requiring a permit which the authorities had broad discretion not to issue. In the ensuing forty-five years only Puerto Rico added itself to this group, while New Jersey reaffirmed its membership and South Carolina repealed its law — the oldest and most stringent of them all. (Two of the original nine had repealed their laws before 1934.)

This dwindling of support for handgun prohibition may seem strange in light of the very one-sided debate on the subject over the past twenty years. The argument for handgun prohibition is a plausible one, and has been forcefully and articulately presented by distinguished political and academic figures. The other side has all too often been represented by people whose intellectual sophistication was insufficient to their argument, and whose manner of presentation did their position more harm than good. But more significant than this debate seems to have been social changes in American life and attitudes since the halcyon years of handgun prohibition in the early part of the century. When handguns were owned by less than 5 percent of the civilian population, it was easy to associate such ownership with groups stereotyped as congenitally or ideologically unfit to own weapons. Fortunately those stereotypes have disappeared — at least to the extent that people of Eastern and Southern European ancestry are accepted as good Americans and good neighbors. Few Americans today would openly argue that any racial or ethnic group should be barred from firearms ownership. Today, also, the innocent pleasures of target shooting and gun collecting are accepted by most Americans, and a less numerous, but still quite large majority, sees self-defense as a justifiable reason for handgun ownership. A major factor in these attitudes is that by the late 1970's nearly half of all American households contained at least one gun, and nearly a quarter contained a handgun. People are unlikely to support confiscation of their own property or of property they know to be owned and deeply valued by their families, friends, and neighbors.

SECTION II: Crime, Suicide, and Accidents: Some Cross-national and Cross-cultural Comparisons

Frequency of Problematic Cross-Societal and Cross-Cultural Comparisons

From the early part of the century, when American handgun restrictions were modeled on European legislation, the debate has continually involved cross-national and cross-cultural comparisons. Thus Congressman Robert Drinan (D-Mass.), the sponsor of several handgun prohibition bills, states that "alone among the Western nations, the United States permits the unrestricted availability of handguns, and alone it suffers an astronomical crime rate." If similar statements did not abound, it would be surprising that anyone — much less a legal scholar like Representative Drinan — could pack so many errors of law fact into one medium-sized sentence. First, the United States does not lead the Western nations in violent crime. Mexico, for instance, has a homicide rate several times greater than ours, though its handgun legislation approximates that urged by Representative Drinan. Second, the United States does not have unrestricted availability of handguns. Federal law bars sale to felons, minors, the mentally unstable, and narcotics addicts, among others. Several states have gone beyond this to impose the same kind of handgun permit requirements that Representative Drinan endorses. In some, these are administered more restrictively than in any other Western nation. In fact, a number of other Western nations have firearms restrictions approximating those of our least restrictive states. The rate of actual firearms ownership in countries like Switzerland or Israel well exceeds that in the United States. Moreover, those countries and several others allow, encourage, or even require widespread civilian ownership of fully automatic (i.e., machine gun type) weapons which have been forbidden to American civilians for almost fifty years.

Value of Cross-Societal Comparisons

Necessarily studies of *American* conditions must provide the primary evidence in any evaluation of firearms in this country. But because foreign comparisons may be enlightening — and because they are so often misused — it is appropriate to preface consideration of the American evidence with some carefully researched and reasoned comparative discussions. For this reason we begin with selections from the writings of British police Superintendent Colin Greenwood and University of California economist Joseph Magaddino.

COLIN GREENWOOD

At forty-six, Colin Greenwood holds the rank of Superintendent in the West Yorkshire Metropolitan Police and is Deputy Commander of a large territorial division based on the town of Halifax. In 1954 he joined the police in the rank of constable after five years in the Coldstream Guards. He has headed a firearms training department, has written widely on firearms for police and firearms technical journals (including a 1976 essay in the Queen's Police Essay competition which was awarded the gold medal), and is generally regarded as Britain's leading authority on sidearms and their use by the police. In 1970 Superintendent Greenwood took a leave of absence to become a Fellow at the Cambridge University Institute of Criminology. There he conducted the only in-depth study of British firearms controls that has ever been done. The resulting book, *Firearms Control: A Study of Armed Crime and Firearms Control in England and Wales*, was sharply critical of England's firearms policies as being fuzzy in objective and based upon inadequate, incompetent, and misleading statistics, and needlessly harsh, inept, and/or inconsistent standards of administration. In general, he concluded that the pistol-licensing system instituted in 1920 had been complied with only because Britain was then so peaceful that few people thought it necessary to keep weapons for self-defense. In terms of coercive enforcement the licensing system has never been successful in denying firearms to those who wished to use them for criminal purposes. Particularly significant is Greenwood's finding that when violent crime began to skyrocket in the 1960s, a frantic intensification of anti-pistol enforcement (and extension of the licensing requirements to rifles and then shotguns) proved unsuccessful in stemming the trend. It resulted only in the diversion of enormous police resources to what Superintendent Greenwood found a useless measure — and an immense inconvenience and harrassment of those wanting firearms for legitimate sporting uses.

Since 1972, Superintendent Greenwood has on several occasions written critically of the attempt — based upon comparisons with the situation in the United States — to extend to shotgun ownership the same restrictive standards now applicable to pistols and rifles. The following is from "Another Syndrome," which appears in the Autumn, 1978, issue of the magazine of the Wildfowler's Association of Great Britain and Ireland. [Note: British spelling has been retained throughout the following]:

The present policy of this Government, and the long standing policy of the Civil Servants at the Home Office (who seem in this context to have more authority than the elected Government) is that the existing system of controlling firearms, and particularly shotguns, is to be tightened as soon as Parliamentary time becomes available. A great deal of comment has been made in public since the publication in 1973 of a Green Paper setting out the Home Office policy.[1] Much of the opposition to that policy has been based on research which tends to show that there is no correlation between the number of firearms in private hands or the degree of control over those firearms and the rate of armed crime. That proposition may be examined on a historical or a comparative perspective. The historical perspective, as it relates to England and Wales, was explored in depth by this writer who concluded:

"No matter how one approaches the figures, one is forced to the rather startling conclusion that the use of firearms in crime was very much less when there were no controls of any sort and when anyone, convicted criminal or lunatic, could buy any type of firearm without restriction. Half a century of strict controls on pistols has ended, perversely, with a far greater use of this class of weapon in crime than ever before."[2]

To date, no-one has attempted a comprehensive comparison, country by country, to relate the type of control exercised and the extent to which firearms are available to the general public (legally or illegally) with the level of armed crime. Such a study would be very complex. It would be very difficult to establish the level of evasion of controls with any precision and any international comparison of crime rates is inevitably complicated by differences in definition and reporting procedures. A good deal of work has been done in various countries and, overall, the amount of information is quite large. It is the process of international comparison itself which creates the major difficulty.

Little research has been done in England and Home Office policy has been criticised as being based on insupportable assumptions rather than sound research. The policy has remained unchanged over the years but the arguments in support of the policy change at frequent intervals. These changes in supporting theories are set out in the comments of Ministers during debates and, most often, in letters sent out from the Home Office in reply to the growing volume of protest. The argument is advanced by opponents of the policy that the use of pistols in crime has grown significantly in spite of strict controls and that the patterns of change in the use of all types of weapon is unaffected by the imposition of controls. The reply currently in vogue to answer all criticisms of the effectiveness of the system is predictable, consistent and repetitive. So repetitive, indeed, that it might be described as the "look-at-what-happens-in-America" syndrome.

A syndrome may be defined as a combination of the symptoms of a disease. In this case the disease is a total failure to understand the problems connected with the control of violent crime, and the combination of symptoms can perhaps best be illustrated by quoting from the debate of the Third Standing Committee on Statutory Instruments on 3rd May 1978 when an increase in charges made under the Firearms Act was being considered. Doctor Shirley Summerskill was promoting the Home Office view. In commenting on the proposition that further controls were unlikely to be effective, she said, "I can only say that in America, where there are no controls, there were in 1974, 197,753 robberies involving the use of a firearm. In England and Wales there were 645 such robberies in that year. In 1974, 128 law enforcement officers were killed with firearms in the United States. It is common knowledge that there is more firearm violence in the United States." Similar views, quoting a whole range of figures about violence generally, and firearms violence in particular in the United States have appeared in numerous letters from the Home Office, usually over the signature of one of the Ministers of State. There we have the syndrome, and its component symptoms are:

1.   A belief that there are no gun controls in the United States.

2.   A belief that the use of firearms in crime is evenly and consistently higher than in England.

3.   The conclusion that No. 2 is a direct consequence of No. 1, and consequently the belief that the existence of controls in Britain is a cause of, or a major factor in the lower rate of armed crime here.

Most Americans would be more than a little surprised to learn that there are no gun controls in their country. In fact there are rather more than 20,000 statutes at Federal, State and local levels which are concerned with the acquisition, ownership or carrying of firearms. Federal controls include the 1968 Gun Control Act which is enforced by the very large sector of the Bureau of Alcohol, Tobacco and Firearms. During 1977 Agents of that Department confiscated some 10,000 guns in the course of their activities. The degree of control exercised is such that they now claim that they can trace about 90% of all guns sold since 1968. At City level, New York has had its Sullivan Law since 1911, giving it a control over handguns far stricter than anything operating in England. [Editor's note: The Sullivan Law is a state law, but it vests the discretion to issue pistol permits in local police. The law is specially tailored to the needs of New York City. Thus a New York City permit is good throughout the state. In comparison a permit issued in some other city (say Buffalo) is good in Buffalo or any part of the state *except* New York City. It is a crime for a Buffalo resident to have his gun in New York City even though he has a Buffalo permit — unless that permit has been validated by the New York City police. This recognizes the historical reality that standards for granting permits differ throughout the state, being perhaps difficult in Buffalo but virtually impossible in New York City.] In 1971 there were in existence [in New York City] only 564 pistol permits which did not relate to people like bank guards who require guns in the course of their employment. This is far below the level of private ownership in any part of England. At least four cities, New York, Chicago, Detroit and Washington, have gun control measures which are much more stringent than anything found in England. Incidentally, over 20% of the country's homicides are committed in those four cities, though they have only 6% of the population.

Despite New York's strict controls on handguns it has been estimated that there are over one million illegal guns in that city.[3] The Homicide rate is well above the national average, as is the rate of armed robbery and other violent crime. The pundits seek to explain this by saying that the shortage of legally held firearms in New York is compensated for by the ease with which firearms can be bought elsewhere and taken into the city. Perhaps, but if that is true it should also apply to cities like Minneapolis, which has a homicide rate of 2.9 per 100,000 against New York's 17.5, but which has no Sullivan Act. It should also apply across the unguarded border in Canada where armed crime generally is very much lower. The United States is a vast country where crime rates vary from the appalling levels of cities such as New York and Detroit to levels far below those to be found in many parts of England. The homicide rate, for example, varies from 0.7 to 21.0 per 100,000. . . .

The situation in the United States is very complicated. Generally speaking it can be said that, in contrast with England, there is a higher level of gun ownership, a higher incidence of violent crime, and a higher incidence of the use of firearms in crime. But these facts are too general and subject to too many exceptions to be capable of use in any comparative analysis. There are parts of the USA which have high rates of armed crime and savage gun controls; there are parts with high armed crime rates and virtually no gun control; and there are parts with virtually no gun control and very low rates of armed crime. The level of violent crime varies dramatically amongst the different ethnic groups. The rate of violent crime and the type of weapon used in that crime has more relevance to the ethnic origins of the offender that to the availability of firearms.

Homicide rates are often used as indicators of the levels of violent crime in international comparisons. The British Office of Health Economics recently published a brief but useful survey of this problem.[4] The comparative homicide rates for 1972 show the United States very much higher in the list than any of the Western

European countries, but very much lower than countries such as Mexico where there is a strict system of gun control. The authors of that report have noted:

"One reason often given for the high numbers of murders and manslaughters in the United States is the easy availability of firearms, which in 1973 accounted (together with explosives) for the deaths of just over 67 per cent of the total 20,465 recorded victims. But the strong correlation with racial and linked socio-economic variables suggest that the underlying determinants of the homicide rate relate to particular cultural factors."

This conclusion is in line with the findings of many other studies. . . . [Citations omitted.]

These comments about the relationship between firearms control or availability and the use of firearms in crime can be applied to all violent crime. It is true that there are more robberies involving a firearm in the U.S.A. than there are in Britain. There are also more robberies involving knives and more in which the only weapon was the hands or feet of the assailant. If it is suggested that the easier availability of firearms is a cause of firearms robberies, is it also suggested that knives are less readily available in England than they are in the U.S.A., or that American criminals have more hands and feet than their British counterpart? What can be shown is that American criminals are more willing to use extreme violence and the causes of this are linked to many ethnic and social factors, but not to the availability of any particular class of weapon.

Any objective look at the wider international scene will show that there is no way in which crime can be correlated with the availability of firearms or the types of control established. In Mexico, for example, the system of firearms control is very much more stringent than is generally the case in the U.S.A., yet Mexico has a much higher homicide rate and armed crime generally is higher. A classic case for comparison can be found in Jamaica where the establishment of the most rigorous system of gun control imaginable, a total ban with all embracing enforcement powers, has been tested as a method of reducing armed crime. The consequences were, to say the least, surprising.

Prior to independence in 1962, Jamaica enjoyed a tolerable level of crime and had a system of firearms control which permitted the private ownership of guns, subject to a system of police permits. Between 1962 and 1973 the homicide rate rose by no less than 450 per cent and other violent crime such as armed robbery rose even more sharply. One particular incident early in 1973 brought in its wake the Draconian gun ban. Following the robbery and shooting of four business men there was enacted a total ban on the private ownership of any type of gun or ammunition. Police immediately seized those held by permit holders. Police were then granted an absolute right to stop and search anyone or any vehicle and to enter any house or other building if they believed firearms or ammunition to be present. They were authorised to arrest without warrant anyone found in possession of even a single cartridge. Anyone arrested was taken before a special 'gun court' and no bail was allowed. Following a delay of anything from hours to weeks, the person was arraigned before a secret court with no representation. Those convicted were imprisoned in a special 'gun stockade' for an indeterminate period. The stockade was surrounded by barbed wire, watch towers and machine guns. The rate of armed crime dropped during the three months following the introduction of this system, and then it rocketed. Jamaica rapidly reached the stage where any political activity was marked by gangs of armed men roaming the streets. Shooting and assassination were common. Elections or other activities required large numbers of armed soldiers to keep order. Armed robberies and other crime involving firearms set new records almost daily, and no-one was safe. Lady Sarah Spencer Churchill and her husband left their home on the island after gunmen broke into her house, shot one of her guests and attacked her. The Commissioner of Corrections for the island was later to admit that the gun ban had in no way affected the hard core criminals. The worst excesses of this system have now been corrected, but the real lesson does not seem to have got across.

At the other end of the spectrum we have in Europe the country which has the highest level of access to firearms and the highest level of private ownership of any civilised nation. In Switzerland, virtually every man remains a member of the armed forces which is primarily a reserve force. He is required to keep at home an assault rifle, a sub-machine gun or a pistol with an ample supply of ammunition. In addition, the rate of private ownership of firearms is exceptionally high. Pistols are subject to a permit system, but permits are issued on demand except to prohibited persons such as criminals or lunatics. Sales from dealers must be recorded in his register but sales between individuals are subject to no records system. Rifles and shotguns are uncontrolled. In virtually every household in the country there are several guns and plenty of ammunition and the guns are usually kept on display. Yet the rate of crime involving the use of firearms is so low that it is not recorded — no other modern industrial country can boast such a situation. These facts seem consistently to be ignored by the "look-at-what-happens-in-America" brigade.

At first glance it may seem odd or even perverse to suggest that statutory controls on the private ownership of firearms are irrelevant to the problem of armed crime, yet that is precisely what the evidence shows. Armed crime and violent crime generally are products of ethnic and social factors unrelated to the availability of a particular type of weapon. The numbers of firearms required to satisfy the 'crime' market is minute, and these are supplied no matter what controls are instituted. Controls have had serious effects on legitimate users of firearms, but there is no case, either in the history of this country or in the experience of other countries, in which controls can be shown to have restricted the flow of weapons to criminals or in any way reduced armed crime. Any superficial examination of either the historical or the international view of the problem will show that there is not one jot of evidence which would in any way support what is being said and done at the Home Office. Ministers of State in seeking to support this programme have to rely on shallow, facile and easily disproved statements which say little for the briefing they receive or the quality of the research underlying them. Perhaps there is some evidence somewhere to support the Government's case. If that be so, they should have it properly researched and presented so that all may see it.

[Superintendent Greenwood offered the following comments on the subject of firearms accidents and other misuse in the British *Shooting Times and Country Magazine* for August 24-30, 1978, under the title "Extending an Error." Superintendent Greenwood is answering an earlier article in the same magazine by a Mr. G. Holderness.]

Mr. Holderness advocates the imposition of a shooting test in addition to (and not as an alternative to) the existing system of police enquiries. He is vague about what such a test would involve and how it would be conducted and financed (another massive increase in fees, perhaps). No doubt the writer had the best of intentions, wishing to support the idea of "law and order" and the police whilst at the same time seeking to improve the lot and the standing of the shooting public. But good intentions alone are adequate only for paving the road to hell. The fact is that the entire article was based on illogicalities and false assumptions.

The first false assumption relates to that oft-made comparison with motor cars. One has to pass a test before driving a car, we are told, then why not a test for the ownership of guns? Well, of course, the first part of that proposition is quite wrong. One does not have to pass a test before driving a car. One may drive a car without passing a test, without a licence, without insurance, without having the vehicle tested and without paying road tax provided the car is used, as a shotgun invariably is, on private property. The comparison must be valid if shotgunners used their guns primarily up and down the High Street or along the M1, but otherwise it is fallacious.

"Dreadful shooting accidents occur every year," we are told. What we are not told is where and how they occur, what proportion of those involved are not certificate holders, and what relevance any test might have to the specific cause of accidents. Many shooting accidents occur in the home when deliberate horseplay is sometimes involved. Other accidents are a consequence of a split second's carelessness. No evidence has been produced to suggest that taking a test on one occasion would affect the accident rate. In any event shooting accidents are very rare indeed in relation to the numbers of guns in use and the numbers of people involved. To suggest that there is a need for a test implies, quite falsely, that shooting is abnormally dangerous. Hazards from other leisure activities are far greater. Deaths by drowning, for example, are very much more common than deaths by shooting. Perhaps we should make it a crime to enter water more than two feet deep unless one has passed a swimming test — that might well save many lives if it could be enforced. And what about riding accidents? Shall we have a compulsory test before a person may hack or hunt?

It seems that the main reason for advocating a shooting test is to demonstrate a sense of responsibility in the hope that the authorities will reciprocate by not imposing other restrictions which might be even more irksome. This somewhat odd bargain seems to be continually sought by some members of the shooting fraternity. Reference to recent events will show that those in authority want no such compromise. They are concerned to reduce the numbers of shotguns in private hands and many say so openly. They move one step at a time towards a goal which in some cases involves a virtual ban on the private ownership of guns. Any concessions are made by the shooting community or their representatives and each of them represents another step forward towards impossible restrictions or a total ban. There are no reverse concessions. Never since controls began has there been any lifting of restrictions in favour of the sportsman.

The last paragraph of Mr. Holderness's article reflects the ultimate nonsense of the sort of thinking which somehow has infected a segment of the shooting public:

> Unnecessary and unreasonable restrictions on the possession and use of arms inhibit and threaten the sport itself and are rightly to be resisted. But do we really want the opposite extreme: a society in which the acquisition of firearms is rendered easy; where, as in America, petty crime can often result in violent death; where human corpses in the street are shudderingly familiar; where, in Shakespeare's words, "Man's life is as cheap as beast's."

Well, now, there is strong, passionate stuff — a frightening prospect eloquently described — but total and absolute rubbish! One wonders how old Mr. Holderness might be and how good is his memory. Perhaps he cannot recall the period before 1968 when shotguns were totally uncontrolled in Britain. Every gun shop, every ironmonger and most second-hand shops had guns openly on display with no security arrangements. Anyone could simply walk in and buy one without let or hindrance. He did not have to go to the police seeking permission, he did not have to ask anyone or tell anyone, he just bought one, two or a hundred if he so wished. The only restrictions applied to persons under 17 or with certain criminal convictions. Now let us think about this carefully. We are not talking about another world or another continent; we are talking about this same Britain. We are not talking about another century or another time, we are speaking of the last decade, within the memory of most people who are now shooting. This was a time and place when, to use Mr. Holderness's own words, "the acquisition of firearms was rendered easy" as it had been for all time previously in this country. Where, then, were those petty crimes which resulted in violent deaths? Where did we experience the shuddering familiarity of corpses in the streets of England? Perhaps Mr. Holderness has not read the many studies which establish that there is no correlation between the numbers of firearms in a community or the degree of control over them and the rate of armed crime. Surely, though, he can accept the empirical evidence of his own experience and that of many thousands of his fellow shooters. The unrestricted sales of shotguns in this country created no problem, and their subsequent control has produced no discernable effect in the armed crime rate.

It would be useful to examine just how shotgun controls came into effect. During the early 1960s there had been occasional noises about shotguns and armed crime in the House of Commons. Questions about controlling shotguns always met with the same response from the police, the Home Office and Ministers. Sir Frank Soskice's reply of February 11, 1965, was typical when he said that after careful consideration and consultation with the police, the Home Office did not propose to control shotguns because "the burden which certificates would place on the police would not be justified by the benefits which would result." That view was repeated many times. Police and Home Office were firmly of the view that shotgun controls were just not worth the effort. The last time the statement was made was by Roy Jenkins in June, 1966. Three months later he had changed his tune completely and announced that he was "endeavouring to draw up plans to end the unrestricted purchase of shotguns. They can be purchased far too easily, by mail order or other means, and there is evidence that the criminal use of shotguns is increasing rapidly." That is a pretty sharp change of tune even for a politician. Search as one may through the evidence, there is nothing to justify it except the shooting, in August, of three London policemen. There was a consequent public outcry and strong demands for the re-introduction of capital punishment. Jenkins, who was a confirmed abolitionist, would not even consider the capital punishment issue, but he did propose shotgun controls which could hardly have been less relevant because the policemen were killed with pistols.

There is no escaping the conclusion that shotgun controls were introduced in the full knowledge that they would have no effect, simply as a sop to take the pressure off the capital punishment issue. The evidence is all there to be found in Hansard and elsewhere. The police and everyone concerned knew perfectly well that shotgun controls would have no effect, yet very soon after they were introduced chief constables were seeking to extend their powers and tighten their grip on all aspects of the ownership and use of shotguns.

Shotgun controls were quite literally sneaked through Parliament wrapped in a controversial Criminal Justice Bill. The controls were virtually undebated in the House and unchallenged outside. The shooting organisations failed miserably in their duty to their members; they were totally unprepared and totally useless when action was needed. Now we see representatives of shooting organisations and apparently responsible shooting men proposing more and more restrictions without stopping to consider the problem to which the legislation is supposed to be addressed, without thought of the masses of hard evidence already accumulated for them.

One wonders what it is about present day Britain which compels people to seek to control and regulate every aspect of life. Whatever it is, shooters are not immune and, indeed, seem to be their own worst enemies. It is sad to see these people rushing like lemmings over a cliff into a mass of controls and bureaucracy which will eventually destroy them and their sport. They ignore not only the evidence of research, but the irrefutable evidence of their own experience. Freedoms lost are not easily regained. Bureaucracy will not give up its stranglehold once established. There is already too much law, too much control and too much bureaucracy directed only at the legitimate shooter. The evidence shows quite clearly that these controls have had, and will have, no significant effect on the rate of armed crime. A cardinal rule of bureaucracy is that it is better to extend an error than to admit a mistake. For the future of the sport we should ensure that, though the Home Office can be relied upon to follow that rule, the shooting community will not.

[Superintendent Greenwood prepared for the Autumn, 1977, issue of the Wildfowlers' magazine "an examination of the effect of statutory controls on the type of weapon used in serious crime." Reprinted here are sections covering homicide and robbery in Great Britain.]

Homicide

Homicide includes murder, manslaughter and infanticide. Until recently, statistical tables attempted to distinguish between these classes but, from 1973, homicide is treated as a single class for many purposes. This change wisely takes account of the fact that the legal position surrounding murder has so changed in recent years that circumstances which, in the past, would have led to a conviction for murder might well now result in a conviction for manslaughter. The interpretation of homicide statistics is complicated by the fact that the figures are adjusted after the end of the statistical year to take account of cases in which a court finds the case to be one of self defence, accident, etc. The figures published in each year's annual statistics are therefore subject to further adjustment and the final figure may not be arrived at for some time. At any one time, the current year's published figure will include some cases which will eventually be removed from the statistics. The number of cases originally recorded as homicide is compared with the numbers finally so recorded in Table 4.[6] The re-classification is not complete for the last two years and those figures may be reduced by a further 0.3% and 14% respectively. The figures in Table 4 are reproduced graphically in Figure 1 to show that the overall trend in homicide is positively upwards.

TABLE 4

HOMICIDE IN ENGLAND AND WALES

Year	No. Originally Recorded as Homicide	No. Finally Classified as Homicide	% + or − on previous years
1967	414	354	—
1968	420	360	+ 1.6
1969	395	332	− 7.7
1970	396	342	+ 3.0
1971	459	407	+19.0
1972	480	411	+ 0.7
1973	465	391	− 4.6
1974	599	527	+34.7
1975	511	451	−14.4

FIGURE 1

TRENDS IN OFFENCES RECORDED AS HOMICIDE

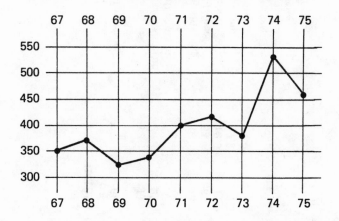

Only a small proportion of homicides involve shooting. Table 5 shows these by the types of weapon used and the percentage use of each weapon.

Figure 2 shows (on a vertical scale five times that of Figure 1) the trend in homicide by shooting and with each type of weapon.

FIGURE 2

TRENDS IN HOMICIDE BY SHOOTING

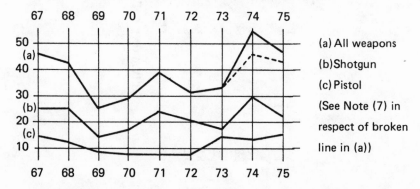

(a) All weapons

(b) Shotgun

(c) Pistol

(See Note (7) in respect of broken line in (a))

Table 6 may help put the matter even further into perspective by showing the methods used in homicides in 1975 by number and percentage. It will be seen that shooting is far from the most popular method. In relation to the chances of being shot, one is about three times more likely to be stabbed to death, twice as likely to be beaten or kicked to death, 50% more likely to be

TABLE 5

HOMICIDES BY SHOOTING IN ENGLAND AND WALES

Type of Weapon	'67	'68	'69	'70	'71	'72	'73	'74	'75
Pistol	12	11	6	8	8	7	14	13	14
Long Barrel shotgun	26	27	13	15	24	21	18	30	23
Sawn off shotgun	8	5	2	2	—	1	—	5	6
Others	8	5	5	4	5	2	—	3	3
Total by shooting	46	43	26	29	38	31	32	51*	46*
Total Offences	354	360	332	342	407	410	391	527*	451*
% by shooting	12.9	11.9	7.8	8.4	9.3	7.5	8.1	9.6	10.1
% by shotgun	7.3	7.5	3.9	4.3	5.8	5.1	4.6	5.6	5.0
% by pistol	3.3	3.0	1.8	2.3	1.9	1.7	3.5	2.4	2.8

(Note * These are unadjusted figures.)[7]

strangled, and about as likely to be beaten to death with a blunt instrument.

TABLE 6

METHODS USED IN HOMICIDE IN ENGLAND AND WALES IN 1975

Method	Number	%
Sharp instrument	140	31.0
Hitting/kicking etc.	95	21.0
Strangulation/asphyxia etc.	71	15.9
Shooting	46	10.1
Blunt instrument	41	9.0
Explosion	9	1.9
Others	43	9.5
Not known	6	1.3

The facts, then, are that the general trend in homicide is progressively upwards. The use of firearms in homicide fluctuates, but during the period 1967 to 1975, we start with 46 and end with 46 and the overall trend is more or less constant or slightly down. For the reasons explained in Note 7 the figures for the last two years may ultimately be 46 and 43 (or even less), reinforcing that point. It is a fact that, each year, shotguns are used in a surprisingly constant proportion of homicides, amounting to about 5%. It is also a fact that the shotgun is used about twice as frequently as the pistol. In respect of neither weapon has the number of cases or their relationship with the total changed significantly. The proposition that the use of the shotgun in homicide is increasing disproportionately is therefore totally false.

To understand the fact that shotguns are used in about twice as many homicides as pistols, it is necessary to examine:

(a)   The relative availability of each weapon.

(b)   The nature of the events which lead to a homicide.

(c)   The effect which relative availability might have on the choice of weapon and on the ultimate result of the incident.

(d)   The effect which legislation might have on the relative availability of a particular type of weapon.

It is very difficult to give an estimate of the numbers of pistols and shotguns in England and Wales. In an earlier study[8] it was estimated that there are about 63,000 legally held pistols, but the evidence suggests that the number illegally held exceeds that total.

As a best estimate, it might be said that there are about 150,000 pistols in the country. About three quarters of a million people hold shotgun certificates and many of them own more than one gun. Taking account of non-certificate holders who still have shotguns, the total number of shotguns in the country might be around 1,500,000. Thus it is probable that there are ten shotguns for every pistol in the country. Furthermore, pistols are usually less readily to hand. The legally held ones are normally for target shooting rather than defence and are subject to a condition that they must be kept in a safe place. Many people such as farmers and gamekeepers see a need to keep a shotgun readily available at all times, and many other people have shotguns on display in cabinets. There is no condition about the manner in which shotguns must be kept. Though the ratio of shotguns to pistols is probably of the order of 10 to 1, their relative availability is more like 15 or 20 to 1.

Though placed in a single statistical category, the events which are eventually classified as homicide are diverse. In one case a bank robbery can result in the shooting down of an innocent bank clerk; in another, a man may find his wife in bed with another man and take the carving knife to them; in yet another, a drunken brawl may result in one man beating another to death with his bare hands. In fact, homicide is overwhelmingly a domestic matter in which killer and victim are well known to each other and the cause of the killing is concerned with the relationship. Table 7 shows the relationship of the victim with the killer for the last couple of years.

The vast majority of homicides occur in a situation of stress between persons well known to each other and for motives of jealousy, rage, etc. In 1975, only 43 homicides were in the course of furtherance of theft, and four were whilst resisting arrest. Thus, only about 10.4% were connected with 'crime' of that sort. In well over 70% of the cases, a domestic situation got out of hand and, in such circumstances, the people involved are likely to turn to whatever weapon is to hand. It seems to be the firm view of the Home Office that the mere availability of a particular type of firearm is a significant factor in homicides of this sort, and in the cases of unlawful wounding which frequently arise in precisely the same circumstances. In their booklet "Firearms in Crime"[9] at paragraph 31, it is said, "Offenders do not normally start out with

TABLE 7

HOMICIDE IN ENGLAND AND WALES, RELATIONSHIP OF VICTIM WITH KILLER

Victim's Relationship	1974		1975	
	No.	%	No.	%
Acquaintance	89	16.6	87	19.2
Spouse/cohabitant	107	20.0	85	18.8
Son/daughter	98	18.3	54	11.9
Lover	36	6.7	42	9.3
Other relative	16	2.9	22	4.8
Parent	18	3.3	18	3.9
Other associate	30	5.6	12	2.6
Total Domestic	394	73.6	320	70.9
Police/prison officer	1	0.2	3	0.6
Stranger	100	18.6	96	21.2
Not known	40	7.4	32	7.0
Total	535*	—	451	—

(Note * This figure is from the 1974 Statistics and so not adjusted to the level in other tables which is from the 1975 figures)

the intention of wounding a particular person and the violence depends on the availability of a weapon. The controls that exists on the sale and possession of revolvers and pistols serve to make weapons of this type less frequently available for spontaneous use." Again, in paragraph 32, it is said, "Violence is likely to be a spontaneous event, relying on the availability of a weapon." The same theory is propounded in the Green Paper[10] and in several other places. The theory, therefore, is that the victim would not have been killed or injured if the firearm had not been present, and that by removing firearms one can reduce the number of killings or the seriousness of assaults. Indeed, it seems that the suggestion is that such crimes are caused by firearms. That hypothesis is difficult to reconcile with the simple fact that shotguns are 15 times more readily available than pistols and yet are used in only twice as many homicides. It is also difficult to relate to the fact that the general trend in homicide is, and has been for many years, upwards. The trend in homicide by shooting, conversely is steady or downwards, but there is nothing to suggest that firearms have become less readily available. In setting forth this theory and maintaining it, the Home Office has ignored the evidence in several standard works, detailed studies, etc.

Professor Marvin Wolfgang is a leading criminologist, and his book "Patterns in Criminal Homicide"[11] reports detailed studies of this very problem. He concludes:

> Several students of homicide have tried to show that the high number of, or easy access to, firearms in this country [the U.S.A.] is causally related to our relatively high homicide rate. Such a conclusion cannot be drawn from the Philadelphia data. Material subsequently reported in the present study regarding the place where the homicide occurred, relationship between victim and offender, motives, and other variables suggest that the many situations, events and personalities that converge in particular ways and that result in homicide do not depend primarily on the presence or absence of firearms ... More than the availability of a shooting weapon is involved in homicide. Pistols and revolvers are not difficult to purchase, legally or illegally, in Philadelphia. Police interrogation of defendants reveals that most frequently these weapons are bought from friends or acquaintances for such nominal sums as ten or twenty dollars. A penknife or a butcher knife, of course, is much cheaper and more easily obtained. Ready access to knives and little reluctance to engage in physical combat without weapons, or to fight it out, are as important as the availability of some sort of gun. The type of weapon used appears to be, in part, the culmination of assault intentions or events and is only superficially related to causality. To measure quantitively the effect of the presence of firearms on the homicide rate would require knowing the number and type of homicides that would not have occurred had not the offender — or in some cases, the victim — possessed a gun. Research would be required to determine the number of shootings which would have been stabbings, beatings or some other method of inflicting death had no gun been available. It is the contention of this observer that few homicides due to shooting could be avoided merely if a firearm were not immediately present, and that the offender would select some other weapon to achieve the same destructive goal. Probably only in those cases where a felon kills a police officer, or vice

versa, would the homicide be avoided in the absence of a firearm.

The problem was also studied, not in relation to firearms but to spears, in E.S. Tanner's report on homicide in Uganda.[12] He concluded:

The existence of weapons does not appear to precipitate homicide. Although there is a constant factor of the accident of availability, it should be remembered that there are no grounds for supposing that, if a particular weapon had not been available, no homicide would have occurred. If spears were prohibited, deep seated hostilities could just as easily be expressed with sticks and stones.

A more recent study in the U.S.A. followed the imposition on 1st April 1975, in Massachusetts, of a mandatory one year's imprisonment on anyone found carrying a firearm outside the home or place of business without a Firearms Identification Card. (The Bartley-Fox Act.) It is reported[13] that the Harvard Law School's Center for Criminal Justice has studied the first year's application of this law and has found that the use of guns in serious crimes such as robbery did not decrease. In unpremediated crimes such as the type of domestic homicide being considered here, the use of guns did decrease, but not the numbers or seriousness of the crimes. Weapons such as knives were substituted for guns with no diminution of the severity of the effects of assaults.

The fact — and it is a well established fact — is that the availability of one type of weapon or another is not a significant factor in the numbers of homicides or the seriousness of assaults falling into the 'domestic' category. The significant factors are the degree of rage or passion generated and the strength of inhibitions imposed, not merely by the law and any possible punishment, but by the norms of society of which the law is, or should be, an expression. Homicide is increasing, and it is suggested that this is related to the fact that society is demonstrating in many ways that it is less ready to condemn and more willing to excuse or condone the use of violence. Persons in stressful situations are therefore less inhibited and are more likely to allow emotion to take control.

To summarise, the rate of homicide is increasing, but the number of homicides by shooting is steady or declining. Shotguns are used about twice as frequently as pistols, but they are about 15 times more readily available. The situation has remained unaltered by the introduction of shotgun controls in May 1968. There are no grounds for thinking that the imposition of even stricter controls would in any way change the picture. The Green Paper[14] suggested (at paragraph 61) that the imposition of stricter controls might reduce the number of people entitled to own shotguns by 20%, but even if this resulted in a reduction of the number of shotguns in the hands of the less responsible, the evidence indicates that the number of deaths would not be reduced. A total ban on the private ownership of shotguns would reduce the number of deaths by shooting (though illegally held shotguns would still feature). However, even this step could not be expected to reduce the number of homicides. It really is too simple and child-like to expect that a complex course of action such as that involved in domestic homicide can be significantly changed by the simple expedient of entangling one means of killing in a web of paper and bureaucracy.

About 18% of homicides are committed by strangers and over 10% are committed in the course or furtherance of theft. It may well be that, if the pattern of this type of homicide were isolated from the greater mass of domestic homicides, a different picture would be presented. As the statistics are currently presented, such an exercise would not be possible, but it is hoped that it might be possible to obtain figures broken down in this way so that the smaller, but nonetheless important aspect of homicide by shooting can be more fully explored. The most significant aspect of the non-domestic homicide is likely to be the proportion which occurs in the course or furtherance of theft — in robbery gone wrong. It is suggested that a study of robberies will allow conclusions to be drawn which are relevant to that problem.

Robbery

Broadly, robbery is theft by the use or threat or force. It is a crime of which violence is an essential ingredient. It is also a 'professional' crime. Various studies[15] show that a majority of offenders graduate to robbery by way of convictions for lesser crimes. A relatively small number of homicides arise from robberies in which someone was killed and these are classified as homicide, and not robbery, in any statistics. It seems reasonable to assume that trends in this small class of homicide will be reflected within the general trend of robbery. It was shown in Part I that the number of burglaries in which firearms are used is quite small and relatively constant. In part this may be due to the fact that in a crime in which a burglar is confronted and uses a firearm in the course of theft the matter will be recorded as robbery. The remaining burglaries will be those where the firearm was used in the escape or where the object was something other than theft (rape, for example). Part of the rise in the use of firearms by persons who might otherwise be called burglars is therefore transferred to the robbery figures. As an indicator of the levels of serious armed crime, therefore, burglary is not very satisfactory and the relatively constant picture created by the figures must be seen as misleading.

Robbery, then, is real crime, hard crime, the type of crime which is mainly planned and deliberate. If one wishes to examine serious armed crime, then robbery is almost exclusively in that class and, indeed, typifies it. Examination of Home Office figures over the years indicates that robbery is more fully reported, and the use of firearms is more certainly documented than in any other class of crime. Analyses of the Home Office figures for indictable offences in which firearms were used is misleading, but from the robbery figures, long term trends in serious armed crime can be clearly discerned.

Table 8 shows the number of robberies in England and Wales, with the numbers in which firearms were used and the proportion which the latter represent of the total.

It is important to keep in mind that the robberies not involving a firearm were nonetheless violent and included offences in which there were used weapons such as blunt instruments, sharp instruments, ammonia, acid and the like. The results of these attacks have been no less serious than most of the cases in which firearms were used.

Table 8 shows that robbery, a serious and violent crime, is increasing at an alarming rate. Within that classification, robberies in which firearms are used have also shown a frightening increase, but the proportion of robberies in which firearms are used remains remarkably constant. The conclusions which might be drawn from this have previously been discussed at length[16]. Briefly, it can be said that the numerical increase in the number of robberies in

TABLE 8

ROBBERIES AND 'FIREARMS' ROBBERIES IN ENGLAND AND WALES

Year	Total Robberies	Firearms Robberies	Firearms robberies as % of total
1967	4564	265	5.8
1968	4815	372	7.7
1969	6041*	463	7.6
1970	6273	475	7.5
1971	7465	572	7.6
1972	8926	533	5.9
1973	7338	484	6.5
1974	8666	645	7.4
1975	11311	949	8.3

(* Part of the change in 1969 was due to reclassification brought about by the Theft Act 1968)

which firearms are involved is not the most significant factor. The real significance of these figures lies in the fact that they are a measure of the broader increase in the willingness of criminals to use extreme violence. There are good grounds for suggesting that the mere availability of firearms of one sort or another is no more significant in these cases than in domestic homicides and assaults, and that nothing would be gained from a complete banning of firearms if criminals simply turned to other weapons which are no less lethal.

There is no indication from these figures that the introduction of the existing shotgun controls in May 1968 produced any results. The basis of the argument in favour of tighter restrictions on shotguns is that they are becoming the preferred weapon of the serious criminal, and stricter controls will make it more difficult for those people to obtain shotguns. Table 9 shows the number of robberies in which firearms were used, broken down to show the relative use of pistols and shotguns.

In examining these figures it should be recalled that pistols have been subjected to stringent controls since 1920, whilst shotguns were completely uncontrolled until May 1968 from when a relatively simple system of control has existed. Further, it will be recalled that shotguns are about 15 times more readily available than pistols. Despite these factors, pistols have been used in robbery about twice as frequently as shotguns and the proportion

TABLE 9

ROBBERIES IN ENGLAND AND WALES
IN WHICH FIREARMS WERE USED

Year	Total Firearms Robberies	Cases involving Pistols		Cases involving Shotguns	
		No.	%	No.	%
1967	265	125	47.1	53	20.0
1968	372	135	36.2	96	25.8
1969	463	168	36.2	94	20.3
1970	475	163	34.3	88	18.5
1971	572	203	35.4	133	25.2
1972	533	175	32.8	116	21.7
1973	484	181	37.3	112	23.1
1974	645	258	40.0	129	20.0
1975	949	365	38.4	184	19.3

of each type of weapon has been surprisingly constant, at about 38% for pistols and 21% for shotguns. The introduction of shotgun controls in May 1968 seems to have produced an increase in both the number and proportion of cases in which shotguns were used, but it cannot be suggested that these are cause and effect. Other year to year fluctuations are just as great. The pattern of use seems to be totally unrelated to or affected by the type of control imposed on the different weapons.

What can be concluded from these figures, it is suggested, is that criminals involved in serious crime such as robbery select the type of weapon they require and are completely unaffected by controls. That a particular type of weapon is freely available, as was the shotgun prior to 1968, does not persuade criminals to use it more readily; nor will a very long period of the most stringent controls produce a reverse effect. All the evidence suggests that there is a large pool of illegal weapons — large enough to satisfy all the criminal demands. The sources of weapons for that pool are many and various and a reduction of flow from one source would be very quickly compensated for from other sources. The pool includes weapons of all types, and the degree of statutory control applied to any type of weapon is shown to have no significance for the criminal.

JOSEPH P. MAGADDINO

Joseph P. Magaddino is Associate Professor of Economics at California State University, Long Beach. His primary research activities have been in the area of law and economics. His 1972 doctoral thesis at Virginia Polytechnic Institute was a comparison study of the various states' handgun control laws compared with their 1970 crime rates, in order to determine whether and how effective each kind of law was in reducing violent crime. As this thesis (a pioneering application of econometric analytical technique) is highly technical and over two hundred pages in length, it is feasible to reproduce only the general conclusions, and also three special sections dealing with the extent of firearms ownership in the United States and with firearms accidents and suicides.

Firearm Availability

In order to analyze the relationship between firearm availability and misuse, it is important to establish the number of firearms outstanding. Unfortunately, no reliable information exists in this area. Estimates of the total number of firearms range from as few as 50 million to as many as 200 million. The National Commission on the Causes and Prevention of Violence attempted to remedy this problem by engaging in a detailed study of firearm production.[17] Theoretically, the total number of firearms is comprised of domestic production and imported weapons less those lost, destroyed or otherwise nonserviceable. The data for domestic production covered the period from 1899 to 1968, while imported weapons covered the period from 1918 to 1968. The estimates of this Task Force are: 102,911,000 total firearms, 27,931,000 handguns, 39,545,000 rifles, and 34,911,000 shotguns. There are several shortcomings in these estimates, all of which were recognized by the Task Force. First, these estimates understate the total amount of firearms since they omit the number of weapons brought into the country by returning servicemen and tourists. Second, they overstate the total since they do not compensate the figures for the number of weapons destroyed, confiscated, damaged, or otherwise nonserviceable. The Task Force merely assumed the amount of understatement was cancelled out by the overstatement, which appears reasonable given the quality of the data. Table 3.1 shows the number of firearms produced domestically and those imported into the United States during the last decade. Inspection of Table 3.1 demonstrates the steady increase in private firearm purchases. The substantial drop in imported handguns from 1967 to 1968 is due to the Gun Control Act of 1968. Imported handguns dropped from 1,155,000 to 349,000 while domestic production of handguns increased from 1,259,000 to 2,840,000. On the basis of this information it is difficult to deduce the effects of the Gun Control Act of 1968. The Gun Control Act did prohibit the importation of cheap handguns; however, the data seems to indicate that domestic handguns are easily substituted for imported handguns.

[Editor's note: Although the Department of the Treasury does not keep exact figures on the number of domestically manufactured and imported handguns sold at retail each year, it estimates this to total 2.5 million per year for each of the years after 1968. Combining this estimate with the Task Force's estimate that there were almost 28 million handguns in the United States in 1968, it would appear that by 1978 the number of handguns in America was well above 50 million. Again, this estimate does not compensate for the unknown number of handguns destroyed, confiscated, damaged, or otherwise rendered non-serviceable during that ten-year period, nor for the unknown number which were illegally imported in the United States, particularly during the Vietnam War. Any attempt to search servicemen returning from Vietnam, or mail coming in from that country, would have faced some constitutional, and insuperable practical, problems. A spot check of the mail during one period, however, revealed to horrified federal officials that soldiers were sending back not only enormous numbers of small handguns, but also of larger weapons, including assault rifles, machine guns, and even bazookas and mortars which had been disassembled for shipment.]

TABLE 3.1

Firearm Production and Imports
for Private Sale, 1960-1969
(in thousands)[a]

Category	1960	1961	1962	1963	1964	1965	1966	1967	1968	1969
Total Firearms	2,163	2,066	2,232	2,523	3,121	3,522	4,087	5,266	6,180	n.a.[b]
Domestic Total	1,508	1,551	1,670	1,949	2,355	2,526	2,879	3,515	5,290	n.a.[b]
Handguns	475	431	453	491	666	700	926	1,359	2,840	n.a.[b]
Rifles	469	529	579	713	790	850	909	1,100	2,450	n.a.[b]
Shotguns	564	591	639	746	899	976	1,044	1,155		n.a.[b]
Import Total	655	516	561	573	766	996	1,208	1,751	890	826
Handguns	128	168	223	253	347	513	747	1,155	349	227
Rifles	402	231	219	182	245	291	239	277	207	237
Shotguns	125	117	120	139	174	192	222	318	334	363

[a]U.S. Department of Commerce, *Statistical Abstract of the United States, 1971.*
[b]Not available.

Firearm Accidents

Many proponents of gun control view firearm availability as a major contributory factor to accidental deaths. Ramsey Clark, former Attorney General, states in his *Crime in America*:

> Several thousand die from the accidental discharge of guns each year. The accidental death rate in the United States is forty times the rate in the Netherlands, fourteen times Japan's, four times Italy's. The mere presence of so many guns insures a continuation of a high death rate caused by their accidental discharge.[18]

While Mr. Clark's statistics may be correct, they are somewhat misleading. Accidental firearm deaths account for only a small number of the total accidental deaths each year. Table 3.2 lists accidental deaths by major type during the period from 1960 to 1970. As can be seen from Table 3.2, accidental firearm deaths account for approximately 2,300 deaths annually. This figure ranks accidental firearm deaths fifth, and well behind the leading

TABLE 3.2

Principal Types of Accidental Deaths, 1960 to 1970[a]

Year	Motor Vehicle	Falls	Fires Burns[b]	Drowning[c]	Firearms	Machinery	Poison[d]	Poison, by gas,
1960	38,137	19,023	7,645	6,529	2,334	1,951	1,679	1,253
1961	38,091	18,691	7,102	6,525	2,204	1,955	1,804	1,192
1962	40,804	19,589	7,534	6,439	2,092	1,922	1,833	1,376
1963	43,564	19,335	8,172	6,347	2,263	1,965	2,061	1,489
1964	47,700	18,941	7,379	6,709	2,275	1,964	2,100	1,360
1965	49,163	19,984	7,347	6,799	2,344	2,054	2,110	1,526
1966	53,041	20,066	8,084	7,084	2,558	2,070	2,285	1,648
1967	52,924	20,120	7,423	7,076	2,896	2,055	2,506	1,574
1968	54,862	18,651	7,335[e]	7,372[e]	2,394[e]	n.a.[f]	2,583	1,526
1969	56,000	17,600	6,900	7,100	2,400	n.a.[f]	2,700	1,600
1970	56,800	17,500	6,700	7,300	2,300	n.a.[f]	3,000	1,600

[a]National Safety Council, *Accident Facts, 1971*, p. 15.
[b]Includes burns by fire and deaths resulting from conflagration regardless of nature of injury.
[c]Includes drownings in water transport accidents.
[d]Solid or liquid.
[e]Data for this year and subsequent years not comparable with previous years due to change in classification.
(Note: Prior to 1968 firearms included death by explosive.)
[f]Not available.

categories of motor vehicle, falls, fires, and drownings. During this period the average death rate per 100,000 for firearm deaths was 1.3. The percentage change in the death rate from 1960 to 1970 exhibited a 15 per cent decrease. During the same period, total firearm sales increased by 300 per cent. These data seem to lend little support to the hypothesis that firearm accidental deaths are related to the total supply of firearms.

In order to determine the nature of firearm accidental deaths, the Metropolitan Life Insurance Company engaged in a study of its policy holders from 1964 to 1966.[19] During this two-year period, there were only 143 accidental firearm deaths reported in the survey, which included all of the Metropolitan's policyholders. The principal conclusions of this study are:

Although firearm accidents prevention programs often emphasize the inherent hazard to hunters in the field, *nearly*

three-fifths, or 1,500 of the 2,600 estimated firearm acci-
dental deaths in the United States in 1966, resulted from
misuse in and about the home. [Emphasis added.] The
weapon most often involved was a long gun, i.e., a shotgun or
rifle.[20]

Table 3.3 summarizes the Metropolitan study. Similar studies by
the Missouri Department of Public Health and Welfare and the
Colorado State Department of Public Health concur with the
Metropolitan's conclusions.[21] The death rate by age-class reaches
a peak for the 15-24 age group. This statistic closely resembles the
pattern of nonpedestrian motor vehicle accidents. Iskrant and
Joliet suggest that this striking resemblance may be related, since

TABLE 3.3

Firearm Accident Deaths in the Home:
A Survey of All Metropolitan Life
Insurance Policyholders, 1964-1966[a]

Activity	Total	Weapon Discharged by				Type of Weapon		
		Victim	Member of Victim's Family	Friend	Unspecified	Rifle or Shotgun	Handgun	Unspecified
Cleaning, oiling repairing	29	24	4	1	—	20	7	1
Playing	26	8	8	9	1	15	10	—
Demonstrating or examining	14	6	3	5	—	10	4	—
Shooting at small animals or target shooting	12	10	—	2	—	12	—	—
Scuffling for possession	5	—	4	1	—	1	4	—
Russian Roulette	4	4	—	—	—	—	4	—
Search for prowler	2	2	—	—	—	2	—	—
Other Specified	15	12	3	—	—	9	5	1
Unspecified	36	15	2	1	18	16	5	15
TOTAL	143	81	24	19	19	85	39	19

[a]Metropolitan Life Insurance Company, *op. cit.*, p. 4.

this age group is characterized by increased risk-taking (playing "Russian Roulette" and "chicken," for example).[22] Since most of the firearm accidents occur in the home, it is unlikely that laws which forbid minors to possess weapons will be effective, unless they also forbid parents from possessing weapons.

Hunting deaths account for eight hundred lives annually. The primary weapon used is the shotgun and rifle, with the handgun accounting for less than ten per cent of these deaths. Although inexperience is mentioned as a prime factor in hunting deaths, the National Rifle Association data indicate that most victims have had at least three years' experience in firearm usage.[23] The common cause of injury and death is unintentional firearm discharge (i.e., stumbling, catching the trigger on some object, inadvertently pulling the trigger, removing from or replacing in vehicle, and crossing a fence with a loaded firearm).

From the viewpoint of economics, laws attempting to reduce firearm accidents through the prohibition of hunting and firearm purchase may be nonoptimal (i.e., the social costs of the laws exceed the social benefits). Individuals, in making choices, evaluate the relative benefits and costs of various alternatives and select those activities which secure them the largest net advantage. In the case of hunting, the individual values the use of his leisure time, the cost involved in the activity and the probability of injury or death. Once he enters the woods to hunt, the economist would infer by his actions that the expected gain exceeds the expected cost. In this case, laws which attempt to protect an individual from himself are nonoptimal since he has all the relevant information and the prohibition would make him worse off and no one better off. This is not to argue that there is no role for government intervention in the area of hunting. Laws holding hunters liable for injuries they cause through their own carelessness may increase the safety level of hunting and thereby benefit all hunters.

The same logic would apply to the possession of a firearm in the home. The consumer evaluates the benefit of home possession against the cost of possible injury to himself or family in terms of accidental discharges. Ownership implies that the benefits exceed the expected costs.

Firearms and Suicide

Suicides account for approximately 20,000 deaths annually. From the viewpoint of ethics, philosophy and emotion, suicide is a difficult and perplexing problem. The question in terms of gun control is whether control will reduce the number of suicides. Table 3.4 lists suicides by type of weapons used for selected years. The figures in Table 3.4 are somewhat distorted due to the aggregation of activities; however, firearms account for almost half of the total successful suicides.

> Although firearms are a highly successful means of committing suicide, a few other methods — hanging, carbon monoxide, jumping, and drowning by jumping — are almost equally effective. The question therefore, is whether persons attempting suicide, if they had no firearms, would turn to equally effective methods that are now used by only a small proportion of those attempting suicide — or whether some would turn to more frequently used, but less effective, alternatives such as barbiturates.[24]

In order to answer the question of weapon substitution, Newton and Zimring compared U.S. suicide rates with those of other countries. In terms of suicide rates per 100,000, the U.S. ranks eighth in the international comparison and first in the percentage of firearms used in suicides. Newton and Zimring concluded that "suicide rates would not seem to be readily affected by making firearms less available."[25] Individuals who seek to end their lives can effectively complete this task by selecting from an array of common weapons.

The case of suicide is closely related to the case of hunting accidents in that the full cost of the activity is borne by the consumer-victim. The absence of spillover costs indicates that there is no economic justification for intervention. The suicide-hunting phenomenon may be compared to cigarette smoking. Although the U.S. Surgeon General has determined that cigarette smoking is dangerous to one's health, individuals continue to smoke. In all these cases, government intervention which protects the individual from himself appears to be an unnecessary restraint on individual choice. . . .

TABLE 3.4

Suicides by Type of Activity:
1960-1968[a]

Activity	1960	1965	1966	1967	1968
			Male		
Poisoning	2,631	3,179	2,970	2,949	2,960
Handgun and hangings	2,576	2,453	2,231	2,112	2,265
Firearms and explosives	7,879	8,457	8,780	8,766	9,078
Other	1,453	1,401	1,435	1,360	1,076
TOTAL	14,539	15,490	15,416	15,187	15,379
			Female		
Poisoning	4,502	2,816	2,618	2,746	2,724
Handgun and hangings	790	744	632	666	834
Firearms and explosives	1,138	1,441	1,627	1,784	1,883
Other	875	1,016	988	942	602
TOTAL	4,502	6,017	5,865	6,138	5,993

[a]U.S. Department of Commerce, *Statistical Abstract of the United States, 1971*, table no. 220.

Conclusions and Limitations

This research began with two hypotheses concerning gun control. On the one hand, gun control is viewed as an efficacious method of deterring violent crimes and reducing accidental deaths attributable to firearms. On the other hand, gun control is viewed *not* as an efficacious method of crime control, but as a program which inherently exhibits a perverse effect on the desired goal of crime reduction. That is to say, an arms build-up by the citizenry, accompanied by knowledge of this build-up, will have a greater effect in deterring crime than an arms limitation. This hypothesis rests upon the observation that: (1) gun control programs cannot feasibly segregate legitimate and illegitimate firearm users; (2) an arms build-up represents an increase in the private supply of protection, which augments the publicly supplied good of law enforcement, and this private supply allows individuals to quantity adjust to the level of the public good supplied; and (3) in a sense, this privately supplied protection represents potential retaliation on the part of the victims of crime and, thus, will influence the criminals' benefit cost calculus. While this research is unable to completely resolve these dichotomous views, a partial justification of the latter hypothesis is supplied. The questions that this research attempted to answer are as follows: (1) are existing state gun control laws a viable method of reducing firearm misuse; and (2) can crime deterrence be better obtained through increases in the clearance rate and the degree of punishment as opposed to increases in the level of gun control laws? The secondary question of the effectiveness of privately supplied protection (i.e., an arms build-up) is omitted from the empirical analysis since reliable data on firearm ownership are nonexistent. While is is not possible to *empirically* evaluate the effectiveness of privately supplied protection, this question is included in the theoretic analysis of consumer choice.

The problem of firearm misuse was defined on the basis of an externality argument. The externality argument employed allows one to outline areas of misuse where government intervention may be economically justified. In the area of firearm accidental deaths and suicide, it was demonstrated that government intervention is *not* justified, since the externality appears to be internalized by the consumer-victim. Alternatively, in the area of the violent crimes of homicide, aggravated assault, and robbery (i.e., crimes where firearm misuse is most pronounced) it was demonstrated that government intervention *may* be justified since the externalities do not appear to be internalized. However, intervention will be efficient if, and only if, the benefit of the gun control law (i.e., a reduction in violent crime) is greater than the "real" cost of the control laws.

In order to limit the scope of this research, only those gun control laws which dealt with the acquisition and ownership of firearms were investigated. These laws were investigated on the basis of their strategy and their effects upon individual choice. In general, these laws attempt to separate legitimate and illegitimate users of firearms. While this goal may be desirable, the actual administration of the law falls considerably short of this goal, since the cost of absolute segregation of consumers is excessive.

Laws cannot feasibly discriminate among potential misusers and legitimate users. Thus, gun control laws simply raise the real "market price" of a firearm (market price plus the cost of compliance or the cost of illegal acquisition) for all consumers. In the case of individuals who engage in criminal activities, it is probable that they are considerably less likely to be deterred from obtaining firearms by price raises than is the legitimate firearm user. If the purpose of gun control laws is to price criminals out of the firearms market, then the price of firearms would have to be substantially increased. It is important to realize that this proposed price increase would also price many legitimate users out of the firearms market.

It is obvious that gun control involves some positive cost. While this present study does not examine the administrative cost of gun control for each state, it does supply cost estimates of various alternatives open to society. The cost estimates deal only with the administrative cost of control programs and do not include the cost of enforcement, the cost to firearms owners, or the cost to the general public. Even on the basis of these administrative cost estimates, the amount of resources devoted to gun control programs appears to be substantial, while, at the same time, it is not apparent whether or not these programs have any benefits.

The Findings of This Study

In order to determine the effectiveness of gun control laws in reducing violent crime, an empirical estimate of the supply of offenses (i.e., the homicide, the aggravated assault, and the robbery, rate) was computed. The empirical approach used in this study differs substantially from previous studies on gun control, since the various gun control laws were treated as dummy variables, and the analysis explicitly incorporated the major variables of deterrence supplied by the public sector (namely, the clearance rate and the level of punishment). On the basis of empirical results computed, the findings of this study are as follows:

(1) Gun control laws, with the exception of dealer licensings, do not appear to be an effective method of controlling the homicide rate.

(2)   Gun control laws, in general, exhibit vague and ambiguous results in the areas of aggravated assault and robbery. Exceptions are prohibition of carrying a loaded firearm in a motor vehicle and government record-keeping of new purchases. Both of these laws appear to provide some level of deterrence on the aggravated assault rate and the robbery rate. In the case of robberies, the prohibition of purchase by addicts appears to provide deterrence.

(3)   The *clearance rate* represents a strong degree of deterrence for all crimes investigated.

(4)   The level of punishment is an important factor in the deterrence of homicide and less effective in deterring aggravated assault and robbery. In the case of aggravated assault, the ineffectiveness of punishment may be due to the fact that these crimes generally occur within the family and among close friends and, thus, there is usually a reluctance on the part of the victim to prosecute. In the area of robberies, the punishment variable excludes juveniles and thus clouds the effectiveness of punishment as deterrence, since a large proportion of robberies are committed by juveniles.

(5)   On the one hand, it is clear that the clearance rate and the level of punishment provide deterrence. However, it does not appear that an increase in the clearance rate or the level of punishment will significantly reduce the level of criminal activity. This premise rests on the observation that the institutional structure remains unchanged. It is possible through institutional change to increase both the level of punishments and the clearance rate at a lower cost. For example, change in the laws which protect the innocent could be reduced and this increased liberty tax would imply a lower probability that guilty individuals would be found innocent. In the case of punishment, an attempt to make prison sentences longer or to make prisons more severe (and shorter sentences) would provide increased deterrence.

(6)   Finally, in view of the cost of gun control, it does not appear that control has any significant positive returns. The effectiveness of gun control remains vague and ambiguous.

Limitations

The limitations of this study are as follows:
(1)   The only gun control laws that were investigated were

those dealing with acquisition and ownership. Laws regulating use were omitted from the analysis.

(2) No attempt was made to account for difference in the level of enforcement among states. If the level of enforcement is significantly different across states it is possible that the empirical results involve a systematic bias.

(3) States which have differential penalties for crimes committed with and without a firearm were not explicitly included in the analysis. While this information may be included in the punishment variable, it was impossible to separate out this information. It does appear that a very strong case may be made for deterring crimes which involve firearms through a system of differential penalties.

(4) The supply of offenses may be considerably more complex than that indicated by the multiple regression analysis employed.

(5) Due to data limitations, no attempt was made to include a time series analysis of the supply of offenses.

(6) An analysis of the logic of the constitutional provision of the right to bear arms was omitted from this study. By comparing the rationale of pre-constitutional choice with post-constituional choice, it does appear that a strong argument may be presented against the philosophical basis of gun control.

SECTION III: Critiquing the Case for Handgun Prohibition

From time to time various types of empirical evidence have been offered to show that Sullivan-type laws in those American jurisdictions having them reduce violence, and that such legislation could be adopted nationally with little real cost. This section of the book contains selections from the writings of two specialists in criminology and criminal law who have evaluated claims that the Sullivan Law is effective and inexpensive to administer and enforce.

MARK K. BENENSON

The first selection is by Mark K. Benenson, Esq., of the New York City Bar, from his "A Controlled Look at Gun Controls," published in the *New York Law Forum* in 1968:

Let us analyze a typical anti-gun argument. It is frequently stated, and it appears to be generally true, that states with minimal firearms laws have a higher percentage of homicides *with firearms*. *The New York Times* on June 17, 1968, for instance, argued in an editorial that three northeastern states, New York, New Jersey, and Massachusetts, with comparatively strict gun laws, averaged but 35% firearms homicides and that three southern states, Mississippi, Texas, and Florida, with lax laws, averaged 68%. From this, the *Times* deduced that the risk of murder was lower in the Northeast. This is certainly not true of Manhattan Island, where the *Times* is published and where the homicide rate was a high 15.13 per 100,000 in 1966,[1] and in any case the comparison is disingenuous. *What is important is not the percentage of gun*

homicides but the homicide rate itself. If the elimination of
firearms would merely result in the substitution of other weapons,
little is accomplished. [Emphasis added.]

This is precisely the point of view of Dr. Marvin Wolfgang of
Pennsylvania University, whose 1958 "Patterns of Criminal Homicide" is the standard text on the subject. Wolfgang, in compre-
hensively analysing four years of Philadelphia criminal homicides,
extensively surveyed, *inter alia*, the use of weapons. Wolfgang has
"rejected the idea that homicide rates are higher in the United
States than in England because of easier access to firearms. . . ."[2]
He wrote:

> Several students of homicide have tried to show that the high
> number of, or easy access to, firearms in this country is
> causally related to our relatively high homicide rate. Such a
> conclusion cannot be drawn from the Philadelphia data.
> Material subsequently reported in the present study regarding
> the place where homicide occurred, relationship between
> victim and offender, motives, and other variables, suggests
> that many situations, events, and personalities that converge
> in a particular way and that result in homicide do not depend
> primarily upon the presence or absence of firearms. While it
> may be true both that the homicide rate is lower in Europe
> and that fewer homicides abroad involve use of firearms, it
> does not necessarily follow that the relatively high homicide
> rate in this country is merely due to greater accessibility of
> such weapons. . . .
>
> Comparisons of a general homicide rate with percentage
> use of firearms is not an adequate comparison. Unless all
> methods and weapons used in homicide are compared be-
> tween two areas or communities, the proportionate use of
> firearms compared in isolation is not convincing evidence of a
> causal relation between a high homicide rate and the number
> of shootings. Moreover, comparison of like cultural areas
> having similar homicide caused by firearms would tend to
> reject an hypothesis of a causal nexus between the two
> phenomena. By way of example, Brearley noted for the years
> 1924-1926 that Pennsylvania had a homicide rate of 5.9 per
> 100,000 population. Using Philadelphia victim data to cor-
> respond to Brearley's use of mortality statistics, we see that
> the rate during 1948-1952 for criminal homicide deaths was

5.7, and for all homicides — criminal and non-criminal — the rate was 6.1. Despite the closeness of these Philadelphia rates with the Pennsylvania rate reported by Brearley, use of firearms in Pennsylvania amounted to 68 per cent of all methods, while use of firearms in Philadelphia was only 33 per cent. The fact that Brearley's figures are for an earlier period of time has no effect on the conclusion. Thus, while the homicide rates for these two population units are similar, the proportionate use of firearms is quite dissimilar, being over twice as high for the state as for the city. The hypothesis of a causal relationship between the homicide rate and proportionate use of firearms in killing is, therefore, rejected.

More than the availability of a shooting weapon is involved in homicide. Pistols and revolvers are not difficult to purchase — legally or illegally — in Philadelphia.[3] Police interrogation of defendants reveals that most frequently these weapons are bought from friends or acquaintances for such nominal sums as ten or twenty dollars. A penknife or butcher knife, of course, is much cheaper and more easily obtained. Ready access to knives and little reluctance to engage in physical combat without weapons, or to 'fight it out,' are as important as the availability of some sort of gun. The type of weapon used appears to be, in part, the culmination of assault intentions or events and is only superficially related to causality. To measure quantitatively the effect of the presence of firearms on the homicide rate would require knowing the number and type of homicides that would not have occurred had the offender — or, in some cases, the victim — possessed a gun. Research would require determination of the number of shootings that would have been stabbings, beatings, or some other method of inflicting death had no gun been available. It is the contention of this observer that few homicides due to shootings could be avoided merely if a firearm were not immediately present, and that the offender would select some other weapon to achieve the same destructive goal. Probably only in those cases where a felon kills a police officer, or vice versa, would homicide be avoided in the absence of a firearm.[4]

Wolfgang's analysis remains the basic work in the field. He should not be misinterpreted as stating gun control would save *no* lives. He has always supported gun control, largely for ethical reasons, as he has told this writer. His view, a scientist's, is that the elimination of guns would not, in a statistical sense, *significantly* decrease the likelihood of homicide. He has recently noted, while remarking, indeed, that "many" lives might be saved, that there has been a steady decline in criminal homicides since the 1930's despite a probable doubling in the number of guns, commenting that "the inverse correlation is not causative, but neither is a reverse interpretation."[5]

A report of the California Department of Justice has supported his views, stating: "[T]he mere availability of weapons lethal enough to produce a human mortality bears no major relationship to the frequency with which this act is completed. In the home, at work, at play, in almost any environmental setting a multitude of objects exist providing means for inflicting illegal death. . . ."[6]

We thus see at the very outset that considerable doubt exists that even the removal of firearms from the homicide environment would affect homicide rates. And anent Wolfgang's comment that the lives of many police officers would be saved, no small consideration, one nevertheless must remark that of 6,998 firearms homicides in 1967, only 71 were of that character,[7] and of course, as the Director of the Federal Bureau of Investigation has remarked, "hoodlums and criminal gangs will obtain guns regardless of controls."[8]

If we go back to the *New York Times'* assertions and try to compare them with what we may call Wolfgang's "Law of Firearms Irrelevance," and look at homicide rates instead of gun death percentage rates, we do see at first glance that the three northeastern states' average homicide rate was 3.8 per 100,000, far below the 9.7 figure for the three southern states.[9] But it does not follow that easy access to firearms was a factor; in three typical northwestern states, North Dakota, Nebraska, and Minnesota, where gun laws were just as lax as in the South, the homicide rate, the crucial factor, was at a national low, averaging 1.9[10] in 1966, the year used by the *Times*.

Of course, whatever the courts have said about the right to bear arms, there is a constitutional right to a free press which the *Times* will defend ardently, and most of us would agree that this right includes the right to publish misleading editorials. To the members of the shooting fraternity who have drawn their own conclusions about the openmindedness of the metropolitan press on this issue, it was not surprising that the *Times* did not publish this author's letter pointing out to the editor the interesting contrast with the northern states, just adverted to.

However, the *Times'* technique was soon emulated in even more official quarters — if that concept is admissible. On July 16, 1968, the Department of Justice released a report, "Firearms Facts." The Department insouciantly adopted the *Times'* partial-statistics trick. In a section of the report entitled "State Gun Laws Compared," the Justice Department claimed that states with strong gun laws tended to have "fewer murders with guns" and "lower overall murder rates" than states with weak gun laws. Curiously, only ten states were compared, Pennsylvania, New Jersey, New York, Massachusetts, and Rhode Island as "strong law" examples, average murder rate 3.1 per 100,000 population, and five "weak" states, Arizona, Nevada, Texas, Mississippi, and Louisiana, where, by golly, the average murder rate was much higher at 9.1.

As we have noted from Wolfgang, talking about the percentage of gun murders is essentially irrelevant; the core question is the homicide rate. Thus, the Justice Department comparison, standing alone, appears to support the pro-gun-law argument that rates go up when the percentage of gun murders climb. But the distortion, again, is in selecting states to support a predetermined conclusion. The Justice Department hand-picked its five "weak" states. Let's pick a transcontinental spread of five *other* states with weak gun laws — Iowa, North Dakota, Vermont, Washington, and New Hampshire — and we find an average homicide rate of 1.8, lower than the rate in the Justice Department's *strong* gun law states. From this counter-example, using the Justice Department's bland effrontery, we might as well argue that the stronger the gun laws, the *higher* the homicide rate.

Why this variation? Analysis suggests possible explanations. We see that homicide rates are indeed very high in the South (weak gun laws), moderately high in the big industrial states (stronger laws), and low through the North, north-west, and upper New England (weak laws). The South has long been stained by a tradition of violence; it was there that the code duello flourished. But the key factor, one suspects, may well be the percentage of black population. In 1967, 53.7% of murder victims were blacks, nearly all of them killed by other blacks, even though blacks are but 11% of the national population. We need not be surprised that this is so. For three hundred years, American society has told blacks that they were somewhat less than really human and crimes against them, whether by fellow blacks or whites, were not treated seriously, particularly in the South. Added to these denigrations have been the hopelessness of the rural South and the bitter pressures of the northern ghetto. Blacks live in the South and in the big industrial states, where homicide rates are high, but not in the northwest and upper New England, where they are low. The crucial importance of this factor shows up dramatically within New York City itself. In Manhattan, the 1966 homicide rate was 15.13 per 100,000 and in Queens, with the identical Sullivan Law administered by the same Police Department, but with a far different population mix, the rate was a low 3.26.[11]

Obviously, an overall survey of *all* the states is required. Only two have been made; neither is ever cited by proponents of gun laws. In 1960, Wisconsin compared murder rate variations as against states with gun laws and concluded:

> The average murder rate does not appear to be appreciably different ... for various reasons, which may or may not include licensing, the licensing states appear to have a slightly better record with regard to the number of murders ... Paradoxically, however, Wisconsin, a non-licensing state, has one of the lowest murder rates in the nation.[12]

Although well-researched, the Wisconsin report did not use approved statistical methods.

However, in 1967, the study was updated by Alan S. Krug, an economist, then at Pennsylvania State University. Krug is now with the National Shooting Sports Foundation, which published his report. His analysis, which was a re-do of the Wisconsin study using formal statistical procedures, found no statistical correlation between crime rates and extent of firearms licensing. Krug's report was made an exhibit to the 1967 hearings before the Senate Juvenile Delinquency Subcommittee.[13] Senator Dodd vigorously criticized the report.[14] Krug in turn has as strongly defended his study.[15] However, Senator Dodd found no computational errors in the Krug analysis and at this writing no contradictory statistical analysis has ever been published by the Senator, the Department of Justice, or any of the groups proposing gun controls which has indicated, using proper statistical methods, that there *is* in fact a correlation between gun controls or gun availability and homicide rates. The reason for this failure, which has led the Department of Justice, as we have seen, to the edge of dishonesty, can be guessed at — perhaps there just is no such correlation.

Perhaps the best proof of this is in another Department of Justice publication — the famed FBI Uniform Crime Reports. For years, a page entitled "Crime Factors" has been included near the head of the Reports; for 1967, it is page VI. On this page are listed what the FBI describes as "[S]ome of the conditions which will affect the amount and type of crime that occurs from place to place. . . ." The long list includes population density, community size, population composition with regard to age, sex, and race, economic status, mores, stability of population, including commuters and transients, climate, including seasonal conditions, educational, recreational and religious characteristics, police effectiveness, standards governing appointments to the police, court and prosecuting official policies, public attitude towards law enforcement problems, administrative and investigative efficiency of the local law enforcement agency.

There is not a word about gun laws, even though the pro-gun commentators have been hugging this omission to their bosoms for years and have frequently cited it. Again, the answer is simple. Whatever the FBI Director's pronouncements about gun control, or his gut feelings on the subject, the Uniform Crime Reports is a professional publication prepared by a professional organization. The Reports are the standard of the world for crime reporting and crime analysis — and there is no room for hot air about the crime-reducing potential of gun control.

It is very difficult for a person unfamiliar with crime and firearms to understand how fewer guns cannot be followed, if not by less crime, at least by fewer homicides. Most people think that a gun is incomparably the deadliest of weapons and that without guns, many murders would not occur, either because the perpetrator would be too squeamish to use another weapon or because it is the only weapon that can kill at a distance. However, this snap judgment ignores many relevant factors. First of all, there is no real evidence to suggest that it is easier, psychologically, to shoot another man than to stab or bludgeon him. According to Wolfgang and many other observers, different population groups differ in their attitudes toward ways of violence; in white against white murders in Philadelphia, for instance, a simple physical beating was the most common cause of death,[16] and many a man who would not hesitate, in the heat of a barroom brawl, to beat another over the head with a table leg would never, under any circumstances, shoot at his opponent. Military analysts like Brigadier General S.L.A. Marshall have noted a tremendous reluctance, on the part of American soldiers engaged in actual battle, to point a rifle at an individual enemy soldier and deliberately kill him, even though their own lives were at stake.[17]

Moreover, a very large number of pistol crimes are committed with so-called cheap "Saturday night specials," mostly in low powered .22 and .25 calibre. The short barrels of these poorly made guns develop low velocity and they leak at the breech.[18] To be shot with one is no more and may be less dangerous than a stab from an ordinary large kitchen knife, or a solid blow to the head with any one of a hundred ordinary household articles. In addition, persons without experience in pistol shooting simply do not realize how hard it is for an untrained person to actually hit a man across the width of an ordinary room — many an attempted homicide with a pistol would have succeeded had a knife been used, requiring the killer to close with the victim.

J. Edgar Hoover asserted in 1963 that guns are "[B]y far the most lethal weapons used in assaults to kill — 7 times more deadly than all other weapons combined. Death to the victims results in 21 percent of such attacks where guns are used where it occurs in only 3 percent of assaults to kill with all other weapons."[19]

Such conclusions are reached by adding gun killings to aggravated assaults with guns, then adding other killings to other aggravated assaults. We then find that the number of gun killings, expressed as a percentage of the total of gun killings plus gun assaults, is several times as high as the number of non-gun killings, expressed in turn as a percentage of the total of non-gun killings plus non-gun assaults. The fly in this ointment is the assumption that every assault is an attempted homicide. Obviously, this is not so, but when a gun is used, even if the shot is missed, there is more likelihood of a willingness to cause death. The knife thrust can be checked, but pulling the trigger is an irrevocable action. Also, when there is any premeditation to homicide, or when the assault is committed in connection with another crime such as robbery or burglary, there is a much larger chance that the assault will be an attempted killing and that the felon will be armed with a gun. Even if we assume that this kind of comparison is a valid method of measuring the deadliness of weapons, we can prove, *reductio ad absurdum*, that in 1966 an assault with bare hands was about 50% more likely to result in death than an assault with a blunt instrument. This is illustrated by the table below. Figures are taken from the 1966 Uniform Crime Reports.

	Gun	Knife	Weapon Used Blunt Inst.	Bare Hands	Misc. & Unknown	Total
Homicides	5660	2134	516	896	346	9,552
Aggr. Assaults	43583	77893	51697	58651	not avail.	231,824
Total	49243	80027	52213	59547	not avail.	241,376
% of homicides	11.5	2.7	1.0	1.5	—	—

. . . If we look at New York City and New York State to determine whether the Sullivan Law has reduced crime, we find both the city and the state ranking high in the 1967 Uniform Crime Reports. The state ranked second generally in both violent and in property crimes. In criminal homicide, it was approximately midway, tied with California, where the gun laws are a good deal less strict. Of the 189 U.S. Standard Metropolitan Statistical Areas, the New York City area was second behind Los Angeles-Long Beach in serious crimes generally. Even though the City administers the Sullivan Law with extra rigor, both the 1966 firearms murder rate and firearms aggravated assault rate were higher in the city than in the state outside the city. The combined rate was in fact five times as great. For the years 1962-1966, the firearms homicide rate in the City was 2.1; in the rest of the state, it was only .8.[20]

As a matter of fact, the firearms homicide rate in the United States, considered over the long term, seems clearly to be declining. In 1937, as noted by the then Attorney General, 70% of homicides involved guns; in 1967, it was 63%; and, although the population had increased by some 70,000,000, the number of homicides was about the same.

As noted in the *Washington Post* of June 23, 1968:

> In the 1920s and the early 1930s, roughly six out of every 100,000 Americans could expect to be murdered by gun each year. Today, fewer than three out of 100,000 can expect the

same fate. There has been a similar decline in the rate of accidental deaths from guns.[2][1]

But this decline took place without a national gun law, and, curriously, a comparison of homicide rates for New York City and the nation across the last fifty years shows a startling symmetry, despite the presumed difference to be made by the Sullivan Law, as illustrated by the graph below.

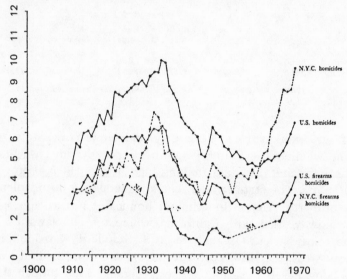

The generally lower gun homicide rate in the city — which is catching up in recent years — is readily explicable as a result of the known cultural fact that fewer people own guns in the East and in large cities.[2][2] The astonishing parallelism in the graph certainly makes one wonder whether the Sullivan Law affects even the rate of gun homicides, not to mention the homicide rate itself. As the graph shows, the overall city homicide rate passed the national rate in 1956, and is climbing much faster than the national rate, again, despite the Sullivan Law. In fact, as the figures in the tables above indicate, this increase is due to more and more pistol homicides, which have more than doubled from 1963 through 1967. . . .

Much incomplete and inaccurate information has been promulgated about the presumed effectiveness of gun legislation. On May 8, 1968, New Jersey Attorney General Arthur J. Sills announced that the 1966 New Jersey gun law was a success because "firearms were used in 44% of all murders in New Jersey last year as compared to 60% nationwide."[23] But according to the FBI figures, for the years 1962-1966 (the New Jersey law took effect in August 1966), the percentage of New Jersey homicides involving guns was only 39.5% — less than it was after the passage of the law. An FBI press release of March 14, 1968, asserted that a gun was used in "58% of all robbery offenses," but the Uniform Crime Reports, released August 27, 1968, corrected this to apply to *armed* robbery, 63% of which involved guns. Thus, the true percentage of gun-armed robberies was only 37%, not 58%, but one wonders how many of the papers announcing the higher figure in March clarified it in August.[24] Again, Harriet Van Horne, in her *New York Post* column on June 14, 1968, asserted that "cities with stern local ordinances against guns (i.e., Philadelphia) have noted a sharp decrease in homicide." It simply isn't so; in the 24 months after the Philadelphia law was passed in April, 1965, there was a 17% increase in homicides as compared to the 24 months before the law's passage — even though in the second city of Pennsylvania, Pittsburgh, which has only the normal Pennsylvania 48-hour purchase delay for handgun sales, there was a 1% decline in homicides for the same periods. Updating the Philadelphia figures, homicides have increased 47.6% in the three and one half years since the law was passed as compared to the same period before its passage.[25] The Philadelphia law, requiring a license to purchase any firearm, not merely handguns, has reduced gun sales in the city by about 75%,[26] but homicides are apparently unaffected.

The anti-gun forces have exaggerated grossly. The Emergency Committee for Gun Control, headed by Colonel John Glenn, Jr., put out a handbill last year which included something called "A Typical Day in the Life of America," which asserted that daily 2520 persons are assaulted, raped, or robbed at gunpoint, 210 commit suicide, 140 are murdered with guns, and that every two minutes someone is wounded with a gun. If the FBI and National Safety Council figures are right, the handbill exaggerated all the figures just stated from 350% to 850%! Assertions are frequently made that since 1900, three-quarters of a million Americans have been "killed by privately owned guns,"[27] the obvious implication being homicide. But the figure, originally taken from Carl Bakal's *The Right to Bear Arms*, is admittedly based upon incomplete records and estimates and includes at least 140,000 accidents and 340,000 suicides.

DAVID T. HARDY

This selection is from an article by David T. Hardy, civil rights litigation specialist, on a report of the Comptroller General, General Accounting Office (GAO), to Congress concerning the desirability of additional federal handgun control legislation.

Winston Churchill once commented that the plagiarist has at least the merit of preservation. By this standard the Comptroller General's report entitled — "Handgun Control: Effectiveness and Costs," has some measurable value.

Released in February [1977], just in time for the next legislative push for stricter firearms control, the report, produced by the General Accounting Office (GAO), essentially summarizes previous literature and states a most general conclusion recommending that "Congress enact further legislation to restrict the availability of handguns." Just what type of legislation, or how much restriction, is not mentioned; presumably, this ideological *carte blanche* is meant to approve anything from reducing the number of dealers to total confiscation. . . .

The report divides its discussions into seven chapters. Two of these function merely as introduction and conclusion, repeating at length data already discussed. The remaining five likewise overlap: the "effect of gun control laws on violent crime" necessarily repeats segments of "the effect of firearm availability on violent crime" and of "the effect of gun control on firearm availability." Accordingly, the report can actually be analyzed under four headings: existing firearms regulations, the relation of firearms to violent crime, the effectiveness of gun control, and the cost of firearm regulation. [Editor's note: David Hardy's analysis of the "effectiveness of gun control" section is omitted because the same material is covered at greater length in the ensuing two articles in the book, Section IV.]

Existing Firearms Regulation

The focus of current legislative debate is not, of course, the 1934 National Firearms Act (aimed mainly at machine guns, etc.). . . . Rather the central question is the desirability of replacing the 1968 Gun Control Act as it supplements local and state regulation.

The Comptroller's report correctly notes that the 1968 Act generally prohibits sale to certain classes of persons, ranging from felons to those who have renounced citizenship or are "an unlawful user of or addicted to marijuana." In a specific effort to assist state gun regulation, interstate transport of firearms is strictly limited, mail order sales are abolished, and sales to out-of-state residents are, with minor exceptions, made criminal. The firearms dealer is required to verify identity and residence, as by driver's license, and to record such identity and the firearms or ammunition sold. These records must be open to inspection by BATF (Bureau of Alcohol, Tobacco & Firearms) agents.

The Comptroller's report complains generally that there is a possibility of use of falsified identification under this system. Nowhere is it shown that this has been a significant problem. It remains, at best, an unverified possibility. The same technology that could produce false drivers' licenses can produce false firearm identification cards, thus evading any proposed system of owner licensing.

The report ignores the fact that the 1968 Act is aimed primarily at implementing state regulation. It dismisses state regulation as "a 'hodge-podge' of differing statutes. . . ." Yet this very "hodge-podge" is the basic virtue of the system. The concept of federalism acknowledges that a single rule is unlikely to be appropriate for a nation as large and diverse as our own. No single gun law could meet the needs both of New York City and of Wyoming or Alaska. In a nation where homicide rates vary from .7 to 21.1 per 100,000, and population densities from .32 to 67,808.0 per square mile, it is impossible to formulate a uniform firearm policy. The balance between liberty and security will necessarily differ when the population of New York City is compared to that of Colorado, Washington, or Vermont. In fact, areas with the highest homicide rates already have strict controls: it has been observed that 20% of American homicides are concentrated in but four cities representing only 6% of the American population (Chicago, Detroit, New York, and Washington, D.C.), all of which have strict firearm controls.[28] That the "hodge-podge" permits such strict controls in these limited areas, without inappropriate restrictions on the remainder of the nation, refutes the Comptroller's casual critique of state power to legislate in this field.

In assessing public attitudes toward change, the study cites a few very general polls. [Editor's note: See discussion of public opinion polls and other indices of public attitudes toward handgun prohibition in the history section *supra*.] It completely fails to inform Congress of the more vital polls among law enforcement officers. It may be anticipated that such officers will have a superior knowledge of law and, from daily contact with criminals, of practical criminology. Recent years have seen two such national police polls. The first is the Crime Control Research Project, conducted in 1977 by the GMA Research Corporation.[29] After analyzing over 6,000 responses from policemen and police officials, the study found overwhelming rejection of gun control. Over three-quarters of the officers felt federal registration would have no effect on crime. When questioned regarding the effect of an outright handgun ban, 91% felt it would have little or no effect in thwarting criminal access to handguns. Less than 9% opined that most or all handguns would be removed from criminals. Conversely, 64% felt an armed citizenry serves as a deterrent to crime.

These results dovetail with those of a 1976 poll entitled "Handgun Control: A Survey of the Leading Law Enforcement Officials in the Country." Conducted by the anti-gun Boston Police Department as limited to high-ranking officers, the poll nonetheless found that "police respondents were strongly against a ban on privately owned handguns. Only 15 (12.3%) of the 122 respondents expressed a favorable response to this measure. . . ."

> A substantial majority of the respondents looked favorably upon the general possession of handguns by the citizenry (excludes those with criminal records and a history of mental instability). Strong approval was also elicited from the police administrators concerning possession of handguns in the home or place of business.[30]

Thus it would appear that police officers, with daily familiarity with crime and illegal gun use, overwhelmingly reject additional firearms controls as an anti-crime measure. So a strong rejection by this group speaks more eloquently than the casual polls presented in the Comptroller's study. No serious indictment of the existing and flexible system of state and local gun controls, backed by the 1968 federal Act, has been established by the Comptroller.

Firearms and Their Relation to Violent Crime

The second section of the report commences with a discussion of firearm use in crime, suggesting that both the number of murders and the murder rate have increased "in recent years." . . . The report mentions in passing that murders did drop "slightly" in 1975 and 1976, but asserts that "firearms have constantly played a large role" in homicide. The facts are somewhat different. Murder rates fell 8% in 1976: robbery rates fell 10%. There had already been a 2% murder rate decline in 1975. The number of murders in 1976 fell to nearly the 1972 level (18,780 vs. 18,670). Moreover, murders committed with handguns fell even more rapidly: 54% of the high 1974 rate was committed with handguns, versus only 49% of the lower 1976 rate. This 49% marks the lowest handgun percentage in nine years. The net result? Murders committed with a handgun fell from 11,183 to 9,202 between 1974 and 1976, a drop of 17%! Thus the trends of "recent years" are almost directly contra to those claimed in the report. It is interesting to note that the Department of Justice had called this to the attention of the report's authors. The Justice Department wrote to GAO that:

> Also on page 21, the report states: 'Recent data indicates [sic] the increasing use of firearms in crime.' UCR data for 1975, and the preliminary UCR data for 1976, show a decrease in reported crime rates for several violent crimes and a decrease in the use of firearms in those crime categories.

To this the authors of the report replied:[31]

> The 1975 and 1976 UCR publication information has been incorporated into the text and figures of these chapters and changes have been made where appropriate. The trend over time has shown an increasing use of firearms in crime over the years. The new data does not change our conclusions or recommendations.

It will be left to the reader's judgment whether the report, in fact, made appropriate changes, and whether a truly objective assessment would conclude that a complete reversal of trends relied on will not have an effect on the findings.

The report then proceeds to compare firearm ownership and firearm murders by region and finds — no great surprise here — that regions with lower firearm ownership have lower *firearm* murder rates. What *is* surprising, (but is not pointed out in the report) is that *firearm* robbery rates are substantially lower in the South, which has far more guns, than in the Northeast, and *overall* robbery rates show no relation whatever to gun ownership: the Northeast suffers nearly twice the rate of the gun-plentiful South, and half again as much as the gun-plentiful West and North-central regions.

The critical question is not, however, whether firearm crimes bear some manner of relation to firearm ownership. The critical question is whether firearm ownership bears a *causal* relationship to *total* crime rates. There is little virtue in being fatally stabbed rather than being fatally shot. Upon this relationship the report is silent. Its crude regional breakdown permits no proper statistical testing. Other studies have been performed on a state level by Krug[32] and Murray[33], which found no relationship between gun laws and total crime, nor between gun ownership and total homicide rates. To the extent that low Northeastern and high Southern homicide rates are claimed to show the effects of gun laws, it might be noted that such differences existed before the Civil War[34] — i.e. long before these states had adopted their gun laws. When preexisting regional biases are factored out, many indicators show a *negative* relationship between gun ownership and homicide rates. The 1973 National Opinion Research Center (NORC) survey, for example, found gun ownership to be highest among rural residents, whites, and high income groups (30% for less than $4,000 per year, 44% for $7-10,000, 58% for $10-15,000 and 55% for over $15,000).[35] Yet all these factors show strong negative relationships to homicide rates.[36] Thus no certain link can be shown between gun ownership and violence rates when analyzed by states, urbanization, race, or income; the last three show strong negative relationships. But the Krug, Murray, and NORC surveys are completely ignored in the Comptroller's report. . . .

We may, in sum, conclude that the Comptroller's report presents an insufficient picture of the purported relationship between firearms and violent crime. The use of firearms in violent crime is in fact steeply dropping, with handgun homicides falling by 17% in the last two years, while five million more handguns entered the market. Regional comparisons between gun ownership and crime are too crude to justify any conclusions, and comparisons based on social, racial, and economic patterns show a strong negative relation between gun ownership and violence. . . .

Costs of Proposed Firearm Regulation

After analyzing the probability of benefit from gun control, the study turns to an analysis of its cost. Since the term "gun control" can mean anything from the simplest registration of handguns to restrictive licensing and virtual "security checks" on the fifty million American handgun owners, assessment of cost is not simple. We shall concentrate here on the report's figures for a Sullivan Law type of system in which all those desiring to buy handguns and all present owners must apply for permits which would be issued only after an extensive background check. (It should also be noted preliminarily that the report discusses only financial costs. Social costs in terms of civil liberties, criminalization of otherwise law-abiding citizens, and so forth are not considered.)

Even as to the purely monetary costs, the assessment is quite inadequate. Only payroll costs, not overhead, appear to be included, and enforcement, as opposed to purely administrative, costs are entirely omitted. The cost estimates appear to be based on computations of worker time consumed, which is then converted to costs at $5-10 per hour. . . . Secretarial, clerical, and higher-echelon administrative staff, buildings, etc., are omitted. Yet it should be obvious that to impose requirements consuming between 1½ and 5 man hours for a background check for each applicant[37] and covering fifty million applicants, would require substantial manpower augmentation and consequent expansion of police force size and office space. To isolate another example, FBI name checks of fingerprint cards are costed at their present charge of $4. Yet present FBI capabilities are but 28,000 checks a day.[38] Merely to keep abreast of new handgun sales each year (at present rates) would require a one-third increase in this capability; to initially process the fifty million handgun owners would require 11,000 days, or about 14 years, of full-time devotion at this rate. It should thus be apparent that existing facilities would have to be expanded, possibly twenty-fold, with consequent expenses ranging from construction to bookkeeping. The $4 per check estimate of present manpower expenses is probably thus a fraction of the true cost.

In short, it appears that the cost estimates ... do not adequately reflect even narrow administrative expenses. Other indications confirm this. Earlier federal commissions estimated purely administrative expenses of background checks at over $70 per application,[39] or about $2.8 billion if applied to all handgun owners. While the report claims the BATF estimates that it could establish full registration for but $21-35 million per year, it is interesting to note that BATF has elsewhere claimed a need for increase in appropriations of about $225 million (with 7,000 added personnel) if they are to fully implement even existing laws![40]

In addition to the administrative expenses, however, enforcement costs must be measured in order to assess true financial cost. Yet the Comptroller entirely omits such cost: indeed, the report expresses doubt that even 500 federal investigators (one per 100,000 gun owners) would be needed, since state enforcement could be counted upon.

This is completely unrealistic. One might as well project the enforcement costs of drug laws based on the assumption that no one will want to violate them, and that simply enacting the laws will be sufficient to cause everyone to turn in their drugs. The effective enforcement of gun laws in high crime areas requires thwarting of the instinct for self-preservation. [Editor's note: The objective effectiveness of self-defense is discussed elsewhere.] Firearms are frequently felt to be necessary by residents of high crime areas, and defiance of laws against their possession is therefore commonplace. Both federal and state authorities estimate illegal handgun possession in New York City alone at two million — or one for every four men, women and children within the city. A study in Florida found that one in fourteen of the persons surveyed carried firearms for protection on a daily basis — the bulk of them illegally. Nor is this purely a "lower class" phenomen. The chief difference is that the more wealthy and powerful individuals generally can obtain permits, and thus carry legally. A private organization in New York City recently discovered that the roster of persons licensed not merely to own, but to carry, concealed handguns in that city included numerous prominent political and social figures, union leaders, celebrities, and even politicians noteworthy as "anti-gun" advocates: allegedly the Rockefeller brothers and former mayor John Lindsay (author of numerous bills to extend the Sullivan Act nationwide) had obtained these carrying permits. Based upon a true appreciation of the incentives for violation, we may proceed to a realistic estimate of some of the financial costs of handgun prohibition:

1. *Compensation: Two to eight billion dollars.* Estimates of civilian handgun ownership range from forty to eighty million; the fair market value of the average handgun has variously been estimated at $50 and at $100. The latter figure appears more accurate: federal undercover agents purchasing guns on the black market in three major urban areas reported average cost of $92.90. A 1976 survey by the Police Foundation of firearms confiscated in New York City found the average retail price at $101.61. Thus we may estimate "one time" compensation costs at two to eight billion, with the latter the more likely figure.

2. *Arrests and Processing: Five billion dollars per year.* Authorities on both sides of the question agree that at least half the handgun owners in the nation would disobey a confiscation order. [Editor's note: The method by which this figure — which is very conservative — is calculated is outlined in Mr. Hardy's article on civil liberties dangers of handgun prohibition, *infra*.] When booking costs, manpower, capital facilities, and court time are considered, "it costs the American taxpayer about $2,000 to arrest someone for a serious crime. Of course, it costs much more than that to convict him." Thus a budget allocation of five billion dollars per year would cover arrest and processing (but not trial or punishment) of approximately 10% of the expected violators. As a practical matter, it is doubtful that 10% of the violators could be apprehended; however, we will here assume *arguendo* that the law would be enforceable. If it is not enforceable, of course, cost estimates are not relevant to the question.

3. *Prosecution and Trial: 4.5 billion dollars per year.* Quantifying prosecution costs is difficult, for the simple reason that

suspiciously few records are kept on costs of criminal prosecution. One local study, undertaken as a means of assessing the cost-benefits of a diversion program, found that actual prosecution costs ranged from $1,769 for a guilty plea with probation to $5,067 for trial ending in conviction and probation. Acquittals were somewhat more economical, since there was no necessity for a pre-sentence report or probation, but still cost $4,712. Due to a 70% guilty plea rate, the average cost was $1,900 per felony prosecution. At this rate, the costs of trying 10% of the violators would amount to approximately 4.5 billion dollars per year. This may be optimistic: if stiff sentences are to be imposed, or the illegal gun owners are atypically willing to go to trial for some other reason the guilty plea rates may not prevail. If even 20% more of the defendants were willing to go to trial, for example, the need for trial facilities would be doubled and costs would drastically increase. Thus 4.5 billion dollars per year is a very conservative estimate.

4. *Necessary Correctional Facilities: .66 billion dollars "one time" cost; .2 billion dollars per year.* The costs of necessary correctional facilities for those defendants imprisoned may be significant. One study of concealed weapons law enforcement, published in the *Michigan Law Review*, concluded that nothing less than actual jail time will deter illegal carrying. It was suggested that a three-day sentence might be sufficient for most "non-criminal" owners. Such a term would theoretically allow 120 individuals to utilize one cell space over the period of a year. At our projected violation rate, approximately 20,000 cells would have to be so dedicated. This would mark a 10% increase in the nation's prison capacity. Current estimates for construction of correctional facilities put the one-time capital costs at approximately $33,000 per cell. The one-time expense would thus be about 666 million dollars. It has also been estimated that the present cost of incarceration is a minimum of $10,000 per year per cell. At this rate, the cost would be approximately 200 million dollars per year recurring expenses. Both these estimates may be regarded as extremely optimistic. Most mandatory sentencing schemes for gun law violations involve much longer terms — from ten days in Chicago to one year in Massachusetts. To increase all terms to the Chicago level would treble the above costs and require a 30% increase in prison capacity.

To summarize the costs of a handgun ban: one-time costs for starting up the system can be estimated at 2 to 5 billion dollars compensation, plus .66 billion for construction of correctional facilities, for a total "one-time" cost of between 2.66 billion and 5.66 billion dollars. Recurring annual costs would amount to approximately 5 billion for arrests and processing 4.5 billion for trial or plea, and .2 billion for correctional facilities, or a total of 9.7 billion dollars per year. Given that total present law-enforcement expenditure (excluding the judiciary) reached 8.5 billion dollars in 1974, it may be recognized that actual enforcement of the proposed ban (assuming that such is a realistic hope) would require a doubling of total law-enforcement expenditures.

As noted above, the fiscal costs are not the only costs: there are also social prices not expressed in dollars and cents. The more important social prices to be paid can be assessed in terms of penalization of otherwise law-abiding citizens, detriment to civil liberties, and reduction in capacity for self-defense and consequent deterrence of crime.

Criminalization and thus alienation of otherwise law-abiding citizens is a primary social cost. Strict gun control is likely to be met with massive defiance. Draconian punishment is a likely response: as the main sponsor of Massachusetts' one year minimum-sentence gun law candidly explained to Congress: "Why so harsh? This we submit to you is preventative legislation. We wish to instill fear into the minds of the 5,700,000 people in Massachusetts, of the legislation."[41]

Other measures currently being used will be discussed below — informants, entrapment, even government bounties for turning in gun-owning citizens. These measures, repugnant to free men, have been abused before, but not against anything like fifty million citizens. The effect on those on the receiving end may be anticipated. Recent writers have commented on the growing rift between the tens of millions of gun owners, traditionally conservative and system-supporting, and the politically decisive elite, who appear to them completely unable to grasp the value and importance of firearms.[42] The wielding against them of legislation aimed at "instilling fear" into their minds, with informants, undercover agents, and bounties, is likely to produce the final, irreparable alienation. Those having registered under state laws, assured by various prominent liberal policymakers that "I know of no member of Congress who wants to impair the legitimate uses of firearms" and that "nobody, least of all Senator Tydings and his colleagues, has ever suggested that any law-abiding person should be denied ownership of a gun," will feel especially betrayed when, as has been proposed, gun registration lists are used to single out those not surrendering handguns: "By keeping track of the serial numbers of collected weapons, the Department will be able to identify owners of registered weapons who have not obeyed the law. Owners of guns not surrendered within the grace period should bear the burden of explaining their loss or disappearance."[43] Given that the fifty million citizens in question compose probably the largest "system-supporting" class left, their alienation is a particularly important problem for the perceived legitimacy of government. . . .

Overall, the Comptroller General's report is, in some instances, seriously deficient with respect to the omission of indicators that firearm control would not prove effective in reducing violence. Numerous statistical studies are omitted, scholarly criticism of the handful of included studies is glossed over, and the defects in the study of 16 cities render it weak evidence for any major change in the present system of flexible state controls. The GAO study, moreover, seriously understates the probable costs, both financial and nonfinancial, incident to the adoption of so questionable a panacea.

SECTION IV: The Effect of Handgun Prohibitions in Reducing Violent Crime

Handgun Prohibition and Homicide: A Plausible Theory Meets the Intractible Facts

DON B. KATES, JR. and MARK K. BENENSON

It may be argued that any legislation that would reduce the number of pistols in circulation would substantially reduce the number of aggravated assaults. The argument rests on two mistaken premises. First, it assumes that restrictive legislation will prevent criminals from obtaining guns. The fact is that experience has shown that legislation such as the New York Sullivan Law does not reduce the number of pistols in the hands of criminals. Second, the argument assumes that guns are used in most aggravated assaults whereas the fact is that they are used only in a small percentage of such assaults.

— Robert V. Murray, former Superintendent of Washington, D.C., police

It is an indisputable fact that a confirmed criminal, even though he may be prohibited by [British laws enforced since 1920] from possessing firearms, can and does buy whatever weapon he wants with the greatest ease. There are countless examples to illustrate the point. Go back to 1952 and the well known case of Craig and Bentley who were convicted for the murder of P[olice] C[onstable] Miles. Only a year earlier Craig, who allegedly fired the fatal shot, had been fined for possessing a .455 Webley revolver without a certificate. At his trial he said that in the previous five years he had had between forty and fifty firearms through his hands. Where had he got them? Swapped or bought them from boys at school. He also said that he had made two of the weapons himself. *And this was a boy of sixteen, prohibited by law from acquiring weapons.*

Harry Roberts, who was convicted for his part in the Shepard's Bush murder of three police officers in 1966, was found to have a small arsenal of weapons. According to the evidence of his trial, his previous record was such as to make him prohibited for life from possessing firearms. Where did he get them? In 1967 a Greek Cypriot was convicted of selling [Roberts] three pistols. Needless to say, this man also held them illegally.

— British police Superintendent Colin Greenwood

Criminals who want to use arms will have access to arms, gun laws or not, especially in this part of the world where there have been weapons readily available for ten thousand years.

— Jerusalem police Commander Shaul Rosolio

[Editor's note: As suggested in the Introduction, the burden of proof rests upon the advocates of a national Sullivan Law. In a free society, it is up to those who propose to limit the liberty of the people — and to severely punish resisters — to demonstrate that the resulting benefit is likely to exceed the cost. The Hardy and Benenson selections immediately preceding this one demonstrate that proponents of a national Sullivan Law have failed to make a case that stands up to searching analysis. In this article Kates and Benenson move beyond critiquing claims made for the Sullivan Law to present the affirmative case against it.]

Hawaii, Michigan, Missouri, New Jersey, New York, North Carolina, and Puerto Rico have laws that prohibit their residents from purchasing or possessing a handgun without a discretionary police permit. As these laws have been in effect for twenty-five to sixty-five years in each state (and, for the past ten years, have been augmented by a federal ban on buying handguns across state lines), any violence-reductive effect should be apparent in these jurisdictions' crime statistics. Six different criminological studies have compared the per capita homicide and other violent crime rates of these jurisdictions in various years to those of states that allow handguns.[1] The conclusion of each study is that, taken together, the handgun-prohibiting states have consistently as high or higher homicide and other violent crime rates as the handgun-allowing states. (For convenience's sake we use the designation "state" to cover Puerto Rico.)

Stated without further elaboration, such findings would seem subject to the objection that the handgun-prohibiting states may simply be more crime-prone than the allowing states. Even assuming this were true, however, it would at least follow that any violence-reducing effect handgun prohibitions have is not significant enough to overcome these demographic differences.

But, on examination, this demographic objection just doesn't turn out to be applicable. It is not the case that the handgun prohibiting jurisdictions, taken together, are any higher in the demographic characteristics commonly associated with crime or violence than are the handgun-allowing jurisdictions. Generally speaking, state handgun-prohibition laws were adopted in what were then rural, unindustrialized and often lightly populated states of the West, Midwest, and South. [Editor's note: See historical discussion in Section I, *supra*.] Although since those days enormous cultural and demographic changes have occurred in all sections of the country, including the handgun-prohibiting states, four of these remain comparatively rural, unindustrialized, and un-ghettoized.

Taken together, the handgun-prohibiting states are widely scattered geographically and are demographically indistinguishable from the national average — except that they exhibit somewhat *less* of the cultural and demographic characteristics that are commonly associated with crime and violence. Yet the substantial equivalency (or worse) of their violence statistics is demonstrated by any number of different comparisons with the handgun-allowing states. Taking each of the handgun-prohibiting states individually, their criminal violence rates are equivalent to (or worse than) those of their handgun-allowing neighbor states or of non-neighboring, but demographically comparable, states. This remains true when the handgun-prohibiting states, taken together, are compared to a similar number of handgun-allowing states that are even higher in the cultural and demographic variables commonly associated with violent crime. It remains true whether these comparisons (or comparisons to the national crime averages) are made on the basis of the latest available yearly figures, on the basis of the last five or ten years, on the basis of the past thirty-five years, or a random selection of years within the past thirty-five.

We do not deny that there are demographic variables relevant to crime rates that differentiate each of the handgun-prohibiting states from each of the handgun-allowing states to which they are being compared. Every handgun-prohibiting state is not only demographically different from every handgun-allowing state, but from every other handgun-prohibiting state as well. It is because of these differences that some handgun-prohibiting states are far above the national average in all kinds of violent crime, while others are only far above in homicide or some other particular kind of violent crime, while yet other handgun-prohibiting states are no worse than the national average as to any species of violent crime and may even be below it as to some. The point is that, though every state in the Union is demographically and culturally unique, there is no pattern of demographic or cultural differences unique to the handgun-prohibiting states that would invalidate the comparisons we have made. The fact that emerges is that, tested over a wide spectrum of demographically, culturally, and geographically diverse states, handgun prohibition laws nowhere appear to have had any reductive effect upon any type of violent crime.

Nullifying the Demographic and Cultural Variables

One way of minimizing possible distortion from demographic and cultural variables is to compare violent crime rates to overall crime rates in both the handgun-prohibiting and the handgun-allowing jurisdictions. For example, if handgun prohibition markedly reduces violent crime, we would expect that, even if New York had a larger population than California, and a greater *overall* crime rate, its ratio of violent crime to overall crime would be less. But, of course, completely the opposite situation exists. Not only does New York have a higher ratio of violent crime to overall crime than does California, it has a higher absolute rate of violent crime, even though it has less population and less overall crime. While such a comparison of individual states is not conclusive, the same pattern emerges when the handgun-prohibiting jurisdictions, taken together, are compared with California and six other handgun-allowing states that, together, are significantly more urbanized, industrialized, ghettoized, and more populous.

A more direct and specific method of excluding possible distortion through demographic variables was that used in a study recently conducted under federal funding at the University of Wisconsin. This is the most massive, extensive, and sophisticated comparison of the crime rates of states with different gun laws ever done. The computerized analysis took into account every demographic, cultural, or geographic variable that was found to have any statistically significant impact upon such comparisons. With demographic bias thus nullified to the extent scientifically possible, the Wisconsin study concluded, "inevitably, that gun control laws have no individual or collective effect in reducing the rates of violent crime."[2]

Laxity of Administration or Enforcement in Permit Law States

Such results cannot be attacked on the hypothesis that perhaps permit requirements are not administered or enforced as stringently as they ought to be in the handgun-prohibiting states. This might explain why these states had higher homicide or other violent crime rates than Britain, which grants fewer permits and (let us assume for the moment) is more efficient in catching, and more stringent in punishing, illegal handgun owners. But it cannot explain why our handgun-prohibiting states have as high or higher rates of violent crime than demographically similar states that do not require permits at all and therefore have no permit laws to enforce. Indeed, although some areas in handgun-permit requiring states are much more lenient, New York City only grants one-seventh as many permits to ordinary citizens as the City of London does.[3] The fact that a very high rate of violence persists in New York (with handguns and with other weapons) suggests that British-type handgun laws may be irrelevant to our own far more violent society.

Actually, the only in-depth study of the British permit system, conducted at Cambridge University in 1971, finds that it has had no ascertainable effect in reducing violence. Noting that "the use of firearms in crime was very much less [before 1920] when there were no controls of any sort," the Cambridge report concludes that social and cultural factors, not gun control, determine violence levels. Demonstrative of these social and cultural factors is the remark of a former head of Scotland Yard that London criminals who wanted handguns in the 1950s could easily get them — but that they knew better than to shoot someone, particularly a police officer, because their own associates in crime

would turn them in. The Cambridge report recommends "abolish-
ing or substantially reducing controls of any sort," because they
are useless and because administering and enforcing them diverts
resources which could otherwise be devoted to viable programs.[4]

It is sometimes suggested that the permit-requiring states would
have even higher levels of violence if handguns were freely
allowed.[5] This seems unlikely although we can never be sure about
might-have-beens. It is noteworthy that homicide and other
violent crime rates in the handgun-prohibiting states appear to
have risen at the same (or even a higher) pace than in handgun-
allowing states during the nearly fifty years in which the FBI has
published national crime statistics. Equally corrosive to the notion
that handgun-prohibiting states would have more violence if they
allowed handguns is the trend in England after 1960, as violence
escalated with the fading of the social and cultural factors that had
previously repressed it. Though the British government frantically
intensified enforcement of its handgun prohibition and extended
the permit system to long arms as well, British homicide doubled
in the era 1960-1975, while American homicide rates have risen
less than 30 percent in forty-five years. Thus there is simply no
evidence that handgun restrictions have resulted in less violence
than the jurisdictions that have them would have experienced if
they had not had them.

The "Adjacent State" Excuse

The refutation most often offered of such statistics might be
labeled the "adjacent state" excuse. It is claimed that evaluating
American state Sullivan-type laws is necessarily unfair because
these laws are so subject to evasion. Any New Yorker who knows
he can't get a pistol permit just goes and gets one in Pennsylvania,
Connecticut, or Vermont, which have no permit requirements.
Where handgun prohibitions are nationwide, it is claimed that they
are truly effective, as exemplified by England and Canada whose
homicide and other violent crime rates are far below ours. Or, to
use an American example offered by Senator Edward Kennedy,
the potential effectiveness of a national handgun prohibition can
be measured against the effectiveness of our prohibition of fully
automatic weapons: "Since enactment of [the National Firearms
Act of 1934] over forty years ago, machine guns have been

virtually eliminated in the United States" — or so Senator Kennedy thinks.[6]

At the risk of belaboring the obvious, we must emphasize that the "adjacent state" excuse is precisely what we have labeled it, an excuse. It does not satisfy the handgun prohibitionists' burden of showing that implementation of their program would provide benefits that exceed the costs. Rather, it is just a possible explanation for the admitted failure of present handgun prohibitions to reduce violence. The "adjacent state" excuse does have the virtue of raising, if only obliquely, one of the most potent arguments against handgun prohibition: that it is inherently unenforceable, at least against that tiny minority of the population who represent a danger with handguns.

The question, then, is whether American state handgun prohibitions have failed because such legislation is inherently unenforceable or only because the presence of adjacent handgun-allowing states makes them unenforceable. Far from supporting the "adjacent state" excuse, the examples of England and Canada undermine it. [Editor's note: Extensive discussion of handgun prohibition in theory, and the English and Canadian experience, is deleted here because the same material is covered in Section II, *supra* (British police Superintendent Greenwood) and in the article on robbery, *infra*. Briefly summarizing the points made in the deleted portion: First, in the short run, prohibition cannot disarm the tiny minority of criminal and irresponsible users, since even a 95 per cent reduction in handgun availability would still leave at least twenty black market handguns for every member of this tiny minority. Second, even in the long run, a handgun ban will not reduce availability to the criminal, the irresponsible, and those who want handguns for self-defense. With the competition of legal handgun manufacture removed, inferior — but equally lethal — handguns can be illegally manufactured and sold more cheaply, yet more profitably, and on a broader scale, than legal handguns are presently sold. In less than a day, a Vietnamese or Pakistani villager can produce a crude, but fully functional, copy of a commercial handgun, using tools far less sophisticated than those which millions of American households presently contain. Though far inferior in long-range accuracy and shooting life to a commercial model, such weapons are adequate for the uses contemplated by criminals, the irresponsible, and self-defense owners.

Third, as hundreds of thousands of "wetbacks" cross the Mexican border annually, and millions of bottles of liquor were imported during Prohibition, despite the most diligent of enforcement, millions of handguns could also cross our borders and shores.]

The "adjacent state" excuse applies far more to Canada, which borders eleven American handgun-allowing states, than to New York which borders only three. Clearly, Canadians could illegally obtain handguns if they wanted to. (In fact they don't have to, since, unlike New York, a handgun license is issued to any law-abiding Canadian almost upon demand.[7]) The fact that Canada's violent crime rates have long been far below ours suggests not that its gun laws are enforceable, but that gun laws are completely irrelevant to the social, cultural, and institutional factors which cause some societies to be plagued by violent crime while others are not. The same is suggested by the English situation, where handgun ownership is minimal in every sector of the population *except criminals.* As the Cambridge University report on English gun control puts it: "half a century of strict controls on pistols has ended, perversely, with a far greater use of this class of weapon in crime than ever before; [there has been] left a vast pool of illegal weapons."

Though cross-national comparisons are fraught with danger, the fact that handgun prohibitions have proven unenforceable even in England is particularly instructive. A host of factors make such prohibitions far *more enforceable* in England than in the United States. England is a relatively small, isolated, and well-policed island that has not had a major war — the source and impetus for so much civilian gun acquisition — in almost thirty-five years. Handgun ownership was comparatively low in England when prohibition was instituted. As the Cambridge study notes, law-abiding Britons willingly complied because the level of violent crime was also so low at that time that few seriously considered it necessary to have arms for self-defense. So sedulously has that attitude been fostered by successive governments that even today, when the incidence of violent crime is much higher, there is no strong public sentiment that victims should be allowed arms for self-defense. As to the enforcement of the handgun ban, there is no English constitution to limit the powers of English police; and public disapprobation of handgun ownership is such that the extensions of search and arrest powers that have accompanied each new Firearms Act have been virtually unopposed.

It should be unnecessary to do more than list the contrasting characteristics which make handgun prohibition far less enforceable in our country: our greater population and much greater land mass, which is much less well policed; our hallowed Constitution with its restraints upon police powers; our very different attitudes about the value of handguns and the right to own them; our history of massive disobedience to banning things (alcohol, marijuana) which substantial numbers of Americans value deeply. In short, if a handgun ban proves unenforceable even in England against those who should be disarmed (while it diverts enormous police administrative and enforcement resources), it seems unlikely to be enforceable anywhere, particularly not here.

We agree with Senator Kennedy that the success of the forty-five-year-old federal laws on machine-gun-type weapons provides an index to the likelihood that a handgun ban could be enforceable in this country. It is noteworthy that even before restrictions of ownership of "tommy guns," civilian sales of these were quite low. The weapon had no legitimate sporting or self-defense use, and its $200 price tag was, for the pre-1935 period, well beyond the means of most honest citizens or even criminals.[8] Though such weapons frequently featured in gang wars of the period, these were not legally purchased, but stolen from police or military armories. But today — unbeknownst to a law-abiding individual like Senator Kennedy — machine-gun-type weapons are much more common instruments of crime than they ever were in the 1920s. There are more of them available on the black market than were legally sold then, and they are available at comparatively lower prices, so that even impecunious lunatic-fringe groups like the SLA easily accumulate them. During a one-month "amnesty," when citizens were allowed to turn in such weapons anonymously and without question, federal officials received 68,000 of them.[9] Indicative of the availability to criminals is a news article about a 1975 Canadian armored-car robbery perpetrated with what one would ordinarily think of as a most unusual weapon — a .50-caliber Browning machine gun on a tripod. Although the weapon was left at the scene of the crime, the St. Louis *Post Dispatch* reported that "police said [it] provided no leads . . . it was a World War II weapon *that could be easily bought in the United States.*" This gun weighs more than

120 pounds and is comparable in size to the average adult human being. If forty-five years of federal regulation is insufficient to prevent a thriving black market in such weapons — of which only a few hundred thousand were ever made, and none for the civilian market — how could we ever hope to enforce a ban on the comparatively tiny handgun, which has been legally sold in this country for five generations and of which there are more than fifty million presently in circulation?

Why Have the Theories Underlying Handgun Prohibition Proved So Appealing?

Having described the empirical data on the success of handgun prohibitions in those jurisdictions that have adopted them, we move on to analyze the theories upon which handgun prohibitions are proposed. It should be noted that this approach is very different from the one favored by proponents of such measures. Admittedly some proponents have attempted to argue that extant handgun bans have produced beneficial effects (see Hardy and Benenson articles, *supra*). But the more sophisticated (and/or scrupulous) of them rely exclusively upon theory, either eschewing any discussion of how handgun prohibition has worked out in actual practice, or admitting that it has failed, and dismissing this by reason of the "adjacent state" or some other excuse.

An approach which relies upon theory to prove that things *ought to work* (and ignores the fact that they don't) is inherently suspect. But the theories of handgun prohibition have been given wide currency, while the facts and studies that refute them have tended to remain buried in obscure professional journals of criminology, mathematical sociology, etc. Though opponents of handgun prohibition tend to blame "the media" for this, they are themselves largely to blame. All too often they have lacked the sophistication to make their own argument — an argument which is intellectually more demanding than the argument for handgun prohibition. Worse, they have often made their argument in political terms which tended to discredit it so completely as to make it "beyond the pale" in the academic world. As a result, they have been excluded from the circles which might have acquainted them with the relevant studies; and the authors of those studies have often found it not prudent or appetizing to advertise the implications thereof.

In contrast, the theories of handgun prohibition have been championed by humanitarians of unimpeachable probity. Those theories present an appealingly simple and apparently common-sensical explanation for the horrifying escalation of violence, much of it involving handguns, that our country experienced in the 1960s and early 1970s. More important yet, they offer a solution to that problem that is relatively easy and cheap, since it is accomplished only at the cost of a group (handgun owners) whose interests those advocating the solution do not understand or sympathize with. Thus, even before describing the theories that underly handgun prohibition, we must admit that they are subliminally irrefutable. People desperately want to understand the reasons for the tragedies that affect their lives and those around them — even if there are no explanations in the present state of our knowledge. It is infinitely more acceptable to scapegoat the easily identifiable handgun than to admit we don't understand the cultural and institutional factors that produce so many more violence-inclined people in our society than in others. It is infinitely more satisfying to focus on England's gun policies (and ignore Switzerland's) than to admit that we don't know how to achieve the relative absence of violence both those countries enjoy.

The bottom line for many, if not most, advocates of handgun prohibition is: "Well, probably it doesn't work, but what does — we've got to do something!" (Moved by the same kind of thinking, the gun fraternity advocates mandatory imprisonment for anyone who uses a handgun in crime. We utterly reject that proposal for reasons we have not space to discuss, beyond saying that they are criminological rather than humanitarian in nature.) Emotionally unsatisfying as it is, we insist that solutions for violent crime must be evaluated on their merits, rather than because they provide a comforting certainty — albeit a false one. We insist that it is better to admit that we do not know the solution — and quite possibly never will — than to acclaim a false one; that the solution can be found only by looking for something that works and not by settling on something plausible that doesn't; and that it is better to expend scarce governmental resources on limited cures than divert them to panaceas that are comprehensive but irrelevant. It is in this spirit that we evaluate the theories underlying handgun prohibition, even while recognizing that such an approach will necessarily fail to convince many.

Theories Underlying Handgun Prohibition

The theoretical arguments generally proceed along three sometimes inter-related lines. First (in order of frequency) is the dangers-of-proliferation approach: "It just stands to reason, the more handguns you have around, the more people will be killed; whereas, if you cut down the number of handguns, you cut down the number of murders." Second is the substitution-of-the-less-deadly-weapon approach: Conceding that taking handguns away won't stop homicidal attacks, it will cause the substitution of knives, clubs, etc., attacks with which will be less likely to result in death. Finally is the "weapons sickness" approach: Handguns are weapons and the mere possession of a weapon alters the consciousness, predisposing the owner to violence. The balance of this article will be devoted to analyzing the validity and relevance of these theories.

Dangers-of-Proliferation Theory

This theory holds the "handgun lying around the house" to be quite literally the cause of domestic homicide. The mere presence of a handgun leads to its murderous use in a moment of rage by otherwise normal, stable householders who would never have thought of ending a domestic quarrel with a rifle, shotgun, axe, butcher knife, andiron, or other potentially lethal instrument that might be lying around. Though ever popular, the dangers-of-proliferation theory is easily refuted by comparing rates of homicide to rates of handgun ownership. If the theory were correct there should be a direct correlation between the two, i.e., the more handguns in a society, the more homicide; the less handguns, the less homicide. But no such correlation can be observed either nationally or locally. In the era 1900-1930 the rate of handgun ownership was quite low and was not growing faster than the rate of growth of the general population. Nevertheless in that thirty-year period the rate of homicide appears to have increased tenfold.[10] In the period immediately after World War II the number of handguns in the country was enormously increased by the influx of millions of war souveniers; in the next fifteen years handgun sales exhibited a steady upward pace which was far beyond the rate of population growth. Nevertheless, during that period the homicide rate remained stable, with occasional upward surges being compensated for by occasional downward trends.

It is true that since the early 1960s both homicide and handgun possession rates have risen enormously. But if there is a causal connection it is the reverse of the handguns-cause-murder argument. That is to say, it is high criminal violence rates that have caused people to buy handguns, not vice versa. After all, since 1974 handgun sales have continued to average about 2.5 million per year, but the homicide rate has steadily dropped and the percentage of homicides committed with handguns has dropped even more rapidly.[11]

This kind of analysis is confirmed by the Wisconsin study mentioned earlier, which could find no correlation when rates of handgun ownership and homicide from all over the country were compared. That is to say that areas with high homicide rates exhibited rates of handgun ownership that varied from quite low to quite high. Conversely, areas with very low rates of homicide exhibited the same random pattern with regard to rates of handgun ownership.

Homicide results not from "proliferation of handguns" among normal, stable citizens, but from the irresponsible actions of a relatively tiny number of sociopathic, highly unstable or otherwise aberrant individuals. This brings the dangers-of-proliferation theory into direct confrontation with the argument of inherent unenforceability. Obviously people who will not obey a law against murder are likely to be the last group in the society to obey a law against owning handguns. If we cannot identify this tiny group of lawless individuals well enough to prevent them from committing murder, how are we going to identify them well enough to divest them of their handguns? (Assuming that we could, would they not murder with any of the other potentially lethal instruments which are "lying around" in every household?)

The Common Citizen As Common Murderer

To avoid such questions, the advocates of handgun prohibition picture the average murderer as just another average citizen who lost his temper and happened to kill "because" a handgun was conveniently available. Were this true, it would seem that the handgun murder rate in a nation with over fifty million handgun owners — all of whom occasionally get mad like any other average citizen — would be in the millions instead of less than ten thousand per year. The evidence adduced for the remarkable assertion that the average killer is just an average householder is that while (a) most "criminals" (i.e., robbers, burglars, etc.) attack strangers, and don't kill them, (b) the people whom most murderers kill are their relatives, friends, or acquaintances. Now (a) and (b) are both generally true, but in no sense do they refute the fact that the average murderer is a sociopath, a disturbed or deranged aberrant whom the law cannot disarm any more than it can keep him from killing. Sociopathic, disturbed, and/or deranged people have relatives, friends, or acquaintances, just as ordinary citizens do. The difference is that while the average citizen — including the average handgun owner — virtually never kills anyone, the sociopathic, etc., aberrant is responsible for most murders (the rest being committed by robbers, rapists, burglars, contract killers, etc.). That the average murderer is not the average citizen can be seen by looking at his pre-murder history. Most citizens do not have even one violent felony on their records. But studies from New York, Chicago, Detroit, and Washington (where over one-fifth of all homicides are committed) find the average murderer has several, and often all of them were against the person he eventually murdered.[1][2] Note that these criminal record figures actually minimize the average murderer's true violence history, because only in highly unusual circumstances do the police arrest for domestic violence that doesn't result in homicide. In other words, for every time the average murderer was actually arrested and convicted for a violent felony, he probably committed three or four that didn't result in any criminal record. [Editor's note: See statistics cited in article on women's armed self-defense, *infra*.] No, the average murderer is not the average citizen.

Typical of the characteristics that distinguish the average murderer from the average citizen is this description of a homicidal aberrant who also dabbled in armed robbery:

A 30 year old man, A.M., was arrested at the scene of a tavern holdup in which he shot and seriously wounded two customers [one of them without any provocation at all]. He had a 4 page police record dating back to the age of 16 with 9 arrests on charge of assault [and had served time in both juvenile and adult institutions for burglary and parole violation].

While on bond awaiting trial he was arrested 6 times on charges of assault, resistance and drunkeness. Over 1 and 1/2 years after the tavern holdup he pleaded guilty to this robbery and was given . . . a suspended sentence.

[Four months later, without provocation, A.M. savagely beat a complete stranger, J.V., who was taking a child to play in a city park.] When J.V. returned to the park to get his car [A.M.] walked up to the car with a gun in his hand, pointed it at him and said "I thought I told you to stay out of the park." J.V. replied, "I'm leaving" [but A.M.] . . . fired his gun seriously wounding J.V. . . . Subsequently, A.M. was arrested and charged with this crime. He was released on bond!

One month later A.M. was arrested and charged with shooting a neighbor who reported that there had been an argument earlier in the day after he refused to lend him money. A.M. was reported to have shot the neighbor's dog twice before shooting the neighbor in the forearm. A.M. was arrested on the scene. There were 6 spent shell cases in his revolver. Once more he was released on bond! [Before he could be tried, again, however, A.M. was found dead in the same park of an overdose of drugs.] [13]

While it is obviously desirable to separate people like A.M. from handguns (or any other conceivable weapon), is it feasible to do so? The A.M.s of this world will be the very last people to obey a national Sullivan Law voluntarily. Since handgun murderers represent far less than one out of every three thousand handgun owners, enforcement would have to exceed 99 per cent effectiveness before we would disarm even one A.M. Since none of our prohibitions of other commodities reaches anything like this effectiveness level, it is unreasonable to think that a handgun ban would. The only effect a national Sullivan Law would have upon crime is to divert enormous law-enforcement resources to taking handguns away from responsible citizens who aren't going to misuse them anyway.

Commonsensical though it seems to be, "the more handguns you have around, the more people are going to get killed" just isn't true. Realistically speaking, A.M. is going to have a handgun if he wants one, no matter how many you take away from responsible citizens.

At the risk of being tiresome, we must repeat once again that handgun prohibitions just don't reduce homicide, because you just can't enforce them against the kinds of people who commit homicide. Many proponents of a national Sullivan Law deal with this problem by simply not discussing it. Their writings begin with the assumption that a law banning the ownership of handguns without a discretionary police permit will result in the magic disappearance of all the unpermitted guns. Without seriously examining that assumption (often without even mentioning the enforcement issue at all), they proceed to theorize rosily about what a world without handguns would be like. But even indulging them in this magical assumption, it turns out that the world would not be all that different — except that it might be even more homicidal.

What if Guns Could be Banned? An Exercise in Thaumaturgical Assumption

Indeed, it would make little difference if not only handguns, but all firearms whatever, magically disappeared. At least so concludes the classic study of Philadelphia homicide by American's leading authority on homicide, Dr. Marvin Wolfgang of the University of Pennsylvania: "It is the contention of this observer that few homicides due to shootings could be avoided merely if a firearm were not immediately present, [because] the offender would select some other weapon to achieve the same destructive goal."[14] Many laymen are intuitively skeptical of this. They respond that the average citizen would find it a great deal harder to bring himself to bludgeon or stab or strangle a person than to pull a nice sanitary trigger. No doubt the average citizen would. But since the ordinary person is never going to attempt a murder, the kind of weapon with which he is not going to attempt it is irrelevant. The fact that the average normal person may be too squeamish to kill in a certain way tells us nothing about whether someone like A.M. is too squeamish. Thus, while certain other aspects of Professor Wolfgang's conclusion have been challenged, most notably by Franklin Zimring (the leading academic advocate of handgun prohibition), criminologists agree that the kind of person who would use a firearm to murder would use some other weapon if no firearm were available.

Substitution of the Less Deadly Weapon

The aspect of Professor Wolfgang's conclusions upon which most criticism has been concentrated is his assertion that potential murderers would be substantially as successful in killing with other weapons as with firearms. Again, though, there is a substantial difference between the lay reaction to this assertion and that of the knowledgeable criminologist. Laymen tend to pontificate to the effect that you can run away from a knife, or defend yourself from it, but not from a gun. This analysis just doesn't accord with the facts that have been developed in homicide studies, including the one in which University of Chicago Professor Zimring has attempted to refute Wolfgang. As Zimring finds, in virtually every shooting the two parties were no more than eight feet from each other.[15] At that range, even if the assailant were armed only with a butcher knife, club, or axe, a victim who turned to run would be stabbed in the back or have his skull broken in. As to self-defense, this is simply not possible for the average person against an attacker who wields such weapons. Moreover, self-defense is not a realistic option to the upwards of 75 per cent of all homicide victims whom coroner's reports find with a blood alcohol level equivalent to blind, staggering drunk.[16] In short, the conditions that prevail in most homicide situations tend to make either flight or resistance impractical for the victim, no matter what weapon the attacker uses.

From his comparative study of gun and knife woundings in Chicago, Professor Zimring offers a different criticism of Wolfgang. Conceding that one who would wound with a bullet would be equally willing and able to wound with a knife, Zimring alleges that knife wounds have a great deal less likelihood of killing. He argues his Chicago study as indicating that, of those wounded somewhere in the head, body, or extremities with a handgun, about 7.5 per cent died.[17] While this 7.5 per cent mortality rate will seem amazingly low to those who get their ideas of handgun lethality from cinematic fiction, it was nevertheless five times the mortality rate Zimring found from knife wounds. But this five to one comparison is not reliable, for the Zimring study is biased by numerous methodological errors tending artificially to minimize the lethality of knife wounds. The most important of these errors is that Zimring's figures are based on an apples-to-oranges-type of invalid comparison. To understand the problem it is necessary to focus on an important distinction between handguns and other weapons. One who shoots another knows that there is a definite danger of death; indeed, given the exaggerated notion of handgun lethality we have received from cinematic fiction, he probably thinks death a lot more likely than it actually is. In contrast, whether there is danger of death in an attack with an edged or pointed weapon depends entirely upon precisely what kind of weapon it is and how it is used. An attacker who uses a small pocket- or penknife, a fork, a beer can opener, can be presumed to want to hurt, to disfigure — but not to think he is going to kill his victim. To determine whether potential murderers would prove substantially less deadly if they were deprived of handguns, a comparative wound study must exclude attacks made with such paltry weapons. It must compare to handgun wounds only wounds made with the kinds of weapons that one who would use a handgun would substitute if no handgun were available — i.e., ice picks, butcher or carving or hunting knives, stilettos, etc., which are used to inflict deep stabs. But since Professor Zimring's study does not concentrate on the kinds of weapons that would be used in homicidal assaults if handguns were banned, its findings are irrelevant. To compare the lethality of handguns to the long-bladed instruments that *would* be substituted, Professor Zimring need not have conducted a new study at all. He could have looked to Professor Wolfgang's classic study of Philadelphia homicide; or to medical journals in which doctors who have studied such wounds conclude that "there is no reason to expect that a sharp knife inflicts less damage than a dull, low-velocity bullet." Among the medical studies is one that gives figures on recovery rates for even the most dangerous wounds inflicted by either handguns or long-bladed knives, i.e., penetrating wounds of the body.[18] Of those hospitalized with penetrating abdominal wounds, 83.2 per cent shot with handguns survived against 85.7 per cent of those stabbed with ice picks and 86.7 per cent of those stabbed with butcher knives. Just as Professor Wolfgang suggests, though the handgun is somewhat deadlier, the difference is marginal. Interesting confirmation of this is provided in a study which finds the homicide rate in thirteenth century England to have been higher than it has ever been in the United States, although, of course, guns did not then exist. Then, as today, the rate varied dramatically by region, with the most peaceful having a homicide rate only two or three times that of our least violent areas (a rate less than half our national rate) and the most violent having a rate two to three times our most violent regions. Just as today, the murderers were restless, disturbed, alcoholic, and poor; the victims were primarily their relatives and acquaintances; the weapons were primarily knives and agricultural implements, and secondarily large rocks.[19] So much for the notion that — without addressing the root causes of violence — a society can greatly reduce the resulting harms just by banning handguns.

In addition to the foregoing objections to Zimring's substitution-of-the-less-deadly-weapon thesis, yet another question must be considered.

Would the Confiscation of All Handguns Actually Increase Homicide By Causing Potential Murderers to Substitute a More Lethal Weapon?

Despite its methodological lapses, Professor Zimring's critique of the Wolfgang conclusion has generally been accepted as definitive by the academic community and is, today, the mainstay of advocates of a national Sullivan Law. The peculiar sanctity with which the academic community has invested Zimring's critique is explicable largely in light of Zimring's own unimpeachable scholarly qualifications, and the fact that subsequent research has not been focused on comparative handgun-knife lethality. Also, of course, academics and intellectuals probably have even less practical experience with firearms than most other people and are fully as steeped in the misleading mystique with which our society, particularly the media, has enveloped the handgun.

It is only this inexperience and misinformation that explains the failure of scholarly criticism to recognize a defect in Zimring's Chicago study which goes beyond any of the methodological errors previously mentioned. This fundamental error is Zimring's failure to conscientiously pursue his own line of reasoning as to the effect upon the homicide rate if other weapons were substituted for the presumptively unavailable handgun. Surely before he concluded that magical disappearance of handguns would reduce homicide by forcing potential murderers to rely upon less lethal weapons, Professor Zimring should have considered the possibility that it would have the opposite effect of increasing homicide by causing reliance upon more lethal weapons. But this possibility is not even mentioned by Professor Zimring, possibly because he is unaware of how much deadlier the most commonly available long guns are than the most commonly available handguns.

The lethality of a firearm is the function of the velocity, diameter and mass of the projectile it fires, and of that projectile's likelihood of hitting a vital area. The common 12-gauge shotgun fires a slug which is more than twice the diameter, and three times the weight, of the uncommonly large .357 magnum handgun bullet — or 11 pellets, each comparable to a .32 handgun bullet. The common 30-30 or 30-06 hunting rifles fire bullets weighing approximately the same as a .357, but at two or three times the velocity. At these velocities, a rifle bullet not only penetrates flesh and bone, but creates waves of hydrostatic shock which crush vital organs far removed from its path. Moreover, because rifle bullets are longer than they are wide, their tumbling action as they move through the body creates horribly destructive wounds.

A pertinent, if perhaps over-dramatic, example is that of the "Son of Sam," whose .44 revolver managed to kill only six of thirteen people it hit one or more times in the head or chest area. A few days before the Son of Sam was captured, a lunatic in New Jersey armed with a rifle in the same caliber (but which developed velocities far beyond those possible in a handgun) shot six people, killing all of them. The comparison is over-dramatic because most shooting victims are not struck in vital places and, in fact, do recover. Thus, where a handgun is used, the mortality rate is only in the 5-10 per cent range, and where a long gun used, mortality is only three or four times as great, i.e., in the 30-40 percent range. But this three or four-to-one comparative figure does not take into account the additional factor of comparative bullet penetration. If a handgun bullet hits a victim it is likely to stay in his body, while a miss is likely to end up harmlessly in a wall. In contrast, a rifle bullet will go thousands of yards and through several walls while still maintaining killing velocity. Even in an armor-piercing projectile, the powerful .357 magnum bullet penetrates only twelve inches of wood, whereas the comparatively underpowered Italian carbine with which John Kennedy was killed has a wood penetration factor of forty-seven inches. One of the bullets which struck Kennedy went all the way through, to inflict upon Governor Connally a wound that would have been mortal had he not been already in an automobile a few blocks from a hospital.

Overall, it must be concluded that, at a minimum, a shot fired from a long gun is four times as likely to kill as one fired from a handgun.[20] To put this in perspective, it is necessary to remember that about 130,000 Americans suffer handgun assaults each year, with about 10,000 of the victims dying and 120,000 recovering. Even had Professor Zimring been right in saying that knives are only one-fifth as deadly, the magic disappearance of handguns would only reduce the homicide rate if it caused prospective murderers to substitute knives. If, on the other hand, it caused them to substitute long guns, the homicide rate would quadruple from 10,000 per year to 40,000. Of course the most likely result, if handguns magically disappeared, would be a combination of substitutions, i.e., some prospective killers would switch to knives while others would switch to long guns. Whether homicide would be reduced or increased would depend upon the exact proportion of the substitutions. But even if 70 per cent switched to knives and only 30 per cent switched to long guns, the result would still be a substantial increase in homicide.[21] If, on the other hand, half of the prospective killers substituted long guns while the other half went to knives, the current homicide rate would double — even if we assume that *none* of the knife-wielders succeeded in killing their victims.

Likelihood of Long Gun Substitution in Homicide

Proponents of a national Sullivan Law with whom we have raised the possibility of increased homicide through substitution of long guns have voiced one or more of the following objections: (1) Long guns will not generally be substituted for handguns by people who now own handguns because long guns are at once far more expensive and far less available than handguns; (2) Long guns will not be substituted because their lesser concealability makes it impossible for them to be used in the vast majority of murders, robberies, rapes, etc.; (3) Handguns are far more dangerous in terms of the "crime of passion" murder because they can be carried on the person and are therefore available in the instant of anger where the long gun is not; and, (4) If long guns are so deadly, then let us ban them as well as handguns.[22]

The short answers to each of these objections (taking them in reverse order) are as follows: (4) Long guns cannot be banned because public sentiment is, and will be for the foreseeable future, overwhelmingly against this. [Editor's note: Section I considers public opinion polls on the outlawing even of handguns and finds that this is supported by a steadily dwindling minority of the population.] That is why the gun prohibitionists have targeted the less popular handgun. But banning handguns without banning long guns is counter-productive since it will increase rather than decrease homicide. As to (3) and (2), studies of homicide uniformly find that most homicides occur in the home, where weapon concealability is irrelevant, and involve weapons that were obtained during the argument, not carried before it. As to (1), the objection is based on factually erroneous premises. Long guns are not more expensive than handguns, and far from being less numerous, they are two and one-half times as plentiful already.[23] Moreover, the predictable result of a magically effective handgun ban would be to explode sales of long guns to those who believe it vitally necessary to have a firearm for the protection of themselves and their families.

Although it is unnecessary to go any deeper into objection (1), it is useful to do so because that objection exemplifies two characteristics which persistently surface all the way down the line in the argument for banning handguns. The first of those characteristics is a profound — indeed a self-righteous — ignorance of firearms, their use, their design, their operation, or the industry that produces them. It requires no great knowledge to realize that objection (1) is factually erroneous. Anyone who knew the first thing about firearms statistics would have known that long guns presently outnumber handguns. Anyone who had followed trends in firearms development and marketing over the past fifteen years would know of the skyrocketing sales and ever-increasing number of models of the cheap "riot gun"-type shotgun and the twenty- or thirty- shot M-1 carbine-type automatic rifles at prices comparable to similar quality handguns. Further, anyone minimally familiar with the subject would recognize that the reason for these skyrocketing sales is not nearly so much the utility of such short-barreled weapons for hunting in heavy brush country as it is the oft-proclaimed advice of gun experts that "for sheer killing power and accuracy the shotgun is unmatched by any weapon. . . . The ultimate tranquilizer," etc.[24]

But not only does the ordinary handgun prohibitionist have insufficient knowledge to realize these things, he is actually proud of his ignorance — because it demonstrates his revulsion at, and disassociation from, the loathsome gun. Unfortunately, this very ignorance disqualifies such people from discussing the regulation of firearms on any level above the purely emotional. An emotionalism so deep as to make ignorance a source of pride is directly connected to the second persistent characteristic we spoke of, a characteristic that psychologists would label projection, while philosophers might call it solipsism. So vehemently does the proponent of banning handguns recoil from the attitudes and beliefs of those who like guns that he is unable accurately to appraise how they will react and instead projects his attitudes on to them. Because he is viscerally repelled by the symbolism of guns and believes them useless for self-defense, he cannot imagine why anyone would own them in the first place, much less defy a law banning them — or, if handguns were not available, go out and buy what he imagines to be an even more expensive long gun. But an accurate perception of what a handgun ban will actually result in requires looking at the beliefs and emotions of gun owners — whose reaction to guns is very different from the gun prohibitionist's. The gun-banning argument is based on a rosy projection of likely conformity to law which is no more realistic than the Prohibitionists' faith that banning liquor would cause drinkers to realize the error of their ways and voluntarily abstain.

Note, incidentally, that we have so far been focusing on the probable reaction to handgun prohibition of the ordinary law-abiding gun owner. Everything we have said goes double for the tiny minority of handgun owners who murder, or the far less than .5 per cent who commit other crimes with them. A sociopath who is not deterred by the pricetag we put on murder is scarcely going to be deterred by a marginal difference in price between a handgun and a long gun. If A.M. feels the need for a firearm, and only long guns are available, he will get one regardless of cost; and if he wants to conceal and carry it in committing a crime, a few moments' work with a hacksaw will reduce it to a handy concealable size.

Moving now to objections (2) and (3), it is necessary first to distinguish robbery, burglary, etc., which often do involve issues of both accessibility and concealability of weapons, from murder, which rarely does. [Editor's note: The utility of a handgun ban in reducing robbery is discussed in the succeeding article in this section of the book.] Most murders are committed in the home, where concealability is irrelevant and where either handgun or long gun will be equally available. Concealment of the weapon appears to be a factor in less than 5 per cent of handgun homicides. Nor, in general, was the murderer carrying the firearm on his person when the dispute maddened him to the point of wanting to kill. Rather, at that point, he went into an adjacent bedroom or nearby automobile to get the gun. In other words, a long gun would have been no less accessible but four times more lethal.[25]

To summarize our objections to Professor Zimring's substitution-of-the-less-deadly-weapon theory: First, banning handguns would not result in potential murderers substituting less deadly weapons because a handgun ban is not practically enforceable against the tiny minority of our population who are most likely to murder. Second, *if* handguns somehow became magically unavailable to such people (and *if* they turned only to knife-type weapons instead), the kinds of knife-type weapons they would substitute are only marginally less deadly than handguns. Third, if handguns magically disappeared, some of the murderous population would turn to the much more lethal long gun instead of the marginally less lethal knife. Assuming that only 30 per cent opted for the former, and 70 per cent for the latter, the result would be an almost 75 per cent *increase* in homicide from the long guns alone — even assuming that none of the knife-wielders killed any of their victims!

So far we have been considering the likelihood of long guns being substituted for handguns in the domestic dispute situation. This is where most proponents of banning handguns think it would do the most good. As to "non-passion" killings, i.e., contract killings, assassins, terrorists, etc., sophisticated proponents of banning handguns concede that these people can never be disarmed.[26] Even if they could be denied handguns, it is generally possible for one who plans a killing or other terrorist activity to find a way of accomplishing it with a long gun. The assassins of Martin Luther King and John F. Kennedy managed to conceal long guns well enough to allow them to perpetrate the crimes and then escape; the Hanafi Muslims managed to descend without detection on a public building in Washington while carrying more than a score of submachine guns, shotguns, and rifles. Indeed professional killers and terrorists generally prefer long guns. For them the easily overcome problems of concealability are outweighed by the major advantages in lethality.

The "Weapons Sickness" Theory of Handgun Prohibition

The "weapons sickness" theory postulates that the mere possession of a weapon corrupts or distorts the psyche, causing the possessor to become more likely to perceive others as threatening and to respond (or initiate contacts) in a bellicose manner. A detailed examination of the evidence suggests two objections: First, the "weapons sickness" theory is factually untrue. Second, if it were true, it would be irrelevant to the issue of *handgun prohibition*, for a handgun is only one of innumerable objects that can be kept as weapons and can, therefore, corrupt the psyche.

Considering the question of factual accuracy, it is necessary only to remember that the Swiss lead the world in the rate of civilian possession of firearms, with the Israelis a close second and the Danes and Finns trailing distantly behind (but far ahead of the United States). If it were true that the possession of weapons corrupted the psyche, these countries should be among the most violent in the world. In fact, however, all of them have very low rates of homicide and other criminal violence. Indeed, their homicide rates are far below those of Japan, which is touted for having the most stringent handgun prohibition in the world.

Just how erroneous the "weapons sickness" theory is can be seen by comparing the purposes of the kinds of weapons kept by the Swiss, Israelis, etc., to the handgun of which Americans are so fond. While it is frequently declared that "the only purpose of handguns is killing," any investigation of the facts demonstrates this to be an emotionalistic falsehood. Though a minority of people do keep handguns primarily to protect their families (not necessarily to take life), the majority of owners are either target shooters or gun collectors. For every handgun bullet discharged at a human being in this country, millions are shot each year on target ranges. In contrast, the fully automatic weapons kept in the house of every military-age Swiss male, and by a large proportion of Israelis (male and female), Danes, and Finns, have *only one purpose*: to kill human beings. It is precisely because their purpose is so limited, and their efficiency in achieving it so great, that for almost forty-five years American civilians have been forbidden to own such weapons by federal law.

Moving now to the irrelevancy of the "weapons sickness" theory, it is necessary only to focus on its difference from the substitution-of-the-less-deadly-weapon theory. The latter postulates that though banning handguns won't reduce the number of murderous people, it will make them less successful in killing. The "weapons sickness" theory follows the almost opposite postulate — that the possession of any weapon subtly changes the psyche causing more people to be murderously inclined than would otherwise be the case. This theory is irrelevant to the banning of handguns, for handguns are merely one of a large number of objects that one who is inclined to do so can perceive and possess as a weapon. Handguns, rifles, shotguns, ice picks, butcher knives, andirons, axes, hatchets, etc., etc., may be more or less deadly when actually employed as weapons. But if the question at issue is simply the psychological effect of keeping something as a weapon, a pocketknife kept for that purpose is no less corrupting to the psyche than a submachine gun.

The "weapons sickness" theory is carried to its logical conclusion by science fiction writer Larry Niven who envisions a future society in which the teaching of karate, judo, boxing, and all other forms of hand-to-hand combat is forbidden. Indeed, the logically consistent application of the "weapons sickness" theory would ban such teaching long before it got around to handgun prohibition. After all, if the mere possession of a handgun corrupts the psyche, what must five to ten hours per week of practicing how to kill with your bare hands do to it? The ultimate absurdity of the "weapons sickness" theory is exemplified (unintentionally) by the knee-jerk-liberal author of a book on battered wives. She actually suggests that wife-beating is somehow related to the effect upon the male psyche of the availability of firearms — and that prohibiting all guns and ammunition would significantly decrease the incidence of male aggression against women. Apparently she is unfamiliar with the conditions that marked human societies in the several millennia preceding the invention of firearms, and particularly the immediate prior centuries that are often called the Dark Ages. Needless to say, humanity was no less violent in general then than now, while violence against women was not only incomparably more frequent, but was, within certain limits, societally acceptable to boot.[27]

Conclusion

To deny the validity and accuracy of the "weapons sickness" theory of handgun prohibition is not to deny that our society is afflicted with "weapons sickness." Conclusive evidence of this is the fact that, though about half the world's nations have higher homicide rates than ours, the other half have lower, some of them as much as 85 per cent lower. Nor is the sickness confined only to those who commit violent crimes; the rest of us, and specifically those who seek to defend themselves against violence, are also deeply molded by the societal factors that create violent people and an atmosphere of violence in our country. The handgun's defenders correctly describe it as a tool like any other, a morally neutral object capable of producing either good or evil depending solely upon the use to which it is put. But the reality of the tool concept is overshadowed by the symbolism of the handgun as the object of death, an object with which Americans (including those who affect to loathe handguns) are so morbidly fascinated. Handgun owners are themselves responsible for much confiscationist sentiment by the gloating, sick way they relate to their weapons — in contrast to the matter-of-fact way in which the Swiss and Israelis seem to relate to their much more deadly ones.

But to causatively associate this sickness with the handgun is at once to trivialize it and to concentrate on the symptom to the exclusion of the disease. The sickness is no less evident in those who eschew the handgun for the shotgun, touting its superiority for self-defense in terms like "the ultimate tranquilizer . . . when you use this baby, you'd better have the sanitation crew ready to come in and clean the remains off the walls." Nor is the sickness limited to firearms, or even to the use of weapons in self-defense, rather than aggression. A cutlery company advertises its utility camping knife as The Ninja, after the legendary bloody assassin-spies of medieval Japan. What kind of a society is it in which sales of an innocent, completely non-violent tool for campers, back-packers, etc., can be spurred by presenting it in terms of the most bloody and vicious of murders?

It is, indeed, a morbid, sick society. But, again, reacting by banning camping knives, handguns, shotguns, or other weapons is to trivialize the illness and to treat its symptoms to the exclusion of its substance. As Bruce Catton, one of our foremost military historians, said in deploring our affinity to the most gruesome weapons:

> Americans did not invent all of this, of course. There is blame enough to go all the way around. But we do need to remember what the trouble really is. It will not do to blame the weapon. We are going to have to begin by blaming ourselves. Then maybe we can start applying a corrective.

Handgun Availability and the Social Harm of Robbery: Recent Data and Some Projections

DAVID T. HARDY and DON B. KATES, JR.

One fact set out in [a British government compilation of data on violent crime] and established by other research, is that serious injuries in robberies involving a firearm are very rare. Far more injuries (of equal severity) are caused by blunt instruments or other weapons. The rather surprising fact is that the risk to the victim is higher in [robberies] which do not involve a firearm.

— British police Superintendent Colin Greenwood

Senator Percy (R-Ill.):
You are currently serving a fifteen-year sentence as a dangerous special offender and you and your former associates
appear to have had access to any weapon that you wanted.
Do you believe current proposals concerning gun control
would be effective in curbing the huge amount of weapons
available on the street today to criminals?

Bowdatch:
I believe the only thing you would accomplish by that is
keeping the people that deserve to have access to guns, you
would keep them from having it. Criminals are always going
to have guns.

Senator Nunn (D-Ga.):
In other words, what you are saying on gun control there is
that no legislation will keep someone like you from getting
guns.

Bowdatch: Yes sir, we will always [get] our guns.
— Underworld figure Gary Bowdatch being questioned
by a Senate subcommittee, August 1, 1978

[A criminal] can easily buy a gun in London's underworld;
[$15.00] will buy you a big revolver; [$30.00] will get a
slender automatic pistol to fit the pocket.
— Sir Robert Fabian, former Superintendent of
Scotland Yard (1954)

Shotgun controls haven't reduced the use of shotguns in
robberies, in fact the use of shotguns doubled over the
previous year [after shotgun controls were instituted]. The
increase in armed crime follows a very distinctive pattern, but
that pattern is in no way related to firearms controls. You
can draw graphs sideways, upside down, any way you want,
but you cannot get the two things to relate. . . . [In the years
since 1969] the number of permits for pistols and rifles has
been reduced by 10,000 a year. And, I regret to say that
there is no evidence to suggest a comparable reduction in
illegally held guns. It's impossible to see where firearms
controls have any effect at all on serious armed crime.
— British police Superintendent Colin Greenwood (1973)

The effect of handgun use in robbery and robbery-murder has often been debated, but little in the way of concrete evidence developed. Only within the last two years have comprehensive studies become available; even now most of those studies are still in the preliminary stages. The most valuable for present purposes are "Patterns of Weapons Use in Robbery," by Wesley Skogan of Northwestern University,[28] "The Effect of Gun Availability on Robbery and Robbery-Murder: A Cross-Section Study of Fifty Cities" by Professor Philip Cook of Duke University, and "A Strategic Choice Analysis of Robbery," also by Professor Cook.[29] These three studies include victimization surveys as well as robberies reported to police (which often under-represent small personal robberies and robberies in areas with little police protection); the samples include several thousand robberies chosen from a variety of cities. Computerization of data enables a more exact scrutiny of the characteristics of the offender, the victim, the weapon utilized, and the probability of injury than has sometimes been possible in the past.

Before reviewing these studies further, it is necessary to note a significant qualification. Comparisons of the kinds of robberies that are committed with handguns to those committed with other weapons at present may be instructive; but great caution must be observed in drawing conclusions therefrom as to the probable effect upon armed robbery of a handgun ban. The problem with such extrapolations is the difficulty in determining how effective a restrictive handgun permit system would be in disarming robbers. Clearly such legislation would significantly reduce handgun ownership in certain sectors of the population, e.g., target shooters. Except for the few privileged to receive permits, this sport would be effectively outlawed and necessarily could be carried on only at such a high risk of detection that few target shooters would continue. Those target shooters who do not see self-defense as a secondary purpose of a handgun would have no reason for not surrendering the weapon, except, perhaps, the hope of being able to sell it on the black market. In contrast, people who make a living through armed robbery would have both a continuing reason to possess a handgun despite the prohibition and less natural inhibition against violating it. We will discuss the extent to which such a prohibition is realistically likely to disarm robbers after reviewing the data provided by these studies as to the effect of handgun and other weapon use in robbery.

Characteristics of Armed Robbery

The studies concur in painting an unusual picture of gun robbery. The gun robber is not the stereotypical juvenile "punk." As a matter of fact, juveniles are far less likely to use firearms in a robbery than are adult, professional robbers. Skogan finds guns used by 11 per cent of juvenile robbers versus 27 per cent of adults. Gun robbers are also more likely to appear in teams of two or more than are non-gun robbers: guns were used by 19 per cent of single robbers and 27 per cent of two-robber teams. Among robbers choosing to use a gun, the choice of victim appears to be altered also. Gun robbers tend to focus upon commercial establishments, while non-gun robbers focus upon attacking individuals: though 19 per cent of individual robberies feature guns, 64 per cent of commercial robberies do. When gun robberies are committed against individuals, the victims are more likely to be males in their prime; non-gun robbers tend to choose the very young, the handicapped, and the elderly as their targets. Gun robbers also tend to make considerably more per robbery, due to their focusing on commercial establishments rather than the less profitable individual robbery, and perhaps due in part to their greater age, experience, and competence.

Injury Comparisons in Armed Robbery

These studies confirm previous British and American statistics showing victim injury to be much more frequent, and substantially more serious, if armed robbery is carried out with some weapon other than a firearm.[30] The reason for this is apparently that both robbers and victims perceive firearms as so dangerous that robbers rarely find it necessary to actually discharge their gun; the threat alone suffices. Robbers displaying knives more frequently have to actually stab their victim. Robbers using "other weapons" (chiefly clubs or heavy instruments) could rarely rely upon threats. Knowing this, they most frequently *began* the robbery by striking the victim. Skogan finds that gun robbers actually wounded or shot at their victims in only 26 per cent of the cases. In contrast, knife robbers actually used their weapons in 46 per cent of the cases, and robbers with other weapons did so in 64 per cent. Injuries were inflicted in 17 per cent of gun robberies, 32 per cent of knife robberies, and 53 per cent of "other weapon" robberies. Cook's study of fifty cities found that medical expenses were incurred by 2.8 per cent of gun robbery victims, 6.6 per cent of knife robbery victims, and an enormous 12 per cent of "other weapon" victims. Serious injuries (defined by medical expenses exceeding $1000) occurred in .3 per cent of gun robberies, .4 per cent of knife robberies, and .7 per cent of "other weapon" robberies. Thus, at least as to non-fatal injuries, robbery with "other weapons" is by far the most dangerous, having an injury rate three to four times that of gun robberies (and about twice that of knife robberies), and a serious injury rate over twice that of gun robberies. (As the data from which these figures come is derived from victim questionnaires, it reflects only degrees of injury less serious than death. Separate figures as to the likelihood of death from robberies with various kinds of weapons will be discussed *infra.*)

Probable Effect of Banning Handguns on Overall Robbery Rate

Both Skogan and Cook go on to speculate as to the result of a handgun prohibition upon robbery rates. Skogan (who assumes only for the sake of argument that such a ban would disarm robbers) notes two diametrically inconsistent possibilities. These are based on the fact that non-gun robberies are less profitable than gun robberies, because the targets tend to be more the vulnerable individual rather than the formidable commercial establishment. He postulates that, if guns were not available, those robbers who would have used them would either: (a) continue in the trade, but have to commit more robberies in order to make the same amount of money; or (b) find the work too hard or dangerous in proportion to their rate of return and so go into other employment (legal or illegal). Professor Skogan's data provide no basis for estimating what percentage of potential robbers would take either course. He does estimate that, to the extent that course (a) were taken, the present rate of robberies would rise by almost 75 per cent as a result of a (hypothetically effective) handgun ban; but if course (b) were taken the present rate would fall by almost 30 per cent.

Professor Cook does attempt to estimate both the extent to which a hypothetical reduction in general firearms availability would reduce gun availability to robbers, and the effect of such a reduction on rates of robbery. He constructs an index of present handgun availability across the nation, based upon handgun use in homicide, suicide, and accidental deaths, and attempts by this to explain variations in rates of overall robbery and firearm robbery. He concludes that any given reduction in the availability of handguns to the general public will result in a reduction of at most one-half that amount in gun robberies. But this will have no reductive effect in the *overall* robbery rate for, he finds, any fall in the gun robbery rate will coincide with an at least equivalent rise in the rate of non-gun robberies.

Hypothesized Effect upon Robbery-Murder of Reducing Handgun Robbery

Nevertheless, Professor Cook supports handgun prohibition as a means of reducing homicide in robbery. Though robbery-homicide is quite rare, Professor Cook concludes that handguns are so much more lethal than non-firearm weapons that armed robberies with handguns are three times more likely to result in death. This seems difficult to square with the numerous and well-authenticated studies previously cited as to the danger of serious but non-fatal injury in robbery. It will be remembered that the rate of serious injury in gun-armed robberies was less than half that in club-armed robberies (.3 per cent to .7 per cent) and slightly lower than in knife-armed robberies (.4 per cent). The disparity between these results and Professor Cook's conclusion that handgun-robberies are three times more likely to kill than armed robberies with other weapons prompts a close examination of the robbery-homicide data available to Professor Cook. At once a major problem is evident. The serious-injury data allows for comparison limited to *armed* robberies, whether by gun, knife, or club (i.e., blunt instrument). But the robbery-homicide data just combines, without differentiation, armed and strong-arm (*unarmed*) robbery. The only armed robberies for which separate homicide figures are available are gun-armed robberies.[31] So Professor Cook has compared the rate of homicides per gun-armed robbery to a combination of homicides occurring not only in knife and club robberies but also in unarmed robberies. Adding in these unarmed robbery-homicides to the rate of homicide per knife and club robbery results in a serious underestimation of that homicide rate, for clearly the number of homicides per unarmed robbery will be far less. This underestimation is particularly unfortunate because the matter under consideration is whether robbery-homicide would be reduced if armed robbers were forced to rely on other weapons than handguns. It appears unlikely that, in the event armed robbers were unable to get handguns, they would decide to give up weapons altogether, rather than adopting knives, clubs, or perhaps sawed-off shotguns (this last a possibility discussed *infra*). Since the homicide data available to Professor Cook doesn't allow an accurate comparison of the number of deaths per knife and club robbery to those per gun robbery, his conclusion that gun robberies are three times more fatal must fall.

Professor Cook takes no note of the underestimation inherent in his homicide data; apparently he regards the knife versus handgun lethality comparison as independently settled by a study of knife and gun woundings which concludes that handguns are several times as lethal as knives.[32] But there are serious methodological flaws in that study, which was done by Professor Franklin Zimring, the leading academic advocate of handgun prohibition. The most serious of these flaws is an over-inclusion comparable to that we have described in the robbery-homicide data relied upon by Professor Cook. Though Professor Zimring purports to be comparing the lethality of gun versus knife wounds, he includes in the latter not only deep stab wounds inflicted with stilettos, ice picks, butcher knives, etc., but also slash wounds and those made with small pen- or pocketknives or even beer-can openers. Doubtless a separate enumeration of such wounds (if Professor Zimring had given it) would be informative as to the unrelated question of extent of injuries where assaults are committed by people who intend to hurt *but not kill.* But it can only be seriously misleading in a comparison of knife to handgun wounds which is used — as both Zimring and Cook do — to suggest that *homicidally intended* attacks would be less lethal if the law banned handguns, so that attempted murderers or robbers had to use knives instead. Reliance on the Zimring study is even more inappropriate as to armed robbers than homicidal attackers. It is conceivable that man who wanted to kill could be so blinded by rage as to overlook a butcher knife or ice pick and go for a pen knife or beer-can opener instead. But the kind of robber who, it is postulated, would have used a handgun but for the law banning them is scarcely going to be so careless. Having his choice of weapons ranging from penknives and can openers to butcher knives and stilettos, he is clearly going to choose the latter. Medical studies comparing the lethality of such long-bladed stabbing weapons to handguns flatly contradict Professor Zimring: "There is no reason to expect that a sharp knife inflicts less damage than a dull, low velocity [i.e., handgun] bullet"; a study of penetrating abdominal wounds finds a recovery rate of 83.2 per cent when inflicted with a handgun compared to 85.7 per cent with ice picks and 86.7 per cent with butcher knives.[33] From this it follows that any reduction in the danger of robbery-homicide if handgun robbers had to use knives instead could not be Professor Cook's postulated 66.7 per cent. At most it would be a 2.5-3.5 per cent reduction.

But note that even this marginal decrease in robbery-homicide would occur only if a robber who is forced to rely on a knife or club actually wounds with it as infrequently as he would do if it were a handgun. The comparative likelihood that different robbery weapons would have to be actually used is an issue as to which the Zimring study provides Professor Cook no support. Zimring concludes that *where handguns and knives are both actually used to wound*, the former are several times as lethal as the latter. Even if that were true, it is clear that a knife or club that is actually used to wound is infinitely more lethal than a handgun that is not. And it is well established that knife and club robbers actually have to wound their victims far more frequently than the gun robber, who can obtain submission by mere threat.

In this context it should be remembered that the statistics indicate club-armed robbers to be even more likely to actually wound than the knife-armed robbers. Unfortunately, the limited evidence that is available suggests that when laws impel robbers to eschew handguns in favor of other weapons, the substitute is most likely to be a club or other blunt instrument rather than a knife. For example, after Florida enacted mandatory sentencing for the use of firearms in certain felonies, gun robberies dropped 38.5 per cent, knife robberies also fell 12 per cent, but robbery with "other weapons" skyrocketed 94 per cent in twelve months. In Massachusetts, following a mandatory sentencing law for carrying firearms without a license, handgun assaults dropped, knife assaults increased only slightly, but "other weapons" assaults increased at several times that rate.[34] This substitution trend has particularly ominous implications, for not only do club-wielding robbers tend to actually use their weapon more — preferably by surprise and against the victim's head — but they also tend to pick victims who are aged and/or infirm. For such a victim population the resulting cranial injuries (complicated by injuries suffered in being knocked to the pavement) may often be fatal. Serious injury is twice as likely in club-armed as in gun-armed robberies, and there is no reason to expect the likelihood to be any different as to robbery-homicide.

In summary, since the available homicide data does not allow a comparison of the lethality of gun-armed robberies to other armed robberies, if such a comparison is to be made at all it must be based upon the data concerning serious injury in robbery with various kinds of weapons. Extrapolating from this admittedly remote data, if a hypothetically effective handgun ban forced robbers to rely upon knives, robbery-homicide would *increase* slightly; if clubs were substituted it would more than double.

In fact, reliance upon the serious injury data probably understates by a considerable degree the extent to which robbery-homicide would increase if a ban actually did take handguns away from robbers. To understand why, we must now examine an assumption that underlies Professor Cook's conclusions but which he never makes explicit or defends. This is the assumption that armed robbers deprived of handguns would substitute knives or clubs *rather than long guns.*

Substitution of the Much Deadlier Long Gun

In making that assumption Professor Cook is guilty of a failure to follow his thinking to its logical conclusion, for which the only excuse is that Professor Zimring has been equally guilty. It is surely incumbent on one who constructs an argument for handgun prohibition based on the idea that less deadly weapons will be substituted to at least consider the alternative that more deadly ones will. Yet neither Cook nor Zimring ever even mention the possibility that handgunless criminals will substitute the four times more lethal long gun.[35]

Professor Cook's failure to consider this issue can not be justified by his finding that 96 per cent of *present* gun robberies are carried out with handguns rather than long guns. After all, his entire argument is based on the hypothesis that banning handguns will compel a drastic change from the present weapons-selection pattern of robbers. Indeed, Professor Cook's lapse in this respect is even less excusable than Professor Zimring's. Zimring's concern is with homicidal assaults, a significant number of which occur without planning and in areas in which the perpetrator may not have ready access to long guns. But Cook is concerned with robbery, a crime which, as to almost any commercial establishment at least, can invariably be planned so as to allow use of a long gun, or one which has been cut down to easily concealable size.

The difference between a long gun and a handgun is essentially ten minutes and a hacksaw. As Professor Kennett notes, "By the mid-1920's the sawed-off shotgun began to find favor in criminal circles. Compact and effective, . . . Clyde Barrow perfected a 'quick draw' with one concealed in a special holster sewn into his trousers."[36] But the most lethal of weapons, the submachine gun, requires no size alteration at all. In size, as well as other design features, the modern submachine gun is patterned after the Israeli Uzi, which is slightly more than thirteen inches long. Imitators include the U.S. Ingram, eleven inches long, designed to replace the .45 automatic pistol as the Army's personal defense sidearm; the Czech Skorpion, ten inches long, a favored weapon for assassinations by the Red Brigades in Italy and similar groups throughout the world; and the Russian Stechkin, 8.8 inches long. A robber can easily and conveniently carry any of these (or a sawed-off long gun) concealed under a sports jacket or in a brief case or flight bag.

In considering the likelihood of long-gun substitution by handgunless robbers, it must be remembered that the purpose of robbery is obtaining money and that robbers are willing, apparently, to endure considerable risk and inconvenience to that end. It must also be remembered that commercial robberies are approximately three times as remunerative as individual robberies, and that robbers are apparently well aware that a knife robbery of commercial premises is much more difficult and dangerous than a gun robbery. Given these considerations, it seems highly unlikely that the minor inconvenience of having to saw off (or find a suitably concealed way of carrying) a long gun would persuade many potential gun robbers to substitute knives or clubs if handguns became unavailable to them.

Moreover, there is evidence that the present preference of robbers for handguns over long guns is based on mere ignorance rather than relative convenience — and that handgun robbers can be redirected toward long guns by circumstances nowhere near as compelling as Professor Cook postulates a handgun ban would be. As to the firearms ignorance of robbers, it is universally attested by police, particularly as to the tyro robber whom Professor Cook believes a ban would most often deprive of a handgun. Studies of armed robbery provide numerous examples of gun-ignorant robbers accidentally discharging their weapons into their victims, their partners, or even themselves. (An example is the serious, though not fatal, injury sustained by the robber who shoved his cocked revolver inside his belt and then assayed to jump over a counter behind which was an open cash drawer. Less dangerous to himself or others was the robber mentioned in Professor McDonald's study who did not know that his automatic pistol had to be cocked in order to fire; when informed of this in the course of the robbery, he did not know how to cock it.)[37]

The likelihood of handgunless robbers substituting long arms is highlighted by a recent incident in Boston, a city in which Professor Cook finds handgun robbery comparatively low because of low handgun availability. Boston has, however, long had a comparatively high proportion of armed robberies committed with sawed-off shotguns. Several years ago Boston police campaigned for a supplemental appropriation to equip their vehicles with shotguns, emphasizing the advantage a robber enjoying the "awesome lethality" of a shotgun has over an officer armed only with the puny pistol. Though the City Fathers proved unresponsive, the publicity was educational for robbers. The number of armed robberies perpetrated with shotguns rose 75 per cent.[38] If this is the effect of mere education, what would a law that supposedly *forced* robbers to give up handguns accomplish by way of promoting shotgun robberies?

Professor Cook speculates (on what evidence we have seen) that if the dimwits he thinks most likely to be disarmed by a handgun ban switched to knives or clubs, the rate of accidental or intentional robbery murders would be reduced by one-third. But, by the same token, if they switched to shotguns and rifles (which are available in quantity, quality, and price comparable to handguns) the danger of homicide in robbery would at least quadruple.[39] What seems most likely is a combination of substitutions, i.e., some robbers would switch to knives and clubs, while others would switch to shotguns. Indulging Professor Cook's belief that non-gun armed robberies will be one-third as deadly, whether a handgun ban would reduce or increase the danger of robbery-homicide would depend upon the exact proportion of the substitutions. But even if 70 per cent switched to knives or clubs and only 30 per cent to long guns, the result would still be a substantially increased rate of robbery-homicide. If, on the other hand, half of the robbers substituted long guns while the other half went to knives, etc., the danger of robbery-homicide would double — even if we assume that *none* of the non-gun robbers ever killed a victim.

In closing this section we should note that our criticisms have been directed against Professor Cook's study only because Professor Skogan's is not vulnerable to them. When Professor Skogan speaks of a gun ban, it is of *all* guns so that there would be no substitution of long guns for handguns. Professor Skogan makes no assertion as to comparative likelihood of victim death in handgun, knife, club, etc., robberies. Finally, Professor Skogan does not suggest that the law can actually deprive robbers of handguns; he simply assumes this for the sake of argument and proceeds to extrapolate on that hypothesis. Whether a handgun ban would actually be effective against robbers is crucial, for if it would not, then it could have no effect upon robbery or robbery-murder.

Would Banning Handguns Reduce the Supply for Robbers?
Examining the Crucial Question

Many people who are unfamiliar with firearms-manufacturing technology assume that a handgun ban would necessarily reduce the availability of such weapons, if not immediately, in the long run, as those now available are surrendered to the police, confiscated, wear out, etc. But, without even considering the possibility of illegal manufacture or importation of weapons, a handgun prohibition might actually increase the number of weapons available to those it is intended to disarm, namely criminals and ordinary citizens who think it necessary to keep a handgun lying loaded around their residences for self-defense. At present such people compete for a very large, but still limited, number of handguns, against a very large number of other citizens who want them for recreational purposes, such as target shooting. It is necessary to differentiate these sub-groups according to their purpose in wanting a handgun, for it is only in direct relationship to those purposes that a handgun ban is likely to effect their conduct. Target shooters are unlikely to disobey a ban (except out of sheer defiance) because the use to which they wish to put their handgun has become virtually impossible without high likelihood of detection. But this does not mean that they will tamely surrender their handguns to the police. Instead, with minimum danger of detection, they can recover a large part of their investment (or even make a handsome profit) by selling their handgun on the black market.[40] Thus, even assuming that the overall supply of handguns is no longer increasing, the pool available to those who want handguns for self-defense or criminal purposes has been substantially increased by the addition of large numbers of weapons previously held by target shooters. At the same time, that pool is no longer being competed for by the former target shooters. Acquisition is thereby made easier for criminals or self-defense types.

But, it is argued, black market sales are inherently more expensive, and so, at the very least, a handgun ban would result in pricing some criminal or self-defense users out of the market. In fact, however, prices will rise only to the extent that the black marketeers' ability to raise them is not frustrated by the reduction in demand resulting from abstention by those who obey the ban on buying handguns. If the handgun ban is successful in compelling large numbers of present gun owners to dispose of their weapons, the result might well be an increase of supply beyond demand, thereby actually decreasing the cost of a black market handgun to a self-defense or criminal user. (Whereas, of course, if the handgun ban is not successful in driving even law-abiding gun owners out of the market, it seems unlikely that it will be successful against any other sector of the population.)

But there is a more telling argument yet against the assumption that banning handguns will at least result in raising their price to the criminal and self-defense types. That assumption rests on an unexamined belief that price is the only elasticity in the handgun market. In fact, the very imposition of a handgun ban produces an alternative elasticity in quality. The purchaser of a snub-nose Colt, Smith & Wesson or other commercially manufactured defense pistol receives a beautifully finished weapon which is highly accurate and has a life expectancy of at least 25,000-50,000 shots. In less than a day a Vietnamese or Pakistani villager can produce a crude, but fully functional, copy of such a handgun using tools considerably less sophisticated than those contained in millions of American households.[41] Made of inferior materials, by a producer with no particular reputation, who does not pay taxes or suffer any of the costs involved in government supervision, such a weapon could profitably be priced far below what is now charged even for cheap imported guns of comparable caliber. Such illegally manufactured weapons would be worthless for target shooting and might have a life expectancy of only a few hundred rounds. But these limitations would not matter to those who want guns for robbery, murder, or self-defense, since such activities are normally conducted at point-blank range and involve at most a few shots.

Only inability to compete against the superior product presently being manufactured, and the lack of an established black market, precludes the revival of handgun manufacture as a "cottage industry" carried on in hundreds of thousands, if not millions, of households and small machine shops across the country. With these impediments removed by a handgun ban, the total annual production by such small entrepreneurs could easily outstrip present annual handgun production and importation. With low-quality materials and no aesthetic frills, such weapons would become available to people who cannot now afford handguns. This raises yet another implication of handgun prohibition. Out of personal responsibility, as well as fear of the law, gun-store owners would not sell a handgun to a fifteen-year-old even if he could come up with the $100 purchase price of a cheap imported or used handgun. Will the illegal manufacturer who produces a "suicide special" for $15.00 and sells it for $40.00 be so scrupulous?

Ineffectiveness of Present Handgun Prohibitions

More compelling than any theoretical extrapolation can be is the actual performance record of handgun prohibition systems where they are in effect — a record of failure admitted even by their most ardent proponents. In 1971 the Mayor of New York, John Lindsay, a lifelong foe of handgun ownership, reported to a Congressional committee that his city contained eight million illegal handguns.[42] Though his precise figure must be dismissed as political hyperbole (it seems unlikely that there is one handgun for every man, woman, and child even in New York City), it is the consensus of informed opinion that the Sullivan Law has been virtually useless as a means of keeping firearms out of the hands either of criminals or of an ever-growing number of New Yorkers who think they need them for self-defense. The rough estimate on which most law-enforcement officials seem agreed is two million illegal handguns in the city.[43] It has been claimed that what this proves is not the inherent unenforceability of handgun prohibition, but the need for a national Sullivan Law that would prevent New Yorkers from buying guns in other states. But such sales are already illegal under both federal and New York law. Yet, if the estimate of two million illegal handguns is accurate, New York City has only half a million less than are legally owned in the entire state of California — and a rate of handgun possession significantly greater than that of the United States as a whole.[44] It is difficult to credit anything but inherent unenforceability for the fact that, after seventy years of rigorously enforced handgun prohibition, handgun-allowing states that are supposedly the source of the problem have lower rates of handgun ownership than does New York.

The attempt to blame the failure of handgun prohibition on the ready accessibility of nearby handgun-allowing states is doomed by evidence from Britain, where the prohibition is national in scope. The only in-depth study, which was done at Cambridge University in 1971, reports that "fifty years of very strict controls on pistols has left a vast pool of illegal weapons." This Cambridge report concludes that Britain's handgun population has remained constant (except for occasional increases), for the number of handguns confiscated by, or turned in to, the police remains about the same year after year.[45] It is true that ordinary respectable Britons do not own handguns, but this proves only that the law is voluntarily complied with, not that it would be enforceable if resisted. As the Cambridge report notes, Britons had voluntarily given up their handguns only because their nation was so violence-free when the handgun ban was instituted, and has remained so, that very few respectable people think they need guns for self-defense. Needless to say, the very different conditions prevailing in this country have generated a very different climate of opinion on that issue.

As he is aware of these considerations, Professor Cook's claims of the effect of a handgun prohibition on robbers are quite limited. He begins with the assertion that "anyone who is determined to obtain a gun will be able to do so, given enough money and effort — the 'professional' robbery will not be deterred. . . ." But under a strict handgun permit system the teenage tyro, the youngster undertaking his first few violent crimes, will not be able to surreptitiously "borrow" one from his father or the collection of someone else he knows. Instead he will have to commit robberies with other weapons (which, as we have seen, juvenile robbers are more likely to do anyway). Though even such a neophyte, if he persists in robbery, will eventually get enough underworld connections to be able to buy an illegal handgun, at least this will be denied him in his early robberies. For reasons already stated, Professor Cook believes that until he gets a handgun the likelihood of his killing a victim is greatly reduced.

Accepting *arguendo* Professor Cook's belief that handgun robberies are more deadly, we have no quarrel with the argument thus made. But in order to avoid misunderstanding as to its importance, it is necessary to correlate it back to the general data on robbery that Professors Cook and Skogan present. Finding that reducing handgun availability does not reduce the overall robbery rate, Professor Cook's argument for handgun prohibition is simply that, given the same robbery rate, less homicides will occur. At present less than 1 in 460 robberies ends in homicide, and such homicides represent less than 20 per cent of all murders. While a sharp decrease in such homicides would be highly desirable, the effect of a handgun prohibition would be slight, even using all of Professor Cook's assumptions. There will be no reduction of homicide at all in run-of-the-mill robberies, i.e., those committed by the experienced robber who concededly will retain his gun, or be able to obtain a new one, notwithstanding any ban. Rates of robbery-homicide can conceivably be effected only in that fraction of robberies that are committed by the teenage tyro or other inexperienced or casual robber. But even in this fraction of robberies a handgun ban will make little difference, because right now the inexperienced or casual are far less likely to rob with a handgun than the experienced robber. Professor Skogan's robbery study dismisses the utility of banning guns as to "amateur" robbers, saying that they "would not be much affected, for they are less likely to employ those weapons. . . ."

Yet another issue suggests that a handgun ban would be of minimal importance in reducing homicide in robbery. This is Skogan's projection (in which Cook concurs) that because gun robberies are two to three times as profitable as non-gun robberies, if a gun ban actually disarmed robbers they might double or triple the number of robberies they commit, in order to maintain their previous profit level. There would be little effect upon robbery-homicide if a handgun ban reduced the *rate* of homicide per robbery by two-thirds but simultaneously doubled or tripled the *number* of robberies.

Victim Armed Self-Defense as a
Factor in Reducing Robbery-Homicide

A final factor is suggested by Professor Cook's discussion of the deterrent effect on the overall robbery rate of victim handgun possession:

> The probability that a robber will be killed or injured by his victim is small but not insignificant, particularly in the case of commercial robbery. Such justifiable homicides almost always are committed with a gun, so that potential victims in cities [with high-density handgun ownership] pose more of a threat to robbers than in low-density cities. [Table setting out comparative statistics omitted.] To put these death rates in perspective, they can be compared to the overall annual death rate for twenty-year-old ˙Negro males of 340 per 100,000. In Atlanta, for example, a robber in this demographic group would double the likelihood of his death by committing seven robberies in a year. The likelihood of a robber being wounded by his victim is presumably some multiple of the likelihood that he will be killed.

The deterrent effect of victim handgun ownership may be illustrated by comparing violent crime rates of states in which shopkeepers are free to arm themselves to those in states whose laws are known to disarm them. New York State, for instance, has less population and less overall crime than California — but significantly more violent crime. While there may well be other factors in this besides the fact that New York bans handguns while California allows them, it remains true that any comparison between the six handgun-prohibiting states and all (or a demo-graphically comparable sub-set) of the handgun-allowing states finds the former to have at best the same rates of violent crime and generally higher ones — though their rates of overall crime are lower.[46] It seems at least possible that criminals feel considerably freer to engage in violent (as opposed to purely property) acquisitive crimes in states in which they know that their victim can not legally have a handgun to resist.

But these reflections on general deterrence of robbery have little importance for the question on which Professor Cook is concentrating, the incidence of homicide in robbery. That inci-dence is so infrequent that it would take a deterrent that enormously reduced the incidence of robbery to put much of a dent in the robbery-murder rate. Moreover, it is at least arguable that the kind of robbers who are going to be deterred by the prospect of an armed victim may be the ones who were least likely to end up in a robbery-murder situation anyway. We may envision four kinds of robbery-murders: (1) The robber deliberately decides either before or during the robbery to eliminate all witnesses; (2) The robber kills through accident or incompetence; (3) The robber panics and starts shooting when a customer or police officer unknowingly walks into the store, or when the victim does something he misinterprets as resistance; (4) The robber kills because the victim resists, screams, or runs. Assuming that these four correlate to four sub-types of robbers, types 1-3 seem inherently more likely to end up killing than type 4, who only kills when it is necessary to the robbery. Assuming that likelihood of victim armed resistance deters some of these types more than others, it is possible that type 3, the panicky robber, will be most likely to stop robbing if he thinks victims may be armed. But on the other hand, types 1 and 2, the murderous and the careless-irresponsible, may be the most unlikely to be deterred. Whatever the truth of these speculations, the fact remains that any deterrent effect the prospect of an armed victim may have upon robbery rates is unlikely to reduce them enough to significantly reduce the incidence of robbery-homicide.

But a question that Professor Cook does not consider is the utility of defensive handgun ownership for allowing a shopkeeper to live through a potential robbery-homicide situation. When a shopkeeper considers the matter (which he must do, at least when the situation is upon him), practical possibilities of using a gun against a robber are limited. If the robber gives himself away by "casing the joint" or acting very nervous while he screws up his courage to begin the robbery, the shopkeeper may frighten him off by displaying his gun. At least the shopkeeper will have it ready and can open fire before the robber has had a chance to more than start unlimbering his weapon.[47] But in most cases the shopkeeper will have no advance warning; the first notice he will have that the robber is anything other than an ordinary customer will come when he is confronted with a weapon. At least if that weapon is a firearm, resistance at that point will seem suicidal. Even if the robber is later momentarily distracted by something (a customer entering, a fire or police siren), the shopkeeper must calculate whether the opportunity is sufficient to allow him to resist successfully — a calculation that shopkeepers seem generally able to make.[48]

It is where the victim is confronted by the type 1 or 2 robber that self-defense becomes most relevant to the prevention of robbery-homicide. When the shopkeeper finds that there is a substantial likelihood of his being killed even if he doesn't resist, he has every reason to pull his own gun and hope that in the ensuing battle he will at worst become one of the 90-95 per cent of handgun shooting victims who recover. For an example of this see *Taylor* v. *Superior Court*, 91 Cal. Rptr. 275, 477 P.2d 129 (1970), in which the apparent intention to kill of a trio of crazed robbers resulted in husband-and-wife shopkeepers (both armed) shooting one to death and wounding another without suffering injury themselves. In a similar recent case from St. Louis, a shopkeeper killed a robber who had indicated his intention of disposing of all witnesses by turning to kill a customer who was lying face down on the floor in response to the robber's orders. How often such instances occur is impossible to determine, but they do recur in the limited available evidence on self-defense. [Editor's note: See detailed discussion of this evidence in the article by Carol Ruth Silver, *infra*, on women's armed self-defense.]

Professor Cook suggests that both the deterrent and self-defense benefits of handgun possession by shopkeepers could be preserved within a handgun prohibition scheme by issuing permits to shopkeepers. But in this he exhibits a surprising naivete, both as to the stated goals of the handgun prohibition movement and to the manner in which handgun prohibitions are actually administered. The several organizations and numerous prominent individuals who are in the forefront of the prohibition movement have reiterated their unshakable faith that handguns are useless for self-defense, and their admiration for England, where self-defense is not an acceptable reason for seeking a handgun permit.[49] In the United States the administrative policy model they point to is New York City where, by conscious design, the number of permits issued to shopkeepers has been steadily reduced over the past forty years almost in direct proportion to the steady increase in commercial robberies.[50] Handgun permits are granted (in general) only upon a showing of "unique need." Special exceptions are granted only to security guards, the very wealthy, the celebrated, the socially elite, political influence-peddlers, and (where sufficient monetary payment is made) to reputable "soldiers" of the Mafia. [Editor's note: See discussions of Sullivan Law administration *infra* in the section on women's armed self-defense.]

Summary and Conclusions as to the Probable Effect of a Handgun Prohibition upon Incidence of Robbery and Robbery-Murder

In sum, the probable effects of a handgun prohibition on robbery are:

1. *Overall Robbery Rates:* Handgun prohibition could conceivably reduce overall robbery rates only to the extent that it disarmed robbers, which neither Professor Skogan nor Professor Cook think it would do in most cases. Even if robbers were disarmed, Professor Cook finds that the overall robbery rate would remain essentially the same, except that it might rise, both because robbers with other weapons would have to make more robberies in order to gain the same profits, and because divesting victims of the means of self-defense would remove a "not insignificant" deterrent to robbery. Professor Skogan, assuming for the sake of argument that a gun prohibition disarmed all present robbers,

projects either an almost 75 per cent increase or an almost 30 per cent decrease in robbery as the result of the lower proceeds from non-gun robberies.

2. *Serious Injury to Victims:* Assuming again that a handgun ban caused all present handgun robbers to switch to knives, clubs, etc., the result would be a rise in serious injury to their victims from .3 per cent, the present gun injury rate, to between .5 per cent (present average injury rate) and .7 per cent (present rate for club-robbery victims).

3. *Effect upon Robbery-Murder:* The variables are so great that it is really quite impossible to predict any effect with certainty. Assuming the best possible case (i.e., ignoring the lacunae in Professor Cook's data and assumptions), the rate of homicide would be reduced by two-thirds in that tiny fraction of robberies committed by tyros who would have used handguns but were unable to get them because of a handgun ban. But this reduction may be fully offset by the effect of such a ban in doubling or tripling the number of non-gun robberies and in reducing the capacity of potential robbery-murder victims to defend themselves. When a crucial variable omitted from Professor Cook's data is examined, it appears that even for this small number of tyros the homicide rate would be reduced only if their lack of a gun induced them to engage in strong-arm robbery. In the much more likely event that they substituted club or knife attacks, homicide might actually be increased, especially as more robberies would be directed against the elderly and private individuals. Examining yet another question Professor Cook omits, to the extent that these robbers substituted sawed-off shotguns the homicide rate in their robberies would be at least quadrupled.

As many advocates of handgun prohibition have recognized, their strongest argument lies not in the likely effect upon robbery, but upon the assumption that domestic and acquaintance homicides would be greatly reduced thereby. The effect of handgun prohibition upon robbery even under the "best case" assumptions would clearly not be significant enough to justify the enormous financial, human, institutional, and constitutional costs of attempting to enforce a confiscation measure against the belief (whether right or wrong) of millions that they urgently need handguns for self-defense and have a constitutional guaranteed right to have them.

SECTION V: Self-defense, Handgun Ownership, and the Independence of Women in a Violent, Sexist Society

CAROL RUTH SILVER and DON B. KATES, JR.

I thought it was a real distinct possibility that I might be killed. I believed he would kill me if I resisted. But the other part was that I would try to kill him first because I guess that for me, at that time in my life, it would have been better to have died resisting rape than to have been raped.

I decided I wasn't going to die. It seemed a waste to die on the floor in my apartment so I decided to fight.

— Recollections of a woman
who successfully resisted rape.

Do you care about freedom? Dreams may have inspired it, and wishes promoted it, but only war and weapons have made it yours.

— Robert Ardrey

Surprisingly, despite the enormous literature on rape and other violence against women (and on firearms for self-defense), there appears to be no detailed treatment of the viability of women's armed self-defense. The widely publicized tracts in which handgun prohibitionists have argued that firearms are useless for self-defense dismiss women and women's issues summarily with the comment that women can't use guns anyway. The other side devotes scant attention specifically to women because it urges armed self-defense equally for both sexes; and gun experts see little difference between male and female capacity for self-defense with firearms.

I do not favor small caliber pistols [for women]. I have taught too many women, girls, and boys to handle [.45s] with ease and accuracy.

— Elmer Keith

If the housewife finds that a 12-gauge [shotgun] is just too strenuous, a 20-gauge is still pretty conclusive. . . .

— Jeff Cooper

During the frequent periods that I am away from home, I don't worry about my family, for my wife has a gun that she could use as well, if not better, than I could; and more important than knowing how to use it, she knows when and under what circumstances to use it.[1]

— Neal Knox

Similarly, the *Women's Gun Pamphlet*, published by a radical feminist group in Berkeley, simply assumes the viability of women's self-defense and proceeds with an excellent treatment of how to master handgun skills.

But we believe a specific discussion of women's armed self-defense is appropriate, because the crimes women fear are particularly deterrable and defendable with handguns. To the extent that the arguments in the anti-self-defense tracts are valid at all, what they demonstrate is that handguns are of little use against burglary and *household* (but not commercial) robbery. Handguns aren't much use against burglars because burglars take care to strike only when no one is at home to shoot them. As to household robbery, this occurs so infrequently that guns are not kept ready and accessible for resistance; in the rare event of a household robbery, the handgun is generally locked up in the basement, closet, or trunk. But proportionately far more crimes that are directed specifically against women (e.g., rape, murder or beatings by ex-husbands or boyfriends, etc.) involve breaking into their homes or offices. Thus a woman who keeps a handgun for defense against these crimes is much more likely than the normal householder to have it ready to confront the attacker — not to mention the fact that an ex-husband or boyfriend is a lot less likely to try to break in if he knows she is armed. But the tracts deriding self-defense deal with crimes against women by just not mentioning them. The most scrupulous and reliable of them, the Eisenhower Commission staff report, devotes to women only one sentence: "[They are] less knowledgeable than men about guns and generally are less capable of self-defense."[2]

We come to a very different conclusion based on a review of all the competent evidence as to successful and unsuccessful firearms defense incidents (by shopkeepers, householders, and, specifically, women repelling male attackers) correlated with the normal fact patterns surrounding crimes against women. As to all forms of male attack, we find that firearms, particularly handguns, offer women a high likelihood of successful resistance with a low likelihood of suffering serious injury, and that no other form of resistance does so. As to rape in particular, a firearm (particularly a handgun) is far superior to any other form of resistance because it is: (a) most likely to stop the attacker; (b) least likely to be taken away; and (c) least likely to be used to injure the woman if it is taken away.

In light of the bitterly controversial nature of this subject, we have attempted (not altogether successfully) to eschew emotionalistic terminology and argumentation and to separately discuss first the moral, and then the practical, issues. Furthermore — though at some cost to readability — we have found it necessary to constantly intersperse the discussion with disclaimers about what we are not saying, and clarifications about what we are. The first set of these can be presented here:

We fully endorse the common-law doctrine that a woman threatened with rape — or anyone else threatened illegally with death or serious injury — may rightfully resist with "deadly force." (The phrase "deadly force" is somewhat misleading, at least as to the relatively puny handgun. Even if an attacker persists to the point of being shot, his chance of recovery is 90-95 per cent, as opposed to perhaps 35 per cent if a rifle is used and 75 per cent in the case of a shotgun wound.[3] Let it be very clear, however, that we are *not* urging women to have handguns for self-defense. Whether a woman should do that is a purely personal decision which must be made in relation to the particular circumstances in her life. The principal factors that must be evaluated are: First, is she willing and emotionally able to use deadly force in defense of herself or others who are threatened with death or serious bodily harm? If not, her only use for a handgun will be target shooting. Second, do the potential dangers of her life situation justify the "costs" involved in having a handgun for self-defense? These costs are not only the monetary expenditures, but the time and effort necessary to familiarize herself with the gun and learn how to use it safely and efficiently. Third, is her environment one in which a gun can safely be kept? As to this, the consideration normally raised is the presence of small children in the household. In fact, it is generally possible to keep a handgun secreted and securely locked, but reasonably ready for use — or, in an emergency situation, on the owner's person where it is at all times under her direct control. Realistically, the presence in the household of a careless or irresponsible husband or boyfriend may create a greater risk of gun accidents than do children.

We do not suggest that a gun will be much protection to a woman who continues living with the person she has reason to think she may need to defend herself against. A gun is not an absolute guarantee of safety even to the most cautious and discreet of owners, much less one who courts danger. A woman who will continue to live with a man she knows to be capable of killing or seriously injuring her needs a miracle, not a gun. By the same token, possession of a gun is no justification for disregarding the litany of sound advice given by rape prevention groups. Rapists are extremely dangerous, and any prospective encounter with them is perilous, whether the woman is armed or not. She is well advised to avoid confrontation if humanly possible, for in this case, an ounce of prevention is worth many pounds of cure. Also, a woman may be confronted with a robber, rapist, or other attacker in circumstances where submission seems "the better part of valor." Having a gun does not compel her to use it any more than she is compelled to scratch, bite, kick, or scream if this would increase her danger. The point is that a gun provides a real opportunity to resist, whereas biting, scratching, etc., have very little likelihood of success and only provoke savage retaliation.

Just as *we* refrain from advising women to own handguns because the decision must be based upon each individual's evaluation of her own situation, so are we unalterably opposed to the so-called gun control laws that seek to substitute government fiat for this individual decision-making. We are opposed to this because we know how that system actually works in New York City, the model of administration that the handgun prohibitionists propose for the entire country. An ordinary woman who seeks a gun permit because she has been threatened or beaten by an ex-husband or boyfriend, or mugged or raped, faces an administrative obstacle course including every technique of discouragement, persuasion, and delay the New York City police can thrust in her path. If an unusually resolute applicant nevertheless perseveres, the permit is automatically denied unless the police are convinced that she will be able and willing to bring a lawsuit. Even when an applicant is successful, the process involves a minimum of six months of red tape — by which time she may have been killed or had to move somewhere else for her own safety. Police bureau-crats — all of whom carry a gun twenty-four hours a day for their own protection, incidentally — work on the principle that if they give a threatened woman a gun permit and she misuses it there will be an immense clamor in the newspapers. Whereas, if they deny the permit and something happens to her, no one will pay attention to her complaints (even if she is still alive to make them).[4] By the same token, such ordinary women — and especially minority and underprivileged women — are considered far too unimportant to receive the limited special protection resources that the police allocate to an elite few city officials and prominent individuals.

Unquestionably there are dangers in leaving to the individual citizen the decision whether to own the means of self-defense — although the far less than one in three thousand handgun owners who uses his weapon to murder is almost always going to be the kind of person whom the law cannot disarm anyway. But we find the dangers of individual choice considerably more acceptable than the arrogation of decision-making to a callous bureaucracy which sees to its own protection (and that of an elite, influential few others), while it cannot and will not provide protection to the ordinary individual to whom it denies a gun permit.

Rape and Other Physical Abuse of Women: The Magnitude of the Problem

For as long as the FBI has been publishing yearly reports of the nation's crime, the incidence of rape has been growing more rapidly than any other violent crime category. The rate (number of offenses reported per 100,000 population) tripled in the period 1933-65, whereas the homicide rate rose less than 25 per cent in the same period. In 1970-75 the rate of reported rapes rose by 48 per cent, while the number of reported murders, aggravated assaults, and robberies rose by 28, 45, and 33 per cent respectively. As violent crime rates (particularly murder) have steadily dropped since 1975, rape rates have continued to rise.[5] (It remains unclear, however, whether this represents an increase in actual incidence of rape — caused perhaps by the greater vulnerability of women as more live independent of men today — or simply the greater willingness of women to report rapes which in earlier years would have gone unreported.)

At the same time, nonsexual violence by men against women continues to account for a large proportion of homicides and an even larger (though often unreported) proportion of aggravated assaults. In New York City "40 per cent of all requests for police assistance and protection come from women who have been battered or threatened by their husbands."[6] (By definition, this figure does not include women murdered by their husbands, or women murdered, assaulted, or threatened by ex-husbands, boy-friends, ex-boyfriends, or other male acquaintances.) A study of St. Louis police reports of aggravated assaults (defined as at-tempted murder or assault resulting in serious injury) found women being attacked by present or ex-husbands or boyfriends in over 12 per cent of all cases (over 38 per cent of the cases where the victim was female). This is a conservative figure, according to Sandy Baker, who did the study for St. Louis Legal Aid, in that it includes only those cases in which the report explicitly so described the man, excluding many others in which the connec-tion was evident but not stated.[7]

Inability of the Criminal Justice System to Protect Women

How effectual is the law in protecting women? "In one city it has been shown that in 85 per cent of the cases, when a homicide occurs in the course of domestic violence, the police had been summoned at least once before the killing occurred; and in 50 per cent of the cases, the police were called five or more times before the actual murder."[8] Or consider the case of Linda Riss, as described in a dissenting opinion in New York's highest court:

Linda Riss, an attractive young woman, was for more than six months terrorized by a rejected suitor well known to the courts of this state. . . . This miscreant, masquerading as a respectable attorney, repeatedly threatened to have Linda killed or maimed if she did not yield to him: "If I can't have you, no one else will have you, and when I get through with you no one else will want you." In fear for her life, she went to those charged by law with the duty of preserving and safeguarding the lives of the citizens and residents of this State. Linda's repeated and almost pathetic pleas for aid were received with little more than indifference. . . . On June 14, 1959 Linda became engaged to another man. At a party held to celebrate the event, she received a phone call warning her that it was her "last chance." Completely distraught, she called the police, begging for help, but was refused. The next day [the suitor] carried out his dire threats in the very manner he had foretold by having a hired thug throw lye in Linda's face. Linda was blinded in one eye, lost a good portion of her vision in the other, and her face was permanently scarred. . . .

[Nevertheless the City has denied all liability, forcing Linda to sue.] What makes the City's position particularly difficult to understand is that, in conformity to the dictates of the law [of New York which forbids any civilian to have a pistol] Linda did not carry any weapon for self-defense. Thus, by a rather bitter irony she was required to rely for protection on the City of New York which now denies all responsibility to her.[9]

Common experience provides innumberable similar examples. A couple of years ago, a friend of ours in San Francisco awakened to find a prowler attempting to break in through her beveled glass front door. Fortunately for her, her screams drove him off — because the police *never* came. Apparently her call just got lost in the shuffle someplace.

Around the same time a male faculty colleague of Professor Kates' was robbed and severely beaten by three teenage hoods in Washington, D.C. After leaving the hospital, he investigated to find out why the police never appeared at the scene, for he knew they had been called by onlookers. He learned eventually that this is standard response by the rank-and-file of Washington officers to any situation involving teenage (as opposed to adult) muggers. The experience of Washington officers is that if they catch an adult mugger in the act he surrenders tamely enough, no matter how well armed he may be. The adult mugger knows that arrest means an hour's detention for booking, followed by release on bond or recognizance, and then, perhaps eight months later, conviction and a suspended sentence. But the poor ignorant teenage mugger, lacking knowledge of court practice, still thinks he is actually going to be punished. When an officer attempts to arrest such teenagers, they resist to the utmost, employing whatever weapons they have. Officers are understandably reluctant to risk life or limb (their own, and those of possible hostages or bystanders) just to send a few more teenage hoods through a forty-five-minute revolving door and out onto the streets again. So when police dispatchers receive a report of a mugging in progress, they are careful to note whether the culprits are teenagers — and, if so, the officers in the area suddenly find themselves terribly busy doing something else.

Police Negligence or Systemic Failure?

Tempting as it is to cast all the blame on the police, or the courts, or some other callous or negligent bureaucracy, the truth is that most of the problems are simply inherent in our system of justice. Often times police are reluctant to arrest a wife-beater, because they sincerely (and reasonably) believe that this will only endanger the wife by making him more vengefully brutal on future occasions when the police will not be there to intervene. Yes, the police can arrest him this time. But they can't stop him from seeing a magistrate after he is booked, and being released on bail or his own recognizance. That is the husband's legal right. The police cannot prevent him from returning to his own house or seeing his own children. Short of a court order, which is time-consuming, difficult, and expensive to obtain, these also are his legal rights. Once on the premises, he can brutalize, maim, or kill his unarmed wife, whether he is armed or not, long before the police can be summoned.

Few, if any, Americans, however great their abhorrence of spousal abuse, would suggest that the police be empowered to drag wife-beaters from their houses directly before judges who would summarily convict them and sentence them to life imprisonment. But it would require this kind of drastic change in our system of criminal procedure to ensure that when the police arrest a wife-beater he won't be out in a few hours, furious and able to wreak vengeance upon her.

Nor is it viable to talk about police protection for the threatened wife, girlfriend, etc. The simple fact is that the police are not staffed and organized (and they cannot be) to provide round-the-clock protection to the tens of thousands of women in communities across the country who are threatened, beaten, or murdered by their husbands each year — much less to the hundreds of thousands of other women who are threatened, beaten, or murdered by ex-husbands, boyfriends, or ex-boyfriends, or even to the women who are attacked by rapists. On this point, note that the facts we quoted from the Riss case were stated in dissent. The other judges of New York's highest court voted to deny any compensation, following hoary and universal doctrines of American law. In California these are summarized in the statutes:

> A public employee is not liable for an injury caused by his ... failure to enforce any enactment [i.e., law] .... Neither a public entity nor a public employee is liable for failure to ... provide police protection ... or to provide sufficient police protection ... [or] for injury caused by the failure to make an arrest or the failure to retain an arrested person in custody.[10]

Neither the courts nor the legislatures of our country are about to impose upon the police liability for not providing protection which they are not equipped or staffed to provide.

The law presumes that a citizen is ordinarily capable of protecting herself. As a practical matter that means a woman has to have a handgun.

The "Morality" of Women Defending Themselves with Handguns

We recognize the force of the conventional response that there must be "some better solution" than a woman threatening or shooting her husband, lover, etc. But in the real world, there all too often isn't any better solution. And musings about better solutions are of very little aid to a woman who is being strangled or beaten to death.

Consider a practical example: Less than a year ago the head of the St. Louis Legal Aid Women's Unit brought a client to Professor Kates for advice on buying and using a handgun. The woman's husband was a huge, powerful man with a long history of extremely violent attacks upon her and others. Her opportunity to divorce him arose only because he was currently hospitalized with two abdominal bullet wounds incurred during a nearly successful attempt to beat his sister and brother-in-law to death.

Let us examine what "better solutions" were available to this woman. Moving to another house in St. Louis and getting an unlisted phone number were of no use, since her husband could always find her at work. An impecunious black woman, she could not afford to quit her job. Even if she had, he could always have tracked her down through her friends. Moving to live with relatives in another part of the country seemed futile, for he knew where they lived, and she was convinced he would follow her. Beyond the immediate practical questions is an ethical one: By what right does anyone say that a woman — black or white, poor or rich — should give up her home, her job, her friends, and move to some place where she does not wish to live, rather than defend herself from a brutal, lawless attacker?

In the actual event, this woman did purchase a handgun and kept it on her person while her husband was visiting with the children. He did attack her, and she sent him back to the hospital with two more bullet wounds. Had she not had the gun, it seems quite probable that she would have been beaten to death. Although her skin is quite dark, the bruises on her face and neck were clearly visible the next day.

The Situation of Minorities and the Poor

This last example raises a question which the earlier ones also suggest: Given what police responsiveness is to violence against Linda Riss or law professors, or to our friend in her beautiful San Francisco Victorian, and to white middle- or upper-class people in general, what must life be like for minorities and underprivileged people living in the high-crime areas of our cities? The St. Louis police hierarchy provided a most reassuring answer when that question was put to them a few months ago by a local reporter doing a series on "gun control." They said that police protection is fully sufficient; blacks and the poor have no need for handguns in St. Louis. But repeating this to rank-and-file officers got the reporter only laughter and ridicule. The officers who actually work the ghetto unanimously and unequivocally told her that they cannot keep order there; self-protection is all that ghetto residents can rely on. More telling than their comments was their reaction to her proposal that some of them escort her into the housing projects while she was doing interviews there. Although she does not ordinarily have difficulty finding male company, she could not get any officer, black or white, to volunteer to enter the area with her while off duty. These men go there at all only because required to do so to keep their jobs — and then only armed, with an armed partner for back-up, in shotgun-equipped squad cars which they rarely leave.

We cannot resist adding a further example of what gun laws mean for poor women. A couple of years ago in Chicago a man literally smashed his way through the thin walls of a tenement apartment, raped the woman he found therein, and threw her out the fifteen-story window. Police arrived too late to catch him, so they arrested her roommate for carrying the handgun she used to scare him out of raping and killing her as well. The prosecutor dropped the charges after the case attracted nationwide publicity. This was probably influenced by his knowledge of what would have happened in the special "gun court" that handles all such cases in Chicago. One of its judges has commented that he rarely gives more than a small fine because, in virtually every case, gun law violators are decent, respectable citizens — shopkeepers, secretaries, the elderly — who carry handguns out of a legitimate desire and need for self-defense. (The real criminals never come before this court, for gun charges against them are only incidental to their trials for murder, armed robbery, aggravated assault, etc.) The judge usually doesn't even add probation to the fines because that would prevent the defendants from buying a new gun to replace the one the police confiscated, and the judge believes they need guns to live and work where they do.

But the leaders of the handgun confiscation movement have the answer. They are going to make it a federal crime to own a handgun, with sentencing to be *mandatory*, so that a prosecutor will not have to drop charges against a woman like this. He will know that the judge has no choice other than to give her a year in prison.

Women's Self-Defense versus the Anti-Self-Defense Tracts

We have already mentioned the several well-publicized tracts in which prohibitionists have argued that handguns are worthless for defense of self and others. It should be noted that none of these involve any attempt to compare how often gun-armed citizens have been successful in defending themselves to how often they have been hurt or killed in doing so. The *only* study collecting data on that has been done by Professor Kates and justifies a conclusion far from what the prohibitionists want. Their tracts rest principally upon the allegedly small number of burglars and robbers actually killed by householders. How appropriate this is as a measure of self-defense (and how they selected their justifiable homicide statistics) is discussed *infra*, along with Professor Kates' study. For the present, we repeat that, taking their figures at face value, all the anti-self-defense tracts show is that handguns have limited utility against: (a) burglars, because these strike when no one is home; and (b) household robbers, because this is so unexpected a crime that comparatively few householders keep handguns readily available to resist them.

This has no bearing at all on the likely success of a woman who keeps a handgun at the ready because she fears rape (which is proportionately far more likely in the home than robbery) or had been threatened by an ex-husband or boyfriend. These tracts have quite literally nothing to say about women's armed self-defense, for, in general, they avoid mentioning the kinds of crimes directed against women; the most thorough and scrupulous of them, as noted, dismisses women and their concerns with one contemptuous sentence. One measure of the likely success where a woman keeps a handgun ready is the success of shopkeepers (including many documented instances of women shopkeepers) in foiling robbers — yet another area the anti-self-defense tracts avoid discussing. A recent Duke University study concludes that in one city where many shopkeepers keep handguns ready for defense the average robber doubles his chance of dying by pulling seven robberies in a year — not to mention raising his chance of being wounded tenfold and taking an incalculably greater chance of being captured.[11]

Deterrent Effect of Handgun Possession

Another significant issue is the deterrent effect that victim possession of a handgun is likely to have on one considering attacking her. The year after Orlando, Florida, instituted a highly publicized training program in which six thousand civilian women mastered handgun combat skills, rape dropped 90 per cent there — though it rose precipitously across the country. We will discuss that and several comparable examples later. Such examples do not prove that handgun possession by individual women will deter crimes like rape or robbery for, in the absence of wide publicity, a criminal contemplating such crimes will not expect his victim to be armed. As to murder and other assaultive crimes, however, the situation is very different, for these are normally perpetrated among acquaintances. One who contemplates assaulting or killing is much more likely to know his victim is armed, and therefore to be deterred, than a rapist or robbery may be.

It is impossible to tell how many murders or assaults have *not* occurred because the victim was known to be armed. Nor can we be certain that such knowledge will necessarily deter the kind of man who contemplates attacking his ex-wife or girlfriend. It is clearly a deterrent to other kinds of violence, however. Surveys among prison populations uniformly find felons stating that, whenever possible, they avoid victims who are thought to be armed, and that they know of planned crimes that were abandoned when it was discovered that the prospective victim was armed.[12] Indeed, in these surveys prison denizens expressed support for handgun prohibition on precisely the same grounds which lead many honest citizens to oppose it, that it would make life safer and easier for the criminal by disarming his victims without affecting his own ability to attack them. Typical of prisoner comments, according to criminologist Ernest van den Haag of New York University, was: "Ban guns; I'd love it. I'm an armed robber."

Another illustration of the deterrent effect of civilian handgun ownership is the contrast between the Albuquerque police strike of 1974 and the Liverpool, England, police strike of sixty years ago. The unprecedented increase in criminal activity in Liverpool while the strike lasted has been used as a classic example of the need for police services.[13] But when Albuquerque police went out on strike, storekeepers openly armed themselves and citizens patrolled their neighborhoods with pistols and shotguns. Not only did major crime not rise — it dropped to lows that Albuquerque had not seen in years.

Quality of the Anti-Self-Defense Tracts

The Eisenhower Commission staff report admits that known handgun possession by a prospective victim can be an important deterrent, but passes quickly over the issue since the crimes it elects to focus on (burglary, robbery) are generally committed by strangers who can't be deterred because they have no idea whether their victim has a gun. Despite the evident bias in its selection of focus, the Eisenhower Report remains the most scrupulous and reliable of the anti-self-defense tracts. The least scrupulous is one that has been widely quoted for the statistic that the number of people killed accidentally by firearms in the home is six times greater than the number of robbers or burglars killed by such firearms. At first blush, this is a very impressive indictment of the keeping of handguns for self-defense. But, upon examination, it turns out that the rabidly anti-gun authors of this study manufactured their statistic by an unannounced transfer of gun suicides into the tiny category of gun accident deaths. Since the number of yearly handgun suicides is about 44 times the number of accidental handgun fatalities, the effect of this sleight-of-hand is to exaggerate the number of accidents by upwards of 4400 per cent, rendering the accident-to-self-defense comparison worthless.[14]

Nearly as misleading is the statement in another such study that "A loaded handgun in the home is statistically far more likely to be used against *family and friends* than as a means to repel strangers." As this study itself notes, about "72 per cent of all murders nation-wide occurred among *family members, friends, and acquaintances.* . . ."[15] Of course a woman who keeps a handgun for self-defense is most likely to end up using it "against family or friends" — because those are the people who are most likely to be trying to kill her!

In striking contrast to the anti-self-defense studies are the measures that their sponsors and publicists take when their own safety is at stake. While the *New York Times* unceasingly advises ordinary citizens that no one needs a handgun for self-defense, its publisher, Arthur Ochs Sulzberger, has a permit to carry a concealed handgun at all times. So, reportedly, have former Congressman and former New York Mayor John Lindsay (author of innummerable bills to disarm everyone else) and the husband of Dr. Joyce Brothers, the renowned pop-psychologist, whose *public* position is that no one needs a handgun for self-defense and that men who have them may be suspected of sexual disfunction.[16] One of the anti-self-defense tracts was issued by the U.S. Conference of Mayors, an organization that lobbies ceaselessly for handgun prohibition. Yet virtually every one of the big-city mayors responsible for this position carries a handgun himself and/or has armed body guards.

Now it will undoubtedly be suggested that public office holders and publishers (but faded ex-mayors and Dr. Joyce Brothers?) have reason to keep handguns for self-defense. But this would seem irrelevant if handguns are useless for self-defense as the tracts say. In any case, it is quite untrue that big-city mayors and newspaper publishers are exposed to greater dangers than many classes of ordinary citizens. For instance, hundreds of thousands of women are threatened by male acquaintances each year; thousands of these women are killed, and tens of thousands severely injured. In contrast, the last big-city mayor murdered in the United States was Anton Cermak of Chicago, who got in the way of a bullet intended for F.D.R. in 1934. Our information as to the murder of newspaper publishers is not so precise, but the last one that comes to mind is Elijah Lovejoy in 1857. If anybody in our society does *not* need handguns for self-defense it is the mayors, the Sulzbergers, the Lindsays and Brotherses, the Nelson, David, Winthrop, and John Rockefellers, and all the other millionaires, socialites, and celebrities who have New York City permits to carry concealed guns while ordinary citizens can't even get permits to own them. If these people — whose lives are spent in mansions, high-security office buildings, and chauffeured limousines — believe that handguns are useless, let them give theirs up first. But, somehow, not only does a handgun prohibition not affect them first, it never gets around to them at all.

Defense of Self and Others With Firearms:
Restoring the Balance to the Calculus of "Gun Control"

One artificial reason for the apparent strength of the case against civilian handgun ownership is an inherent lack of balance in the information available. The FBI publishes each year a national crime report from which anti-handgun propagandists draw endless statistics of the misuse of handguns in crime. But no state or federal agency, and very few localities, collect evidence of the lives saved and/or crimes foiled by civilian handgun possession. As we shall see, however, the evidence that is available on this suggests that such incidents numerically far exceed the incidents of handgun misuse. In short, we hear only about the bad that handguns do and not about the good. (Of course, much of that good is not quantifiable anyway. There is no way to determine how many assaults or murders do not take place because the prospective victim is known to be armed. Likewise, there is no way to quantify the innocent pleasure collectors or target shooters get from their weapons, or the feeling of security people get from having a gun handy, though in fact they never need to use it.)

The largest available sample of incidents in which civilian handguns were used against crime comes from the magazine of the National Rifle Association. But this sample is both biased and incomplete. It is biased because the NRA confessedly prints only those instances in which civilians were successful in using handguns against criminals, not those in which they were unsuccessful. It is very incomplete because the NRA prints only a page each month of the far more numerous incidents sent in by its readers from newspaper clippings. Newspapers report only a fraction of the armed self-defense incidents that occur. Moreover, NRA members do not read every newspaper in the country, they do not spot every incident reported in the newspapers they do read, and they do not clip and send in every report that they spot.

To obtain a less biased and more comprehensive sample, Professor Kates has for a year and a half had students clipping out, from thirty daily newspapers available in university and public libraries in St. Louis, reports of both successful and unsuccessful use of firearms in repelling criminal attackes. Some 296 incidents were analyzed, which allowed an interesting comparison between the success rate of armed civilians against criminals and that of the police and uniformed security guards. With success defined as the criminal being driven off, captured, or killed, armed civilians were successful in 84 per cent of the cases, while police and security officers were successful in 73.3 per cent. As to the danger of such resistance, 11.3 per cent of the civilian defenders, and 15.1 per cent of the officers, were wounded, while 6.5 per cent of the civilians and 6 per cent of the officers were killed. (The differential between the success of civilian defenders and the somewhat lesser success of police may be due to the fact that victims are likely to encounter criminals at closer range than are police. Alternatively or cumulatively, it is also true that the average police officer has little interest in developing firearm skills, and the encouragement, training, and opportunity to do so afforded by most police departments are meagre at best,[1 7] whereas shopkeepers and residents in high-crime areas often have great incentive to perfect their firearm skills.)

The difficulties inherent in a study based upon newspaper reports are numerous. Newspaper reports are not always accurate and complete. Some unsuccessful self-defense attempts may not have been recognized as such, e.g., because the robber snatched up the defender's gun after killing him, so that one does not thereafter recognize that the defender even had a gun. On the other hand, for reasons that will be described later, most successful self-defense examples are either not reported by the police or at least not thereafter carried in newspapers. Finally, the newspapers available in St. Louis do not cover anything like the entire country. With those deficiencies acknowledged, it remains true that this study represents the only attempt ever made to compare successful to unsuccessful self-defense incidents and to determine the percentage of times in which a defender was injured or killed.

In contrast, the anti-self-defense tracts contain concealed biases far more inappropriate than those that are apparent even in the NRA's totally unscientific monthly column. These tracts make no attempt to compare the numbers of successful and unsuccessful self-defense instances or to measure the percentage of danger that a defender may be injured or killed. They just belittle the value of self-defense by stressing the small number of burglars or robbers *killed* by *householders* in Cleveland, Detroit, Los Angeles, etc. Assuming that killings were the appropriate standard, no explanation is given for omitting the numerically far more frequent killings of criminals by *shopkeepers* who, after all, will also be denied handguns by a national Sullivan Law. Similarly, no explanation is given for these studies' reliance upon unofficial police "guestimates" of justifiable homicides from cities like Detroit and Los Angeles that do not keep actual records. At least some of the authors must be aware that the Chicago police department has been keeping records of justifiable homicides by civilians and by police for over forty years. These records show the number of criminals justifiably killed by civilians in each year to have equalled or exceeded the number killed by police — and in the last five years the civilian total has been almost three times that of the police.[18]

This comparison of civilians to police gains particular significance in light of the fact that "of the five largest cities in the United States, Chicago has the highest incidence of killings by the police." Professor Harding's study "Killings by Chicago Police,"[19] from which this figure is taken, prompts some other comparisons between police killings and justifiable homicides by civilian gun owners. Every one of these civilian homicides was declared "justifiable" only after the most rigorous scrutiny by the Homicide Section of the Chicago police. But when the killings are by the police, rather less rigorous investigative techniques are employed. Professor Harding concludes, "the collaboration between or the inertia of [Chicago police officialdom and the Prosecutor's office] has erected an almost impenetrable barrier to effective testing of questionable police conduct." Working only from materials made public by the authorities (i.e., without any attempt to find or question witnesses independently), Professor Harding categorized 14 per cent of the police killings he investigated as "apparent prima facie cases of manslaughter or murder. Several other [cases] presented factual anomalies sufficient to suggest that a thorough investigation [by the police at the time] might well have revealed such prima facie cases." Needless to say, in not one of these cases was an officer charged with any crime; in only one of them was an officer even disciplined by the department, although in almost 20 per cent of them Professor Harding found there to have been prima facie violations of such rules as not to shoot from a moving automobile or through apartment doors at unidentifiable targets.

At the risk of melodrama, it seems that possession of a Chicago badge is the equivalent of James Bond's "license to kill." Nor is Chicago atypical in the way in which it investigates killings by the police. A study by the Police Foundation finds the same pattern prevailing in seven other major American cities.[20] One may well wonder which represents the greater danger to public safety, handgun possession by citizens who know that if they are caught misusing their weapons they will be punished — or by police who know that they will not be?

Returning now to the anti-self-defense tracts, the most unfair of all the improprieties in their methodology is seizing on the number of criminals killed as a way of minimizing the "success" of civilian self-defense. Citizens keep pistols not to kill with, but to defend themselves. Success is measured as much by the number of criminals wounded, captured, or driven off without a shot being fired, as by the number killed. After all, we measure the success of the police not by how many criminals they kill, but by how many arrests they make and/or how many crimes they stop. The unfair minimization when kills alone are used as an index is not a minor one. From ten to twenty times as many criminals will survive handgun wounds as die of them,[21] and the number who flee or surrender without a shot being fired may well exceed the number of wounded survivors.

Admittedly, it is very difficult to quantify the amount of non-kill success against criminals. While many such examples appear in Professor Kates' newspaper sample, there is good reason to believe that the majority of such incidents are nowhere recorded. The unfortunate fact is that crime has become so commonplace that many major newspapers do not consider newsworthy an item about a citizen driving off or even capturing or wounding a criminal.[22] Moreover, it appears that many incidents in which prowlers, burglars, or muggers are driven off by civilians are never reported to the police, in part because most incidents occur at night, and the civilian has no very good description to give, and in part because the civilian may have owned or carried the gun illegally.

Only one sample with which we are familiar (and that a highly flawed one) provides comprehensive evidence as to the use of civilian handguns in defense of self or family. This is a survey taken for the California Department of Justice, in which 58 per cent of those admitting to handgun ownership claimed that they or a member of their family at some time used that handgun in civilian self-defense.[23] Such self-reporting statistics must be used with great caution. The respondent may simply have invented an incident for the delectation of the poll-taker. Or the incident may have occurred, but it may have been the handgun user who was in the wrong and who illegally threatened or harmed another person. Because the question asked contained no time limitation, the respondent could be referring to an incident which happened in his household thirty or forty years ago. A drastic but effective way of excluding bias through invented or misreported or ancient incidents is to arbitrarily exclude from consideration 90 per cent of the self-defense uses claimed by the respondents, and to assume that the incidents in question occurred not in the two years immediately preceding the survey, but in the entire preceding fifteen years. Assuming, therefore, that only 5.8 per cent (rather than 58 per cent) of America's handgun owners used their weapons in defense of self or others during years 1960-75, it still appears that the number of instances in which handguns were used in defense exceeds the number in which they were misused to kill in those years by a factor of 15-1.

The Effort to Dissuade Women From Keeping Firearms for Self-Defense

We are well aware of the deluge of advice to women that resisting a rapist with a firearm is both futile and dangerous. If this be accepted, it must be concluded that women should make no physical resistance to rape, for unarmed resistance would be even more futile and at least as dangerous. If an armed woman cannot resist a rapist, surely it would be futile for an unarmed woman to try. As to likelihood of injury or death from resisting, if rapists would be inspired to homicidal fury by the mere experience of wresting a gun away from a woman (as they are supposed to be able to do so easily), what will their reaction be to a woman who screams, scratches, bites, kicks, etc.? It seems that a woman who doesn't have a male around to protect her had better just "lie back and enjoy it" — and hope that her attacker does not have it in mind to mutilate or murder her afterwards.

Before accepting such a posture, women should be informed that there is no evidence that the projected scenario of a rapist taking a woman's gun away from her and shooting her with it has ever occurred outside of cinematic fiction. To eliminate any question of biased research on our part, we took this conclusion to Lorraine Copeland, an acknowledged authority in the area of rape. While director of the Queen's Bench Foundation Rape Victimization Project, she did three major empirical studies,[24] including one on resistance techniques, and familiarized herself with the vast corpus of studies and other literature available on rape. Though there were women who successfully used firearms in self-defense in Ms. Copeland's sample, their number was too small to justify any conclusion. But in none of those cases did the woman have her gun taken away and used against her; and Ms. Copeland confirms our conclusion that a review of the entire corpus of rape literature reveals no such case.

In contrast to this unsubstantiated scenario, there are hundreds of documented examples of women successfully using firearms against male attackers. The following from the *St. Louis Post-Dispatch* from March 25, 1976, provides a particularly ironic counterpoint to the propaganda with which anti-gun police officials have deluged women:

> George Kensey can't be sure whether he has poor judgment or bad luck — but he can be sure that he has bullet wounds in the shoulder and back. The woman whom Kensey attempted to pull from an outdoor phone booth near Gardena, California, early yesterday turned out to be Barbara Sherwood. And Ms. Sherwood turned out to be a sheriff's deputy, armed with a .38 revolver. She shot Kensey twice, took him to the hospital for treatment, and then moved him to the Los Angeles County jail where he is being held on suspicion of attempted rape.

Or consider this item from the *St. Louis Globe Democrat:*

> "Get off or I'll shoot you," said the 60-year-old woman as she yanked a gun from under her pillow and ordered the rapist to stop. He obeyed. While continuing to point the gun at her assailant, the woman, whose identity was not disclosed, telephoned police yesterday. They arrested Robert Thomas, 27, and charged him with [attempted rape and various other crimes]. Police said Thomas came to the woman's apartment seeking a friend who was not there. He allegedly flashed a

straight razor, ordering the woman into her bedroom, and told her to undress.

This incident recalls an earlier one in which a Chicago woman confronted by a rapist in her apartment pretended to faint. When he carried her to her bed she reached under a pillow, pulled out a revolver, and shot him dead.

Many of the thousands of examples printed in the NRA magazine over the years have involved gun-armed women routing male attackers. Typical are the following that appeared in just one randomly selected issue (January, 1978).

Oklahoma City, Oklahoma — a knife-armed burglar who backed a 77-year-old woman into her bedroom fled when she grabbed a handgun from under her pillow and fired a shot over his head.

Richmond, California — a woman called the police about a shotgun-armed prowler. When he broke into the house before they arrived, she killed him with a pistol.

Shreveport, Louisiana — a burglar who tried to force his way into the home of an 84-year-old woman at 2:30 A.M. fled after she shot him with a handgun.

Lennox, California — two men raped a woman who was five months pregnant; they fled when she secured a gun after they had gone into the kitchen to get some beer.

As isolated instances, such anecdotes prove little. We recount them to exemplify the hundreds of such cases we have reviewed. These are to be considered in the context of the general facts on armed self-defense and on the psychology of rapists and the circumstances of rape that are described in the immediately preceding and succeeding sections. Our conclusion from all this evidence can be stated in two sentences: First, women who prepare themselves to repel rape with a firearm stand a very good chance of success, and very little chance of being injured as a result. Second, if someone nevertheless considers self-defense with a gun too risky, the only rational course is complete submission, since any other form of resistance is at once far less likely to succeed, and at least equally likely to provoke a rapist into violent retaliation. A further point is that about 80 per cent of· the documented successful armed resistance examples involved women using handguns. These are safer, easier to handle, and much less lethal, than long guns. As to karate, judo, or other martial arts, achieving and maintaining the necessary defensive preparedness with a handgun is far less arduous. At the same time, a handgun is a far more effective defensive weapon against even one attacker, much less several. Although Ms. Silver has a brown belt in one school of karate, and a purple belt in another, she believes it far safer to have a firearm to resist an attacker, regardless of whether, or how, he is armed.

Although we will be devoting considerable space to the likelihood that a rapist can disarm his victim, it may be useful to enter another set of disclaimers and clarifications here: We are not claiming that never out of thousands of instances of resistance by armed women will a rapist get a handgun away. We are saying that such an occurence will be very rare, and that when it occurs it is highly unlikely that the rapist will shoot her.

First, a rapist who is confronted by a woman who is armed and ready to defend herself will generally flee; what rapists seek is a helpless victim upon whom they can take out their hostilities — not someone who stands a substantial chance of seriously injuring or killing them. Second, if the rapist chooses to attack, the most likely result is that he will be shot until he desists; police combat instructors advise their pupils never to attempt to manually disarm a person with a handgun unless they are convinced he is about to shoot them anyway. Third, assuming that a rapist does wrest a gun from a woman after considerable struggle, he will be no more (and perhaps less) inclined to kill her or injure her than if she had bitten, scratched, kicked, or otherwise resisted without a weapon; if the gun has been fired during the struggle, the rapist will probably depart rapidly to avoid the police. Assuming that rapists could wrest guns away as easily as movie and TV scripts suggest, they are likely to be considerably less annoyed by such resistance than biting, scratching, etc. In the one case we know of where a rapist did get a woman's gun, he did not brutalize her thereafter. She stated, incidentally, that she lost her gun only because she could not bring herself to shoot him, though she had the opportunity. However humanitarian her reluctance, the result is that this so-called East Area Rapist has continued to rape scores of women in Sacramento, California, over several years' time.

Characteristics of Rapists and Rape Situations

Despite centuries of romanticization, it is by now well recognized that rape is not primarily a sexual act. This is emphasized by a survey Lorraine Copeland took among convicted rapists in California's Atascadero State Hospital.[25] More than three-quarters of the inmates stated that, on the day of their crime, they were feeling frustrated, upset, or depressed about something (other than the woman whom they victimized). Their primary concern was not sexual release, but venting these hostilities and antagonisms on a helpless victim. Indeed, almost 40 per cent of these men were frustrated or depressed in general, and not because of conflict with a particular woman or women or all women. It seems that these men would have been equally happy to take out their frustrations by brutalizing a man they knew to be helpless; and some rapists have records of non-sexual, but extreme and unprovoked, violence against children.

The theme of power and helplessness — as opposed to sexual arousal — runs like a leitmotif through every study of rape. Despite the romantic myths, it is quite untrue that rapists concentrate upon conventionally attractive women. Victims are chosen primarily because their situation is perceived by the rapist as foreclosing effectual resistance; it is more important that the victim be helpless than desirable. Though over 60 per cent of the Atascadero rapists were frustrated, angry, or depressed because of problems with some particular woman, they chose instead to brutalize some other female acquaintance or a complete stranger. They were getting back at a woman who had them "by the short hair" — but they could do so only by striking at one whom they perceived as helpless. Incidentally, when the rapist is confident that it will be futile, he often actually enjoys the woman's resistance. Many of the Atascadero rapists expressed disappointment that their victims had not struggled more. Very violent rapists often gratuitously brutalize unresisting victims in order to provoke them to futile resistance which can be even more savagely suppressed.

As to time and geography, a recent Denver study finds that "the greatest proportion of" rapes over a two-year period "occurred [between] midnight and 4 A.M., while the victim was asleep in her bedroom."[26] A study of almost 650 Philadelphia rapes in the late

1950s found over 38 per cent of them occurring in the victim's own home, with another 11.6 per cent occurring in automobiles, and the rest in "open spaces." Of the Philadelphia rapes, 71 per cent are characterized as "planned" and 11 per cent as "partially planned," though the evidence for this is somewhat shaky, since it relies primarily on victim perception.[27] In a New York study, some 60 per cent of the rape offenders questioned indicated that they acted upon immediate impulse with no prior planning.[28] As to means of intimidation, various empirical studies of rape disclose from 10 to 15 per cent of the offenders using guns, from 20 to 55 per cent using knives and other weapons, with the remainder relying on brute force.[29] The fact that only a small minority of rapists carry guns, and that a very large proportion carry no weapons at all, should not be misinterpreted as suggesting that rapists are not dangerous. If anything, it suggests the reverse. A gun-armed criminal (whether rapist, robber, or burglar) brings to bear against his victim the weapon which is most likely to secure obedience by mere threat. A criminal who relies on some lesser weapon is more likely to actually have to use it, either gratuitously, because he fears that threatening with it will not be enough, or because the victim actually does resist. For that reason, numerous studies of robberies both in this country and in Great Britain find injury to occur most frequently and be most serious when no weapon is used, or when the weapon is not a firearm.[30]

In contrast to rapists, robbers are significantly more likely to be carrying some kind of weapon, which is most likely to be a firearm. Doubtless one reason for this is that robbery occurs far less often than rape on the spur of the moment, when the perpetrator is likely to be armed with nothing more than a pocketknife, if that. In contrast to the robber, the rapist feels more free to act on momentary impulse, because he is confident of his physical domination over women. By the same token, even when a rape is pre-planned, the rapist may not think it necessary to use a firearm (or, perhaps, not any artificial weapon at all) to overawe his victim.

Also, many rapists eschew firearms (or other weapons) for exactly the same reasons that robbers adopt them, i.e., the likelihood that their mere display will cow the victim into submission. While a robber wants to obtain money, and as easily as possible, a rapist is seeking psychological satisfaction. Because this is enhanced by victim resistance (if obviously futile), rapists generally opt against the gun, which will ensure compliance, thereby depriving them of the opportunity to savagely suppress resistance. Moreover, as a means of suppressing resistance, a gun is too distant and impersonal. Extremely brutal rapists almost always prefer a knife, or even better, a bludgeon or their unaided hands and feet.[31] Rape-murderers very rarely shoot their victims, preferring to stab them as did Richard Speck (though he also had a gun). But often even the knife-armed rape-murderer eschews the weapon, preferring to get down and beat, kick, and/or strangle his victim.

The Mechanics of Women's Armed Self-Defense

The notion that women cannot defend themselves with firearms is the last apparently respectable (to "liberals") remnant of the sexist mythology about women and machines. In fact, women are at least equal to men in mastering combat firearms skills. In addition to its police training, the Chattanooga, Tennessee, Police Academy has initiated a short combat pistol training course for civilian women. The Academy's head reports that "most of the women had never [before] held a revolver, much less fired one." Nevertheless, he was astounded to find that, after two hours of classroom instruction and one hour on the range, they were consistently outshooting experienced police cadets who had the benefit of eight times as much instruction and practice.[32]

Of course the average rapist whom an armed woman will face has nowhere near the training or experience even of a police cadet. The phenomenal incompetence of criminals with weapons is something often and thankfully commented upon by police.[33] In addition, about 85 per cent of rapists facing an armed woman will have the distinct disadvantage of not having a gun themselves.

Many rapists confronted with a gun will not even attempt to attack the woman, but will retreat or surrender if the opportunity is open. Empirical studies of sexual assault find a substantial proportion of would-be rapists backing off from even unarmed victims who show confidence and belligerence, rather than the timorous submission that the rapist expected. A fortiori, the number of rapists backing off will be greater yet where the woman's confident belligerence is supported and emphasized with a pistol. Of those rapists who would attack despite the woman's possession of a gun (or because they don't realize she has one until too late), many would be stopped cold by absorbing one or more bullets. Even if the rapist manages to close upon, and grapple with, a gun-armed woman without being shot, her screams and/or the weapon's discharge is likely to summon help, or at least to cause the rapist to depart for fear that police may come.

Confronting the Gun-Armed Rapist

A commonly heard objection to these arguments is that they apply only as long as rapists are less well armed than their victims. But (it is said) when women start defending themselves with guns this will prompt rapists to begin carrying guns, and the victim with the gun will find herself in more trouble than she would have been without it.

There are so many holes, both factual and theoretical, in this objection that it is hard to know where to start. Probably it is best to begin by reiterating a point made earlier which applies to resistance by a gun-armed woman in any situation, no matter what kind of weapon her attacker has. The idea that having a gun puts the victim in a worse position than if she had no weapon depends on the perverse assumption that somehow a woman with a gun must attempt to use it even if she thinks it will endanger her life. But nothing requires a woman to pull a gun against a rapist who has "the drop on her" or has grabbed her and placed a knife against her throat. The whole purpose of having a weapon for self-defense is to increase, not to diminish, the victim's options. A gun-armed woman may still submit if this seems advisable. The gun simply gives her the capacity to resist if that option seems open, or if the rapist appears to be one of those who kill or mutilate their victims regardless of submission.

This raises a point of significance for the question of any kind of resistance to rapists. We have said that there is no evidence that rapists have ever injured women because of armed resistance, while there is every reason to believe that other forms of resistance are at least equally likely to enrage them. But, while women who resist without weapons are sometimes injured because of it, it must also be noted that far more terrible injury has often been suffered by women who submitted abjectly. Many rape-murderers make up their mind to kill their victim before they ever focus on a specific woman, and regardless of whether she resists. Many victims are maimed or murdered for no apparent reason at all, or even because they had submitted, thereby cheating the rapist out of the satisfaction of savagely suppressing their resistance.[34] Faced with such an attacker a woman can only be better off for having a gun, whereas with a less brutal rapist she is no worse off.

Nor can the full range of the opportunities to resist be comprehended by a scenario in which the rapist "gets the drop" in a completely unexpected initial encounter. Most rapists apparently observe their victims for some time before making any move, and often the victim observes them as well. Many rape victims indicate that they anticipated the attack before it came but were unarmed and therefore unable to do anything about it.[35] An armed woman could forestall attack in such a situation by simply making it apparent that she had a gun. Even if he has a gun himself, a rapist has nothing to gain and everything to lose from attacking rather than fleeing at this point. The woman can pull her gun at least as quickly as he can pull his, and she will be far more willing to actually shoot because of the police attention which the resulting noise is likely to attract. The best he can hope for from an exchange of gunfire is to escape from the situation unscathed — which is precisely what he could have accomplished by leaving without pulling his gun. If she shoots him, he is plainly the loser. Even if he manages to shoot her in return, she goes to a hospital where 90-95 per cent of handgun shooting victims recover, while he can go there only at the risk of being apprehended.

Assuming now a different scenario, in which a rapist takes an armed victim completely by surprise, her firearm may still give her the opportunity for effectual resistance at a later time. Often rapists encounter their victims at locations where it is impossible to search or disrobe them, and therefore have to transport them to more secluded areas. During the movement phase there will almost always be moments in which the attacker's attention is distracted, so that the victim may draw and (if necessary) use her own weapon. This will be particularly true if, as often occurs, the rapist attempts to transport her in his automobile.

Above, and apart from, the foregoing answers to the objection is a simple factual problem with it: The growth of an expectation among prospective rapists that women are going to resist them with guns will not result in more rapists arming themselves with guns but in fewer rape attacks. A rapist who thinks armed resistance is likely will not rape, for what he wants is "a sure thing," a helpless victim who has no real chance at all. When a victim arms herself she raises her chances of injuring her attacker by an infinite quantum, i.e., from virtually nil to substantial. Even if the rapist believes that by getting a gun himself he shifts the odds back into his own favor, the chance of loss is still unacceptably high. It is no longer "a sure thing"; he can get hurt or killed.

The accuracy of this analysis is demonstrated by the actual results in communities which have adopted defensive firearms training for victims as a strategy for reducing violent crime. Faced with a dramatic increase in forcible rape, Orlando, Florida, police instituted in 1966 a well publicized program in which 6,000 civilian women received firearms defense training. In 1968 Orlando was the only city of 100,000 population in the United States to report a decrease in violent crime. Rape dropped by 90 per cent, while aggravated assault and burglary dropped by 25 and 24 per cent respectively.

In Highland Park, Michigan, armed robberies dropped from a total of eighty in a four-month period to zero in the succeeding four months, after police there instituted a highly publicized firearms training program for retail merchants. In Detroit such a program was carried on by a grocers' association over the opposition of the police chief. The program received extensive publicity, first through the chief's denunciations of it, and subsequently when seven robbers were shot by grocers. Grocery robberies in Detroit dropped 90 per cent. In 1971 publicity for a firearms training program for New Orleans pharmacists was credited by police and federal narcotics agents with causing pharmacy robberies to drop from three per week to three in six months there.[36]

By no means are these statistics offered for the proposition that armed civilian self-defense represents a panacea for violent crime. It is certainly conceivable that the dramatic crime reductions noted were purely coincidental, being caused by factors that had nothing to do with the highly publicized civilian firearms training programs. More likely is the possibility that at least part of the criminal activity that would have been committed in Orlando, Highland Park, Detroit, and New Orleans was transferred to neighboring communities, where victims were perceived to be less well armed.

Moreover, a strong argument can be made that the Orlando, etc., examples are of limited relevance to the subject under discussion here. These examples involve widely publicized community firearms training programs which might have come to the notice of persons considering committing violent crimes in those communities. In the short run, at least, even a very substantial increase in the percentage of women who keep firearms for self-defense is unlikely to generate enough publicity to become a factor in the calculations of prospective rapists. Obviously, they are not going to be deterred from rape by the increased likelihood of victim armed resistance if they do not perceive that increased likelihood. By the same token, however, rapists who do not perceive an increased likelihood of armed resistance will not react to that likelihood by increasingly carrying firearms themselves. But increased carrying of firearms by rapists was the harm which it was postulated would follow from an increase in the incidence of women's armed self-defense.

In sum, women are not constitutionally incapable of mastering armed self-defense as has been postulated. The possession of a firearm gives a woman decisive superiority over the 85 per cent of rapists who are either unarmed or armed with a weapon which is markedly inferior. A dramatic increase in incidents of gun-armed women repelling rapists will not dramatically increase the proportion of rapists who attack with firearms. If it has any effect, it will be to dramatically decrease the overall number of rape attacks, at least against women who are perceived as likely to be armed.

Conclusion

In closing it seems pertinent to ask why so many men have expended so much effort toward convincing women that they cannot defend themselves with guns. At least part of the answer, we submit, lies in the fact that the handgun, both symbolically and in reality, is the ultimate expression of the difference that the Age of Machines has made in the relationship between men and women. In prior ages, that relationship has been largely fixed by the differential in strength between the sexes. But the fact that most men can easily bench-press a hundred pounds, while most

women would have difficulty with seventy-five, fades into insignif-
icance when women have access to machines that lift tons. Even
for men who accept this (and the continuing mythology about
women and machines shows the extent of male resistance to it),
the sticking point is the idea of women having access to guns to
protect themselves with.

For men know that throughout all the prior ages of history the
bottom line in male-female relations has always been woman's
need for male protection. Women could not live alone for fear of
predation by males. So they lived with a male protector and
accepted his dictation of their role, either as a condition of
receiving his protection, or because he would impose it upon them
by physical force, or both. Access to firearms gives women, for the
first time in history, the capacity to live independently and apart
from men in safety and freedom.

We are not suggesting that it is right (or wrong) for women to
live separately and apart from men. What we are suggesting is that
women must have the freedom to choose with whom, and under
what conditions, they shall live. That freedom is made possible by
the opportunity to possess a handgun. To paraphrase a saying
from the Old West: God didn't make men and women equal,
Colonel Colt did.

SECTION VI: Constitutional and Civil Liberties Implications of Handgun Prohibition

The Second Amendment as a Restraint on State and Federal Firearm Restrictions

DAVID T. HARDY

The ultimate authority . . . resides in the people alone [under our Constitution, due to] the advantage of being armed which the Americans possess over the people of almost every other nation.
— James Madison

Guard with jealous attention the public liberty. Suspect every one who approaches that jewel. Unfortunately, nothing will preserve it but downright force. Whenever you give up that force, you are ruined. . . . The great object is that every man be armed . . . Everyone who is able may have a gun.
— Patrick Henry

. . . and what country can preserve its liberties if its rulers are not warned from time to time that this people preserve the spirit of resistance. Let them take arms.
— Thomas Jefferson

The Second Amendment: Individual or Collective Right?

The Second Amendment's simple statement of a need for a militia and the existence of a right to bear arms has engendered considerable controversy among courts and commentators. The major dispute in its interpretation concerns the question of whether this Amendment creates an individual or a collective right. The United States Supreme Court in *United States* v. *Miller*, as well as many commentators,[1] have adopted the collective rights approach. This position views the Second Amendment as a guarantee only of the right of state governments to maintain organized militia units free from federal disarmament. The effect is to interpret the Amendment as stating "the right of the state to arm organized militia formations shall not be infringed." Under this view, since the Amendment protects the interests of the state alone, individuals cannot invoke its protections, and it confers no right to bear arms aside from uses necessary to the maintenance of the organized state military units. The basis for this interpretation rests upon the view that the Amendment's initial clause, "A well regulated Militia, being necessary . . . ," strictly limits the following phrase, " . . . the right of the people to keep and bear arms shall not be infringed." It is argued that the framers used "the people" to signify "the states," and certain statements of the framers emphasizing the interest of the states in their militia tend to validate this.

In contrast to the collective rights theory, a minority of commentators have adopted an individual rights approach.[2] This view emphasizes the positive grant contained in the second clause of the Amendment that "the right of the people to keep and bear Arms, shall not be infringed." The initial militia clause is viewed as a statement of the object that the framers hoped to achieve by guaranteeing an individual right to bear arms, the creation of an armed citizenry. By guaranteeing the existence of such an armed citizenry, which would itself constitute the militia (as the term was employed by the framers),[3] the framers are seen as intending to create a base, secure against federal control, from which the states might fashion organized units. Whatever end the framers desired to achieve, the right they created is viewed by individual-rights theorists as residing in individual citizens and it may be invoked by them as a protection of their right to keep and bear arms.

Language of the Second Amendment

In attempting to determine the better view, resort may be had both to the literal content of the Second Amendment and to the extrinsic evidence as to the meaning attached to those words by the framers. An examination of the Second Amendment should focus upon three critical phrases: "the right of the people," "to keep and bear Arms," and "A well regulated Militia, being necessary to a free State."

Some commentators have suggested that the choice of the words "the right of the people" indicates that the right conferred was collective in nature.[4] These authorities argue that the framers employed the terms "citizens" or "persons" to describe rights intended as individual, and "the people" to describe rights intended as collective. This argument seems deficient for two reasons. First, it does not correspond with the interpretation given other constitutional provisions of similar wording. The Fourth Amendment refers to the "right of the people" to be free from unreasonable searches and seizures, yet it has been construed as a right invokable by individual citizens. The First Amendment employs similar language in recognizing the right of association, a right which, though collective in nature, has been construed as protective of individuals. The Ninth Amendment also refers to rights of the people, and on the few occasions when it has been applied it has been viewed as barring government intrusions upon individual rights. In addition to conflicting with interpretations given similar phrases in other amendments, the view that "the people" connotes "the states" fails to account for various indications that the framers distinguished between these two terms. In the Tenth Amendment, the framers reserved non-delegated powers either to the states "or to the people," suggesting that they viewed the two as different entities. Moreover, major disputes in the ratifying conventions centered upon whether the phrase "We, the people" in the Preamble implied that the Constitution originated from the people rather than from the states, which suggests that the framers did not consider the terms interchangeable. Thus the view that the right "of the people" to bear arms is really a right "of the states" must involve inconsistent constitutional interpretation and also fails to consider evidence of a distinction made by the framers between these terms.

In contrast, the view that "the people" indicates the recognition of an individual right does not conflict with interpretations given other rights of similar wording and recognizes a distinction between the people and the states. The terms employed to describe those to whom the Second Amendment rights belong thus seem to support the individual and not the collective approach to the Second Amendment.

The framers' description of the right "to keep and bear Arms" also seems more favorable to the individual approach than to the collective rights view. Two specific rights were established, the right to keep arms and the right to bear arms. If the framers' intent was only to protect organized state militias, and insure against a professional army, this dichotomy would be neither necessary nor appropriate. It would not be necessary, since a right to bear arms in the field would have sufficed to enable the militia to carry out its duties, regardless of where the weapons were kept when the members were off duty. The provision of a right to keep arms is also more appropriate to an individual than to a collective right. It is possible to construe a right of the people to bear arms as a collective right to engage in military service, viewing the bearing of arms as a term of art relating to service in the military. But the keeping of an object is not often used in other than its most natural meaning, to retain or preserve that object. It is much more difficult to conceptualize a collective right to keep firearms, residing at once in the entire people and yet in no individual. The individual rights approach, on the other hand, neither renders the right to keep arms superfluous nor inappropriate, as each citizen has a right to possess and to utilize firearms. Since an interpretation which gives meaning to all terms is favored over one which renders some provisions meaningless, it would appear that the individual rights approach is preferable to the collective approach in terms of giving meaning to the rights recognized in the Second Amendment.

The Second Amendment's initial phrase, "A well regulated Militia, being necessary to the security of a free State . . . " has been the source of considerable dispute. The collective approach views this phrase as a strict limitation on the right to keep and bear arms which is conferred in the following phrase, while the individual rights view treats it as a statement of purpose, an explanation of the rationale behind the absolute right to keep and bear arms. Here, too, the individual rights approach seems superior to the collective rights stand. First, as used by the framers, the term "Militia" referred to all citizens capable of bearing arms, and not merely to those persons enrolled in formal state military units.

Thus, even should the Second Amendment be construed to protect only members of the "Militia" its protections would extend to all persons capable of bearing arms. To the extent that "Militia" refers to an armed citizenry rather than formal units, the collective approach has the same effect in practice as the individual approach. Any citizen physically able to use firearms may do so.

A second difficulty with the collective rights interpretation of this phrase is that it creates a conflict between constitutional provisions. Construing the Second Amendment to bar federal interference with the armament of formal militia units places that Amendment in conflict with another constitutional provision that creates a federal power to regulate the armament of formal militia units.[5] This conflict does not exist, however, if the individual rights interpretation is adopted. Under this approach, the Second Amendment is viewed as creating an informal militia, an armed citizenry, with which the federal government may not interfere. From this armed citizenry the states might create formal, organized militia units and these formal military units would then be subject to federal regulation. Thus, since an interpretation harmonizing constitutional provisions is favored over one that creates conflict or implies repeal, the individual rights approach again seems superior to the view that the Second Amendment creates only a collective right.

A third reason for the superiority of the individual rights construction of the militia phrase is that this view gives meaning to the qualifier "well regulated." Under the collective rights view, the right to bear arms phrase is dependent upon the militia phrase. In effect, the Second Amendment is seen as stating that "to the extent necessary to the existence of a well regulated militia, the right to keep and bear arms shall not be infringed." This interpretation renders the qualifier "well" both meaningless and superfluous. It renders this term meaningless, since it is obvious that prohibiting federal disarmament of militia units does not ensure that they will be well-regulated, as armament and organization have at best a most tangential relationship. A guarantee against disarmament may ensure the existence of an armed militia, but not a well regulated one. The collective interpretation also renders the term "well regulated" superfluous; if the states sought protection of their militias, a simple reference to the necessity of a militia, whether regulated or unregulated, would have sufficed. The individual rights approach, in contrast, gives meaning to this qualifier and should therefore be favored. This view construes the militia phrase as a statement of the objective which the framers hoped might be accomplished by the creation of a general, individual, right to bear arms. The right would create an armed citizenry from which the states could fashion well-regulated units which would form the foundation of their security and freedom. Taken as an independent statement of fact, the claim that a well-regulated militia is necessary to a free state is not without reason. Taken as a provision of limitation, the statement that a right to be armed exists only to the extent it is necessary to a militia which is well-regulated seems to have little meaning.

Finally, the fourth flaw in the collective rights interpretation of the militia phrase results from the contention that a statement of purpose together with a pronouncement of a right results in a right strictly limited to activities having a direct connection with the stated purpose. This position is inconsistent with the interpretation given a similar constitutional provision, the right of assembly. The First Amendment right of assembly resembles the Second Amendment both in its pronouncement of a "right of the people" and also in its statement of the purpose for assembly: "to petition the Government for a redress of grievances." Despite this structure, the right has been successfully invoked by private organizations as well as individual citizens, and held to bar indirect hindrances to assembly as well as direct imposition of criminal penalties.[6] Despite the express purpose of permitting assembly "to petition the Government," courts have applied freedom of assembly to labor unions whose primary purpose was economic[7] and which are barred by statute from most political activities. Freedom of association has also been held to bar limitations on anti-union pamphleteering by Chambers of Commerce,[8] and to limit restrictions upon political groups not likely to petition the existing government structure.[9] These decisions are consistent with the principle that constitutional restrictions on government power are to be construed liberally rather than strictly,[10] but they seem difficult to reconcile with the collective rights position that a statement of a right is limited by a statement of purpose. The individual rights approach, in contrast, would construe the Second Amendment in a manner consistent with the construction of the right of association. In both cases the framers would be seen as recognizing a broad right, not strictly limited by a purpose clause, and a right which, while it may as a practical matter be exercised on a collective level, nevertheless protects any individual. It appears, therefore, that the choice of the phrase "A well regulated Militia," like the use of "the right of the people" and "to keep and bear Arms," lends greater support to an individual rights inter- pretation of the second amendment than to the collective rights approach.

Original Meaning of Second Amendment Terminology

Beyond analyzing the terms used to structure the Second Amendment, an examination of the meaning attached to these terms by the framers provides further insight into whether the Second Amendment creates individual or collective rights. The meaning of these terms to the framers may be gathered from evidence concerning usages of the terms when the Amendment was drafted. In this respect, the wording chosen by the state conventions which, in ratifying the Constitution, made the original proposals for a Bill of Rights, seems to be strong evidence of prevailing usages. If these proposals referred to other rights which are now accepted as individual in character in terms similar to those employed to express the right to bear arms, then it seems likely that the phrasing of the Second Amendment was not seen as creating a right of a nature distinct from other clearly individual rights. Proceeding from this premise, a survey of proposals for the Bill of Rights makes it clear that provisions protecting the right to bear arms employed language very similar to that used in pro- visions now accepted as creating individual rights. Ratifying conventions in Virginia, New York, North Carolina, and Rhode Island used the following terms to delineate the rights later embodied in the First Amendment:

> The people have a right to freedom of speech and of writing and publishing their sentiments, that freedom of the press is one of the greatest bulwarks of liberty, and ought not to be violated.

The Virginia proposal for a right to bear arms, which was virtually identical with those of New York, North Carolina, and Rhode Island, utilized a similar format:

The people have a right to keep and to bear arms, that a well
regulated Militia composed of the body of the people trained
to arms is the proper, natural and safe defense of a free State.

The similarity of phrasing suggests that the structure of the
Second Amendment — a statement of a right of the people,
together with a statement of the relation which that right bears to
freedom and a democratic government — was not understood at
the time of the framing to create a right different in character
from the freedom of speech or of the press.

The meaning of the terms employed by the framers in expressing the right to keep and bear arms may also be clarified by
examining the practical construction given those terms by state
constitutions in existence during the ratification process. Provisions guaranteeing a right of the people to keep and bear arms
were present in the constitutions of Massachusetts,[11] Pennsylvania,[12] Rhode Island,[13] and North Carolina.[14] These provisions would be meaningless if it is assumed that the phrase "the
right of the people to keep and bear Arms" refers only to the right
of a state to form a militia. A state can hardly infringe its own
rights; a guarantee in its constitution that it will not do so would
border on the absurd. The propriety of protecting the right
embodied in these words against both federal and state interference indicates that it is a right capable of infringement by both
levels of government. Given the structure of the federal system,
the process of elimination indicates that the "right of the people
to keep and bear Arms" must inhere in the individual. Consideration of the words employed in the Second Amendment, when
viewed in light of evidence as to the meaning attached to those
words when the Amendment was drafted, suggests that the
framers intended to create an individual right, and not one
protecting the states alone.

Statements of the Founding Fathers

Attempts have been made to interpret the Second Amendment
by an examination of the writings of the more notable framers and
their contemporaries. It is argued that the framers' motive in
creating the Second Amendment was to prevent the formation of
a professional standing army. Since under this view the motive was
to replace the standing army with the militia, the Second Amend-

ment should be construed to do no more than protect the existence of an organized militia, the modern citizen-soldier organization. This argument appears to overlook the distinction between motive and intent. To interpret a constitutional provision in terms not of intent, as gathered from the document, but in terms of the motive inspiring that intent, as gathered from the statements of a few of the drafters, is a most questionable procedure. This approach becomes a speculative attempt to apply not the measures the framers had resolved to implement, but instead the measures the commentator thinks they should have implemented in light of their goals. Whatever the motive, the intent of the framers, as nearly as can be discerned from statements in the state conventions,[15] the writings of the more noted contemporary authorities,[16] and the early commentators,[17] was to ensure that the federal government would have no power to disarm the militia — the body of the citizenry capable of bearing arms. The motive, whether or not it was to prevent a standing army, should not obscure nor control this intent.

Even should the motive be considered of importance, however, there is strong support for the view that a primary motive behind the guarantee of a well-armed citizenry was to enable the populace to arise in armed rebellion should the newly formed government prove oppressive.[18] This motive would be inconsistent with any construction of the Second Amendment which would allow federal disarmament of the general population. There is also evidence that right to bear arms proposals were not viewed at the time of the framing of the amendment as being aimed at the prevention of standing armies. Alexander Hamilton, in a contribution to *The Federalist*, noted concerning the state constitutions that "*two* only of them contained an interdiction of standing armies in time of peace; that the other eleven had either observed a profound silence on the subject, or had in express terms admitted the right of the legislature to authorize their existence."[19] At the time of Hamilton's statement, four states possessed constitutional right to bear arms guarantees.[20] This can hardly be considered a "profound silence" unless the right to bear arms provisions were considered to have no necessary connection with the standing army limitations. Additional evidence supporting a motive to create an individual right to bear arms is found in proposals for a bill of rights made by several state ratification conventions. New Hampshire proposed that "Congress shall never disarm any Citizen unless such as are or have been in Actual Rebellion."[21] Members of the Pennsylvania convention proposed a bill of rights which failed to gain majority approval but inspired and greatly influenced suggestions for amendments made by other states.[22] The Pennsylvania proposals included a provision that "no law shall be enacted for disarming the people except for crimes committed or in a case of real danger of public injury from individuals . . ."[23] A motive aimed at creating an individual right to bear arms is also suggested by the very wording of the Second Amendment. That amendment does not prevent or even limit the use of standing armies. Nor does it establish the militia as the sole or primary defense of the United States. If the framers meant to avoid the dangers of standing armies by this amendment, it can only be observed that they chose a remarkably inefficient way of doing it, when more direct and positive measures had been proposed.[24]

In summary, the framers seem to have intended to create a right which would protect individual citizens against disarmament by the federal government. Since this right is an express exception to the enumerated powers of Congress, it is not limited by any federal "police power." The individual rights approach has the virtues of consistency with interpretations given other amendments and avoidance of conflict with other provisions, and it appears to be in accord with the intent of the framers of the Amendment.

Application of the Second Amendment to the States

There is also reason to believe that the Fourteenth Amendment should be construed to apply the Second Amendment as a restriction on state authority. This issue has not been considered by the Supreme Court in modern times, but the legislative history for Fourteenth Amendment incorporation of the Second Amendment is considerably stronger than that for virtually any of the provisions of the Bill of Rights that the Court has held applicable to the states.

The purpose of the Fourteenth Amendment was to guarantee the fundamental rights of the newly emancipated slaves. In particular Congress desired to place the principles of the recently passed Civil Rights Act of 1866 into the Constitution, so that they could not be easily repealed when the Southern delegations were readmitted to Congress.[25] The question then is, were those fundamental rights deemed to include the right to keep and bear arms? To answer this it is necessary to consider the history of Southern legislation against blacks bearing arms, both under slavery and after emancipation.

Before emancipation the laws of the Southern states made it a serious criminal offense to supply firearms to blacks, whether slave or free, and for blacks to own them. As soon after the end of the Civil War as the white Southern legislatures could reassemble, they enacted Black Codes to fix the social, economic, and political position of the new freedman as perpetual serfdom. Among the most obnoxious provisions of these Codes, according to the Special Report of the Anti-Slavery Conference of 1867, was that blacks were "forbidden to own or bear firearms, and thus were rendered defenseless against assaults."[26] The Black Codes were the immediate occasion of the Civil Rights Act and the Fourteenth Amendment. These were intended to strike the Black Codes down, guaranteeing to the freedman "the right of personal security": the Congressional debates are replete with references to the freedman's "right to defend himself and his wife and children; a right to bear arms . . ." (Rep. Raymond); "the right to keep and bear arms in his defense" (Rep. Dawes); "the right to keep and bear arms" (Sen. Howard). Addressing this aspect of the Black Codes specifically, Rep. Clarke (R.-Ka.) declared: "I find in the Constitution of the United States an article which declared that 'the right of the people to keep and bear arms shall not be infringed.' For myself, I shall insist that the reconstructed rebels of Mississippi respect the Constitution in their local laws."[27] Given this debate, plus the specific Congressional intent to overturn the Black Codes and the expressed intention to guarantee to the freedman the fundamental rights of human beings (which then were deemed to include the right to self-defense and to possess arms for that purpose), it is difficult to see how the Second Amendment could not be considered incorporated against the states by the Fourteenth.

Modern Functions of The Second Amendment

It is sometimes argued that the collectivist interpretation of the Amendment is to be preferred, even though it is not faithful to the original purpose, because changes in weapons technology have rendered the original purpose obsolete. Since it is no longer possible for the armed populace to overthrow a despotic government as the Founding Fathers intended, the Second Amendment is an anachronism which Congress and the states need no longer respect. Conceding for the moment that the Second Amendment is obsolete, the argument nevertheless proves entirely too much and is entirely too dangerous. It is trite but necessary to reassert that, in our constitutional system, rights guaranteed the people may be divested or diluted only with the consent of the people through the process of constitutional amendment. Allowing government to flout any of those rights in the interest of supposedly useful social legislation starts us down a rocky road. After all, technological changes since the Bill of Rights was adopted affect all our constitutional rights, not just the Second Amendment. It might equally be denied that a right to individual free speech has meaning in an age of the mass media; the time when an individual "soap box" speech could alter governmental policy is long past. The right to assemble and petition the legislature is likewise of doubtful value in an age when policies are determined at the mass level by lobbying and public relations campaigns, and actual petitions are few and ineffectual. If a right is recognized by the words and apparent intent of the framers, judgments by government as to its present value can hardly be accepted as reason to release government from its restrictions.

Further, even if it were assumed that such implicit repeal could occur, we might ask what body has the power to decree the repeal. The Constitution and the Bill of Rights were not granted by the national government; rather, they are the charter under which the people have permitted that national government to exist and exercise power. Thus, if the Second Amendment is to be rendered into a meaningless collective right, it must be by a concerted public perception of it as such. But the general populace apparently has a considerably more favorable view of the individualist interpretation of the Second Amendment than do government policy makers. A 1975 public opinion survey found 78 per cent of the population responding that the Constitution gave them the right to keep and bear arms; when asked whether the "right to keep and bear arms" applied to the individual citizen or only to the National Guard, the 78 per cent indicated the individual citizen.[28]

Moreover, it is far from clear that the Second Amendment no longer serves the purposes for which it was enacted. The original understanding indicates a double purpose: protection of the nation against governmental tyranny imposed by a monopoly of force; and protection of the individual against non-governmental threats. It cannot seriously be argued that firearms are useless for self-defense in a nation in which the number of justifiable homicides by civilians approximates, and often greatly exceeds, those by police. [Editor's note: See discussion in the article on women's armed self-defense, *supra*.] It is frequently argued that a man should submit to robbery (or a woman to rape) rather than resisting and thereby taking a chance on being injured or killed. How persuasive this is may depend upon whether you are a well-to-do white liberal rather than a laborer or welfare mother who stands to lose several weeks' irreplaceable family food money. Similarly, the reasonableness of the risks involved in self-defense may be different to the manager of a bank, with its federally guaranteed deposits, than to a black shopkeeper in an area where robbery insurance is unobtainable and getting a reputation as an easy mark is tantamount to being run out of business. But however the decisional factors be evaluated, the Second Amendment dictates that the power of decision remain in the hands of the individual, and not be usurped by government.

As to the prospect of an armed citizenry overthrowing a despotic government, it is clear that the balance of power has entirely shifted since the eighteenth century, when Madison and Hamilton envisioned an army of perhaps 25,000, equipped with essentially the same arms as the civilian populace. Today, government armaments, in terms of every kind of heavy weapon, air power, and even atomic weapons, far exceed the combined firepower of the armed citizenry. Recent events in Nicaragua, Lebanon, and Vietnam, and more remote events in Budapest (1956) and the Warsaw ghetto (1943), demonstrate that armored units, given time and a completely free hand, can suppress concerted urban resistance — albeit at the price of reducing the area in question to a mass of burning rubble. Thus, in terms of resistance to an army in the field, the armed citizenry no longer serves the original purpose of the Second Amendment. [Editor's note: Events in Iran since this was written may make it necessary to re-evaluate even the limited concession that the Second Amendment is obsolete because rebellion is impossible.]

The Armed Populace as a Deterrent to Dictatorship

But this does not end our inquiry — for knowledge that the citizenry is armed may *deter* a potential military dictator from acting on his ambitions, just as knowledge that a prospective victim is armed may deter a robber. Though both the general and the robber be fairly confident of emerging from the contretemps relatively unscathed, the decisive question is whether what is likely to be left to him after the struggle is worth the risk of injury. A general may have pipe dreams of a sudden and peaceful take-over and a nation moving confidently forward, united under his direction. But the realistic general will remember the actual fruits of civil war — shattered cities like Hue, Beirut, and Belfast, devastated countrysides like the Mekong Delta, Cypress, and southern Lebanon. Is that what he wants for San Francisco, Milwaukee, and Philadelphia; for the San Joaquin Valley, Iowa, and Mississippi? However some generals may despise the country's current civilian leadership and policies, most will be realistic enough to recognize that the situation would be far worse with the country wracked by the civil war that would inevitably follow a military take-over. Even if a general is certain that he could eventually win such a civil war, he must also evaluate its effect in leaving the country vulnerable to foreign invasion.

Because it leads any prospective dictator to think through such questions, the individual, anonymous ownership of firearms is still a deterrent today to the despotism that it was originally intended to obviate. The prospect of attempting to impose a benevolent dictatorship upon a people possessing, mostly anonymously, upwards of 160 million firearms may prove discouraging to even the most optimistic of potential dictators.

Implicit in the Bill of Rights, as in the entire structure of our Constitution, are the twin hallmarks of traditional liberal thought: trust in the people; and distrust in government, particularly the military and the police. We are apt to forget these constant principles in light of our government's generally quite good record of exerting power without abusing it. But the deterrent effect of an armed citizenry is one little-recognized factor that may have contributed to this. In the words of the late Senator Hubert

Humphrey, "The right of citizens to bear arms is just one more guarantee against arbitrary government, one more safeguard against the tyranny which now appears remote in America, but which historically has proved to be always possible."

The Necessity of Access to Firearms by Dissenters and Minorities Whom Government is Unwilling or Unable to Protect

JOHN R. SALTER, JR. and DON B. KATES, JR.

Among the many misdeeds of the British rule in India, history will look upon the Act depriving a whole nation of arms, as the blackest.

— Mahatma Gandhi

The most foolish mistake we could possibly make would be to allow the subject races to possess arms. History shows that all conquerors who have allowed their subject races to carry arms have prepared their own downfall by doing so.

— Adolf Hitler

From a contemporary German commentary on Hitler's Firearms Act of 1937:

[No civilian is to have a firearm without a permit and these will not be issued to persons] suspected of acting against the state. For Jews [too] this permission will not be granted. Those people who do not require permission to purchase or carry weapons [include] the whole S.S. and S.A. [storm troopers], including the Death's Head group [and officers of the Hitler Jugend.]

DON B. KATES, JR.

As a civil rights worker in a Southern state during the early 1960s, I found that the possession of firearms for self-defense was almost universally endorsed by the black community, for it could not depend on police protection from the KKK. The leading civil rights lawyer in the state (then and later a nationally prominent figure) went nowhere without a revolver on his person or in his briefcase. The black lawyer for whom I principally worked did not carry a gun all the time, but he attributed the relative quiescence of the Klan to the fact that the black community was so heavily armed. Everyone remembered an incident several years before, in which the state's Klansmen attempted to break up a civil rights meeting and were routed by return gunfire. When one of our clients (a schoolteacher who had been fired for her leadership in the Movement) was threatened by the Klan, I joined the group that stood armed vigil outside her house nightly. No attack ever came — though the KKK certainly knew that the police would have done nothing to hinder or punish them.

As a civil rights worker, I saw how possession of a firearm could shrink the threat of ultimate violence into just another more or less innocuous incident: When Klansmen catch you in some deserted area and open fire, you take cover and shoot back — if you have a gun. Then both sides depart with great speed, because no one wants to get shot. If you don't have a gun, however, the Klansmen keep on shooting and moving closer, and your only hope is that their aim is poor and that you can outdistance their pursuit.

I also learned what value to place on the pseudo-pacifism (I have too much respect for genuine pacifists to call this real) of those who see no difference between aggression and self-defense. Driving South, I had been accompanied by another new civil rights worker bound for another state. Proclaiming himself an ethical pacifist, he was appalled that I carried guns for self-defense. When we met a few months later, I still believed in self-defense. He now believed in terrorism and assassination. The philosophy of self-defense prepares one to evaluate realistically a potentially violent world and respond with a minimum degree of violence necessary to cope with it. His philosophy having not so prepared him, he had perforce to abandon it. People who are unable to discriminate between defensive violence and aggression are unlikely, if they come to believe violence necessary, to be very discriminating about its use. A little-remembered fact is that all the white members of the Symbionese Liberation Army started out not as "macho gun nuts," but as pacifists of the flower-child type. The failure of their rosy dreams that all obstacles can be surmounted, all prejudices and differences of viewpoint reconciled, through "good vibes" and effusions of love, led them to equally unrealistic dreams of salvation through blood and death.

In 1976 I debated in the *Civil Liberties Review* with Rep. Robert Drinan, S.J., a distinguished liberal Congressman and scholar who sponsors handgun prohibition legislation. The civil rights experience played a major part in my remarks:

Advocacy of controversial political or social views frequently provokes violent antagonisms. Although they are usually unwilling or politically unable to overtly suppress these views, officials can covertly withdraw police protection, leaving the job to such groups as the Ku Klux Klan, the White Citizens Council, the Storm Troopers, the Cherry Society, and the Black Hand.

What might have happened to civil rights workers if there had been strict gun control in the South is exemplified in the 1969 machine-gunning of several hundred marchers by right-wing extremists in Mexico City. Both the possession of automatic weapons and the act of murder are as strictly forbidden by law in Mexico as they are in the U.S. Nevertheless, the police made no arrests — either on the scene or when the attackers later invaded hospitals to finish off the wounded.

Even assuming that gun prohibition would be enforced against right-wing extremists also, the effect is to render dissenters defenseless without meaningfully preventing lethal attacks upon them. A group of Klansmen or other neo-fascists will hesitate to attack someone they know to be armed, or to fire-bomb his house, because they don't want to risk injury or death. Even though they may be unarmed, they will not hesitate to attack if they know that their intended victim is also unarmed and that the police will not defend him. No one had guns in the hostile mob which burned the headquarters of the Marxist W.E.B. DuBois Club in 1966 while New York City police looked on. But the DuBois Club member who had to pull a pistol on the mob in order to get out of the burning clubhouse was immediately arrested for gun possession. Needless to say, no members of the mob were arrested.

During the civil rights turmoil in the South, Klan violence was bad enough; it would have been worse with gun control. It was only because black neighborhoods were full of people who had guns and could fight back that the Klan didn't shoot up civil rights meetings or terrorize blacks by shooting at random from cars.

Moreover, civil rights workers' access to firearms for self-defense often caused Southern police to preserve the peace as they would not have done if only the Ku Kluxers had been armed. I remember how Klansmen broke up a series of marches in a Louisiana town with hideous violence and head-bashing while the police looked on in benevolent neutrality. The unarmed marchers' appeals to the governor for state police protection were in vain. After many weeks of heavy injuries to the marchers, a black man shot one of several Klansmen who attacked him with clubs. The state police arrived the next day, and there was no further violence.

Contrast an incident that occurred in Madrid on November 6, 1975. A meeting of opposition reform parties was broken up and its participants severely beaten by right-wing gunmen. The victims could offer no resistance, since Spanish law strictly forbids civilian possession of handguns (except by right-wing thugs with permits). Falangist policy follows the gun laws of Nazi Germany and fascist Italy, under which Jews and political opponents were disarmed and left helpless against mob violence in the early 1930s. As Hermann Goring said in 1933, "Certainly I shall use the police — and most ruthlessly — whenever the German people are hurt; but I refuse the notion that the police are protective troops for Jewish stores. The police protect whoever comes into Germany legitimately, but not Jewish usurers."

Though Rep. Drinan's reply was principally devoted to other issues, he offered the following remarks about the civil rights experience:

> Prof. Kates' admirable efforts to aid in the fight for civil rights in the South in the early 1960s have apparently exerted a great influence on his views regarding gun control, dissent, and self-defense. The experience of confronting an armed mob acting with the tacit approval of the local police

is certainly a powerful and searing memory, and one which can be expected to instill strong feelings in support of the right to purchase arms for self-defense. It must be conceded, however, that such abdications of responsibility by the police are highly unusual, particularly in the light of civil rights progress in the South.

For each example of attacks on unarmed minorities by armed people against whom the police did not enforce anti-gun laws (and most of these instances cited by Prof. Kates occurred in foreign countries), one could list hundreds of deaths caused by the unlimited availability of handguns. The solution to the problem of occasional, isolated non-enforcement of the law is not to advocate, as Prof. Kates apparently does, a society in which everyone goes armed in the interest of self-defense, but rather to embark on the far less dangerous and far more sensible course of drafting an impartial and fair law and then seeing to it that the law is enforced with strict objectivity.

The *Civil Liberties Review* allowed me to respond and once again I concentrated much more heavily on the civil rights experience:

Rep. Drinan's complaint against my discussion of foreign countries comes rather strangely from one who relies so heavily upon foreign examples himself. He claims that handgun prohibitions increase dissenter safety by denying terrorists arms — something which will certainly come as news to the IRA in Northern Ireland and Britain and the Montenaros in Argentina.

If anti-government terrorists cannot be disarmed, how effective will firearms prohibition be against those, like the Klan and the right-wing Argentine and Brazilian death squads, whom army and police support? I cannot concede, as Rep. Drinan requests, that "abdications of responsibility by the police [in the South or even the North] are highly unusual," because they are not. Those who view the situation from the perspective of today's federally enforced civil rights gains can have no idea what the South was like in the 1950s and early 1960s when over a hundred civil rights workers were murdered while our federal government would do nothing to offend the South's all-white electorate. Under strict gun control the slaughter would have been immeasurably worse, since we could not have defended ourselves. The movement would have collapsed, just as it did during the Reconstruction when the army was withdrawn, leaving the blacks (who had no firearms) to the mercy of the Klan.

Nor is police refusal to protect the unpopular confined to the South. The inaction of New York State police when Paul Robeson's Peekskill concert was mobbed, and of the New York City, Boston, and Oakland (California) police when hardhats and Hell's Angels attacked peace marchers, are only the most famous examples. Any reader of black newspapers knows how Northern police react when mobs attack blacks who move into all-white neighborhoods.

Rep. Drinan would substitute for the right of self-defense the "far more sensible course of drafting an impartial and fair law and then seeing to it that the law is enforced with strict objectivity." Such Panglossian unwillingness to abandon *theories* of government in the face of experience with it is reminiscent of the replies invariably given by those two anti-gun attorneys general, Robert Kennedy and Nicholas deB. Katzenbach, to letters begging federal intervention against Klan violence: "Shootings, beatings, arson, and mayhem are not within our jurisdiction. Please refer to your local police department."

If Rep. Drinan really thinks he can coerce recalcitrant police to do their duty, I respectfully suggest that he direct his legislative attention to enforcing the Fourth Amendment. Until he demonstrates a capacity to control police behavior as neither the Constitution nor the courts have done, a more realistic appraisal is contained in this 1968 letter to a pacifist group from the national coordinator of the American "Minutemen":

> I was certainly happy to see your ad in the *New York Times* urging your people to dispose of their guns.
>
> I hope all of you left-wing dopes dispose of your guns.
>
> We are not going to dispose of our guns.
>
> Please urge your members to turn their guns into the local police department rather than just throwing them in the river — it is better publicity for your anti-gun drive that way — and besides, we have members in most local police departments who are able to pass many of these guns on to us.
>
> Eventually you pro-communist peace punks will have no guns.

We'll have lots of guns.

What then?

(The letter-writer, who has for years been wanted on federal firearms charges, attributes his ability to elude the FBI to information given him by Midwestern police.)

JOHN R. SALTER, JR.

Shortly after the publication of this debate, I received a letter from an old friend with whom I had lost contact since the Movement years, Professor John Salter. John was a renowned civil rights organizer in the early sixties; his face still bears the evidence of a nearly successful attempt by the Klan to kill him in Mississippi. Enclosed with John's letter to me was a reply he had recently sent to one of the many organizations soliciting funds to lobby for a national Sullivan Law. He has graciously consented to my printing it here:

Several times recently, I've received copies of your appeal. I'm not surprised — I belong to and support a number of liberal causes involved with civil rights and liberties — and very likely you have gotten my name from several mailing lists. I would like to ask that you send me no more appeals. I do not support your view and have no intention of doing so.

I come out of a racially mixed background — Indian and white — and my roots go deep into this land. The Native American side of my heritage comes from the woodland hunters of the Northeast; on the other side, I draw from Western pioneers. Trained as a sociologist, I am currently a professor in the Graduate Program in Urban Regional Planning at the University of Iowa and am also the UI's Advisor and Counselor to the American Indian students. I come from a long line of hunters — back to the very beginning of Creation — and I have hunted consistently since I was five years old. I have had many firearms and currently have seven, including a handgun for target-plinking purposes. Two of my sons and I are life members of the National Rifle Association.

In the early 1960s, I taught at Tougaloo College, a black school in Jackson, Mississippi. I was a member of the statewide board of the NAACP, and was Chairman of the Strategy Committee of the Jackson Movement during the massive demonstrations in spring and summer of 1963. I was beaten many times and hospitalized on a couple of occasions. This happened to many, many people in the Movement. No one knows what kind of massive racist retaliation would have been directed against grass-roots black people had the black community not had a healthy measure of firearms within it.

When the campus of Tougaloo College was fired upon in December of 1962 by Klansmen, my home was shot up and a bullet missed my infant daughter by inches. We received no help from the Justice Department, and we guarded our campus — faculty and students together — on that and subsequent occasions. We let this be known in a calm and sensible manner and the racial attacks on Tougaloo slackened considerably. Night riders are cowardly people, and they take advantage of fear and weakness.

During most of the 1960s I did civil rights work in various parts of the South and almost always had with me a .38 special Smith & Wesson 2-inch-barrel revolver — what you would erroneously call a "Saturday Night Special." I remember an FBI agent coming to my home at Raleigh, North Carolina, in 1965 and telling us that an informer in the local "klavern" had reported that an attack was imminent on our home which was located in a black neighborhood — but that the FBI could do nothing. Again, we guarded our home and neighborhood, and let this be known in a quietly effective fashion. The attack never came.

In 1969-73, I was Southside Director of the Chicago Commons Association, a large, privately funded social service agency. Our major focus involved assisting minority people in developing multi-issue block clubs involved with schools, civic services, housing, police-community relations, etc. — in the context of racially changing neighborhoods and reactionary white groups, including the American Nazi party and miscellaneous youth gangs. My staff and I received many death threats, and on one occasion, men came to my home with weapons in their hands, and in broad daylight, to tell my wife and children that they intended to kill me. (I happened to be at work.) The police were not much help — were tired and overworked. Again I was glad that we had firearms to guard our home, and again we made it known that we were doing so. We responded to hate calls on the telephone by telling callers that we were prepared for them. The would-be assailants never returned.

I noticed something else in Chicago. The police, honorably committed as the vast majority of them are, could not begin to deal with the crime situation in the city. Large numbers of people — certainly the low-income minority people with whom we worked — were glad when they had personal firearms protection. Outlaws can always get guns. They can make them if necessary, or they can use knives, a hatchet, or a vast number of other things.

The taking of handguns that you propose is, in my opinion, morally and legally wrong and quite unenforceable. We're a free people and have a natural right to possess firearms. We have the Second Amendment whose intent is quite clear to any objective person. (As liberals, we take a sound view of the First Amendment; why do you not take the same honest view of the Second?) A huge number of our people, particularly poor and minority people, are not going to give up the only security they and their families have, no matter how often they are told they will be safer by well-to-do white gun-banners living in suburbs and high-security buildings.

The causes of crime are complex and involved: racism and ethnocentrism, poverty, urban congestion, and inter-personal and value alienation. They can't be constructively touched by gimmicky legislation, but gimmicky legislation can hurt good people and seriously damage the libertarian traditions of this country.

The Potential for Civil Liberties Violations in the Enforcement of Handgun Prohibition

DAVID T. HARDY and KENNETH L. CHOTINER

I want the state to take away people's guns. But I don't want the state to use methods against gun owners that I deplore when used against naughty children, sexual minorities, drug users, and unsightly drinkers. Since such reprehensible police practices are probably needed to make anti-gun laws effective, my proposal to ban all guns should probably be marked a failure before it is even tried.

> — Aryeh Neier, Executive Director of the American Civil Liberties Union

Enforcement of present firearms controls accounts for a large number of citizen-police interactions, particularly in the handful of states like Missouri, Michigan, or New York where it is illegal to purchase or own a handgun without a discretionary police permit.[29] The extension of such permit systems nationwide has frequently been advocated as a means of reducing crime and is the subject of numerous bills introduced into Congress each year. It may therefore be rather surprising that there is little literature dealing with the impact of such controls upon constitutional freedoms other than the Second Amendment right to keep and bear arms. Indeed, many committed civil libertarians seem little interested in the potential dangers to traditional civil liberties and privacy of a national handgun confiscation effort.

Our purpose is to explore in depth those constitutional interests (outside of the Second and Fifth amendments) which enforcement of firearms regulations is most likely to threaten. These liberties can be grouped into four categories: rights against unreasonable search and seizure; rights to privacy; risk of selective enforcement for political, cultural, or racial reasons; and the risk of unduly harsh and punitive statutes. In order to objectively assess each of these categories of rights and risks, the present degree of impairment caused by existing controls will be assessed and then compared to foreseeable results of future legislation.

Fourth Amendment: Illegal Search and Seizure

One index of whether serious enforcement of a national handgun prohibition would require illegal search and seizure is the extent to which such unconstitutional police conduct is engaged in to enforce present federal, state, and local gun laws, in the states having Sullivan-type permit systems. It is not possible to determine the precise number of illegal searches that are presently conducted for firearms, since local police do not care to record and neatly classify these. Similarly, though the FBI publishes nationwide crime figures annually, this compilation does not include any category of crimes committed by police against the Fourth Amendment rights of citizens. Nevertheless, available data suggests that illegal searches are a common, perhaps even the primary, means of enforcing present firearms laws, particularly in the states approximating the proposed national permit system. A Detroit study found that 85 per cent of dismissals in cases of carrying concealed weapons were due to illegality of search. This far exceeded even the 57 per cent for narcotics dismissals, where illegal searches are frequent, and their existence is often the only feasible defense.[30] A Chicago study noted motions to suppress for illegal evidence being filed in 36 per cent of all weapons charges, with 62 per cent of these being granted by the court.[31] In Ohio, a former prosecutor has opined that 50-75 per cent of weapons arrests resulted from questionable, if not clearly illegal, searches.[32] A Chicago judge who presides over a court devoted solely to gun-law violations has commented:

> The primary area of contest in most gun cases is in the area of search and seizure. . . . Constitutional search and seizure issues are probably more regularly argued in this court than anywhere in America. . . . More than half these contested cases begin with a motion to suppress. . . . These arguments dispose of more contested matters than any other.[33]

It must be understood that these suppression-hearing figures represent only a tiny fraction of the actual number of illegal searches that occur in the enforcement of current gun laws. A suppression hearing occurs only if the illegal search has actually turned up a gun and the citizen has been charged with some offense based on this evidence. If the illegally searched citizen has no gun there is no court case in which a suppression motion can be made. But there has still been an illegal search and a violation of the constitutional rights of a completely innocent person. Some idea of how many illegal weapons searches never even come to light in suppression hearings can be gleaned from the experience in one major city that has a Sullivan-type handgun purchase permit requirement. The ACLU notes that police there made 25,000 illegal searches in recent years "on the theory that any black driving a late model car has an illegal gun" — but these searches produced only 117 firearms.[34]

Methods of Enforcement Expected by Advocates of Prohibition

Despite the inauspicious experience with the enforcement of present gun laws, at least one Congressman who has repeatedly introduced national handgun prohibition bills strongly denies that their enforcement will require or result in significant Fourth Amendment violations:

> Given the enormous number of items currently prohibited by law, it seems highly unlikely that the addition to the list of one more illegal commodity would lead to a significant increase in the incidence of police searches. Gun control advocates do not envision or support massive police intrusions into private homes in search of handguns; the constitutional requirement of a specific warrant obtained as a result of corroborating evidence and signed by an impartial magistrate would remain enforced to preclude unreasonable searches.[35]

The author of these comments, Representative Robert F. Drinan (D.—Mass.), is a distinguished legal scholar and civil libertarian. His remarks evidence the curious disinclination of some civil libertarians to look closely at the potential constitutional costs of a handgun prohibition.

Other civil libertarians take these costs much more seriously —

even though agreeing (in the abstract) that handgun prohibition
would be desirable, if constitutionally enforceable. The views of
ACLU Executive Director Aryeh Neier have already been quoted.
Similar is the appraisal of Dr. Donald T. Lunde, a professor of
psychiatry and of criminal law at Stanford University, (after
asserting his belief that banning all firearms would significantly
reduce homicide):

> ... but how would we go about disarming the most heavily
> armed population in the world? [The passage of such legisla-
> tion would not produce compliance among] the millions who
> are opposed to gun controls or the millions who currently
> possess guns obtained illegally. Enforcement of non-
> voluntary provisions would be unworkable: The search and
> seizure aspect of such provisions would infringe on civil
> liberties and would require vast resources of manpower and
> money which are unavailable.[36]

One reason why other civil libertarians are facing the dangers to
which Representative Drinan is so blind is the evidence accumulat-
ing daily to refute his confidence that "gun control advocates do
not envision or support massive police intrusions..." Unfortunately, that is precisely what a growing number of prominent
handgun prohibition advocates do envision and support. On
October 7, 1977, federal appellate Judge Malcolm Wilkey published in the *Wall Street Journal* a guest editorial urging the
Supreme Court to abandon the exclusionary rule which it has
adopted to enforce the Fourth Amendment. His argument centered on the rule's effect upon gun laws, though he was concerned
with drug laws as well:[37]

> the exclusionary rule has made unenforceable the gun control
> laws we have and will make ineffective any stricter controls
> which might be devised. ... *Unless a police officer has
> "probable cause" to make a reasonable search*, nothing found
> during a search — [whether illegal long gun or] automatic
> pistol — can be introduced as evidence ... it is virtually
> impossible to be convicted in the U.S. of carrying a weapon
> illegally. ... No laws on gun control will work if they can not
> be effectively enforced. No gun control law can be enforced
> [while the exclusionary rule keeps] out the most reliable
> evidence necessary for conviction. [Emphasis added.]

It is only when closely compared to the ordinary criticisms of the exclusionary rule that the unique, and uniquely ominous, character of Judge Wilkey's criticism becomes apparent. For only then does it become clear that it is not the exclusionary rule of which Judge Wilkey wishes to be rid, but the Fourth Amendment. As Judge Wilkey himself says, it is the requirement of " 'probable cause' to make a reasonable search" that defeats gun control laws. But that requirement is not part of the exclusionary rule, but of the Fourth Amendment. It *is* the Fourth Amendment. The exclusionary rule merely provides that when police obtain evidence by violating the Fourth Amendment, that evidence cannot be used in the trial. This rests upon the Supreme Court's common-sense realization that police are much less likely to break into houses, etc., without probable cause if they know in advance that they cannot use any evidence they obtain this way. Most critics of the exclusionary rule argue that it is unnecessary because (they say) the police can be adequately deterred from illegal search by the prospect of being criminally prosecuted or of civil liability. Judge Wilkey is unique among the critics in that he *agrees* with the Court that the exclusionary rule is the only really effective way of curbing police violations of the Fourth Amendment. The very thing he condemns about the exclusionary rule is that it does work, that it does prevent the mass searches without probable cause that he believes are necessary to make a gun confiscation law effective. What Judge Wilkey seeks is a judicial repeal of the Fourth Amendment, so that, while it would remain in theory, in fact it would be unenforced. So much for Representative Drinan's assurance that under handgun confiscation "the constitutional requirement of a specific warrant [based on probable cause and] signed by an impartial magistrate would remain in force to preclude unreasonable searches."

Judge Wilkey's views do not represent an isolated aberration among the advocates of handgun confiscation. A few months before his article appeared, the *Detroit Free Press* published a guest editorial by police Inspector John Domm. He called for "reinterpretation" of the Fourth Amendment to allow police to swoop down on strategically located streets, round up pedestrians en masse, and herd them through portable airport-type gun detection machines.[38] The same idea was heralded in the September, 1977, *Harpers* by a leading handgun prohibitionist who has elsewhere urged that local police and federal agencies should model gun law enforcement after the manner in which drug laws are enforced.[39]

Though we have concentrated on recent expressions of such views by prohibitionists, they are by no means new. In a book that prohibitionists have quoted and endorsed ever since its publication in 1970, Norval Morris and Gordon Hawkins advocated the prohibition of all firearms. To enforce this they called for the development of "portable and discriminatory monitors capable of secretly searching anyone passing through a door or along a footpath to ascertain if he carries a concealed gun." They continued: " . . . there are surely no 1984 fears in this. There can be no right to privacy in regard to armament." Professor Morris is now Dean of the University of Chicago Law School and was recently nominated to head the federal Law Enforcement Assistance Administration. On September 27 and 28, 1978, under exceptionally severe questioning from members of the Senate Judiciary Committee, he retreated from the quoted statements, describing them as "stupid simplifications," "inept overstatements," "an author's aberration," "rather science fiction," and "Utopian views." Needless to say, Dean Morris' Utopia is not that of the traditional civil libertarian. Neither, apparently, is it that of the Senate, which failed to approve his nomination.[40]

Factors Bearing on the Necessity of Massive Illegal Search and Seizure as the Means of Enforcing Handgun Prohibition

Our projection that any serious attempt to enforce national handgun confiscation would have to involve a veritable campaign of illegal search and seizure is not based solely on the expectations of the more candid handgun prohibition advocates. The matter ought to be plain to anyone who considers it in light of traditional American attitudes toward guns and traditional American reactions to the banning of any commodity deeply valued by a substantial portion of the public. We do not mean to suggest that no commodity ban can succeed in this country except by illegal search and seizure. It is possible to ban things that few people own or have ever owned or deeply desired to own, because, as to these things, the ingredients necessary to an atmosphere of widely condoned defiance are lacking. A high proportion of the public, including most of the present owners, will voluntarily comply with the ban; there will be little incentive for black market manufacture or sale, and the few resisters can be controlled by ordinary, constitutionally acceptable, means of enforcement.

Even where a commodity or activity prohibition is widely unpopular, it is possible, without exceeding constitutional limits, to enforce it against those aspects that are necessarily highly public. A ban on handguns will deter most people from target shooting, as a ban on marijuana will deter people from growing the plant, since such activities can be carried on only with a high risk of detection. But the keeping of marijuana or a handgun in home, office, auto, or on the person is virtually impossible to detect except by searching those things. In general, the Fourth Amendment allows such searches only if there is probable cause to believe contraband will be found. But if ownership of the banned item is sufficiently widespread, and/or the incentive to acquire sufficiently great, the number of searches that can *legally* be made will simply not be enough to deter continued violation. To give the ban any chance of substantial success, the police must use random or other illegal searches, which it is hoped can provide enough evidence against enough violators so that they can be convicted and severely enough punished to frighten the unapprehended majority of violators into voluntary compliance.

Having laid out these general considerations, we proceed to apply them to the question of whether handgun prohibition and confiscation could have any hope of success except by a veritable massive campaign of illegal search and seizure.

Likelihood of Voluntary Compliance

Laws restricting handgun possession rank poorly in terms of the likelihood of voluntary obedience by any sector of the population. Federal undercover agents making "buys" to set up prosecutions in handgun-prohibiting jurisdictions like New York, Boston, and Washington, D.C., have noted that used-model guns of inferior brands are selling for 60-100 per cent more than what they would bring if such sales were legal.[41] But these exorbitant prices have not extinguished demand. New Yorkers willingly pay the same price for a used RG or Rohm that buyers in most other states pay for a fine used Colt or Ruger. Federal and state authorities recently estimated the illegal handgun population of New York City at two million. This is half a million less than the estimated number of handguns *legally owned* in California, and represents a significantly higher rate of handgun ownership than exists in the nation as a whole.[42]

Although it is obviously impossible to predict precisely how many present handgun owners would defy confiscation, an approximation may be gathered from the results of a 1975 poll in which respondents across the nation were asked how many gun owners they thought would comply. Some 92 per cent of the respondents estimated that 50 per cent or more of handgun owners would defy a confiscation law.[43] Another possible measure is the amount of non-compliance that has been shown in cities or states that have recently imposed the less onerous requirement that all handgun owners register their weapons. When Illinois so legislated in 1968, the Chicago police estimated the rate of defiance at over two-thirds; statewide the rate was estimated at over three-fourths. In 1976, Cleveland authorities estimated the rate of compliance with their city's new handgun registration law at less than 12 per cent.[44] At first blush these figures are surprising, in view of the findings of repeated public opinion polls over the past forty years that a majority even of handgun owners has consistently supported mandatory registration laws. The paradox disappears, however, when we focus on the co-finding of the polls that the vast majority of handgun owners oppose confiscation.[45] Handgun owners associate confiscation with registration in the sense that a result of the latter is to identify the handgun owner to the authorities, thereby facilitating confiscation. In short, 75 per cent of the handgun owners in Illinois, and 88 per cent of those in Cleveland, will not comply even with a registration law in which they believe, because they have no assurance (quite the reverse, in fact) that it will not facilitate confiscation. A prohibition law they are apparently prepared to disobey, if they think that they can get away with it. Thus the 1975 poll's estimate of 50 per cent non-compliance with a national handgun prohibition appears to be an extremely conservative one indeed.

The nature and location of probable violation is likewise suggestive of a great need for government to trench upon Fourth Amendment rights in order to enforce a national Sullivan Law.

The average citizen who keeps a handgun will generally keep it in his home or business. As to those who murder with handguns, studies repeatedly find the vast majority of such crimes being committed in a house or other building. Comparatively few citizens habitually carry firearms (even murderers, robbers, etc., are unlikely to do so except to and from the scene of their contemplated crime), so that neither "stop and frisk" laws nor Inspector Domm's streetside airport-security-machine system are likely to keep pace with the infusion of new black market handguns, much less to decrease the overall total. Any serious attempt at that would require an immense number of searches of residential and business premises. (One idea that was kicked around at the last national conference held by the handgun prohibition groups was to start off by searching the house of every person that some kind of official record indicates may ever have purchased or owned a handgun.)

The projected model for abuse potential thus gives a picture discouraging to those who value freedom from illegal search and seizure. A national Sullivan Law is likely to be met with massive violation, which can be conservatively estimated at half of all handgun owners, i.e., approximately twenty-five million citizens. Enforcement must, of necessity, involve intrusion into residences where firearms ownership is suspected — with, of course, the potential "bonus" that officers may seize any other kind of contraband they find. The bulk of these intrusions may well be directed against racial minorities, whose possession of arms the enforcing authorities may view as far more dangerous than illegal arms possession by other groups.

To the extent that the police conscientiously attempt to enforce the law against the entire population, they will have a strong incentive to initiate drastic search procedures from the very beginning, and these will provide precedent for later excesses. If a handgun prohibition is to be universally enforced, common sense calls for extremely strenuous enforcement to accompany the institution of the ban. After all, it is at that time that faith in the law's efficacy is likely to be greatest among the populace, and therefore compliance is likely to be greatest. If that part of the population that defies the law is not ferreted out and punished when the spirit of compliance is greatest, it will prove increasingly impossible to do so as time goes on. Those who initially defied the law will certainly not become more inclined to comply when time shows that they are part of a large group of successful disobedients. By the same token, those who at the outset reluctantly gave up what they conceived as the means of protecting their families will become ever more bitter and angry as it becomes evident that millions of others have not done so and are getting away with it. Predictably, many of these will eventually find a black market source to replace the gun they initially gave up. So would many people who had never owned a handgun. (Although the experience of Prohibition and of our drug laws has proven the impossibility of preventing black market imports of handguns across our thousands of miles of shore and borders, most people do not realize that a cheaper, and therefore more likely, source for the black market would be illegal domestic manufacture. With only the most primitive tools, villagers in Vietnam and elsewhere have managed to produce perfectly functioning copies of regulation military handguns, at a rate of from one to several per day. In this country, without even considering the small machine shops whose staffs could produce handguns on an assembly line basis, literally millions of household hobbyists have the equipment in their basements or garages to produce handguns fully as useful for self-defense purposes (though not for long-term target shooting) as those made by the commercial manufacturers, who would not be competing with them to supply the now illegal civilian market.)[46]

In short, any hope for effective handgun prohibition must be based upon the demonstrated capacity of the authorities to confiscate, voluntarily or involuntarily, virtually all the handguns in the country within the first few months. To deter non-compliance, the law must have penalties sufficiently Draconian to cause the populace — even that in the most violent inner-city areas where police protection is non-existent — to fear the law more than the consequences of being unarmed. To show that such a penalty scheme is more than a "paper tiger," it will be necessary for the police to unearth, and begin prosecuting, a substantial number of disobedients. Since the bulk of defensive firearms are kept in private premises, this will require a massive campaign of house searches; since, after the law is enacted, those who carry handguns outside the house will be concealing them, large numbers of personal searches will be required. The only practical way to insure the initial universal compliance that an effectual handgun ban requires would be something tantamount to suspending civil liberties and declaring martial law; enforcement activities would focus on the high-violence inner-city areas where the maximum non-compliance could be expected; police activities would include a house-to-house "clean sweep," complemented by random and dragnet searches; workers going to and from their jobs would be herded into long queues and processed through metal detectors; those found with firearms would receive harsh sentences designed to be more terrifying than the violence feared by inner-city residents. Such a system has all the civil liberties appeal of the swastika.

Individual Privacy and Weapons Permit Laws

A secondary constitutional consideration relevant to domestic firearm control is that vague area often identified as a "right to privacy." Legislation involving confiscation of handguns is most frequently combined with a permit system under which police have discretion to issue or deny permits to applicants whose records and backgrounds have been thoroughly checked. There are also non-discretionary systems, varying from the minimally intrusive (e.g., excluding persons with felony/violence conviction records) to the greatly intrusive (e.g., excluding citizens because they have had psychiatric care or been convicted of any crime, including non-violent misdemeanors, or just because they have been arrested even without conviction). In view of the repugnance with which civil libertarians have reacted to the idea of national computerized data files (or the national ID-card proposal) it is surprising that many have so easily accepted comparable or even more extensive proposals as to gun owners, who make up about half the households of the nation. Even former Justice William O. Douglas, no friend to governmental intrusions, has advocated laws forbidding handgun ownership to anyone with "a police record" and requiring a governmental psychiatric examination as a prerequisite.[49]

By themselves, the usual concomitants of licensing — fingerprinting, photographing, psychiatric reports, and some manner of background check — rarely excite much interest, save among the individuals actually required to submit. The extension of such a program nationwide, however, should be a cause for greater concern. The dossiers to be compiled would cover about 25 per cent of the households in the nation, if limited to handguns, and about 50 per cent if extended to all firearms. At a minimum, to prevent fraudulent application, they would require cross-indexing with criminal records, records of mental treatment, and psychiatric admissions. Beyond these items it would be necessary to have information as to even more specialized matters. Thus, under the 1968 federal law, renunciation of citizenship, undesirable military discharge, or being "addicted to, or an unlawful user of" marijuana disqualifies one from buying a gun. This level of information gathering would be adequate only for a non-discretionary or permissive licensing system (i.e., one in which every applicant who meets certain statutorily specified criteria is entitled to a license to own a gun). Under the Sullivan-type discretionary licensing power urged by the advocates of national handgun confiscation, police will have authority to reject applications for any reason or none at all. Anti-gun activist Carl Bakal approvingly notes that New York police revoke Sullivan Law permits "if you are arrested" or found to "hang around drinking places"; a person with a spotless record was reportedly denied a renewal in New York City because his son "had been in trouble with the police."[48] With such criteria being utilized, dossiers will have to be extensive indeed.

As part of the application procedure, some jurisdictions require generalized investigations described as inquiries into "moral character,"[49] or a thorough background investigation of each applicant, including questioning of references and employers.[50] The computerization of such information, together with identity, fingerprints, and photograph, when applied to one-fourth of the populace, raises serious privacy issues. As one Massachusetts official proudly described that state's firearm permit computer program:

> All inquiries are kept as history. Nothing is purged from the system, the information becomes history. At the present time we have approximately 550,000 licenses on file, 150,000 of which are active. All these bear fingerprints and photographs of the applicant. . . .[51]

Such data must be available for instant access to law-enforcement officials considering a permit application:

> You cannot look at a man and tell whether he has been

convicted of crime in another state. You cannot look at him and tell whether he has renounced his citizenship. . . . But with registration you can have virtually instantaneous information that would bring the situation under control.[52]

In addition to the national data-banking necessary to keep tabs on all those who receive (or even just apply for) handgun permits, there will be the tactics necessary to catch those who are suspected of having illegal guns. Three alternative or cumulative methods exist whereby the authorities can obtain the necessary information to ferret out and convict violators: (1) Professional informers, acting undercover, could trick suspected handgun owners into convicting themselves out of their own mouths; (2) Bounty payments could be made to encourage private citizens who have been in the confidence of suspected gun owners to inform on them; or (3) Electronic or other technology could be developed and used to effectively "search" people and premises without direct physical intrusion.

The Police Foundation has suggested that gun-law-enforcing state and local agencies use informers and follow the methods now used to enforce drug laws.[53] David Hardy has had some experience in investigating undercover enforcement under existing federal gun laws. The results are appalling. Agents are required to meet what are, in effect, quotas of guns seized and arrests made. To do so they frequently skirt the edges of entrapment or even outright frame-ups. In one case, a heroin addict was hired for $2,000 in advance, plus a per diem fee and a $1,500 bonus. The informer was never clear about the terms of the bonus, sometimes suggesting it was payable if a case went to trial, sometimes inferring it was payable *only if his testimony resulted in conviction.* The upshot was nine arrests. The only felony conviction obtained was that of the informer who, midway through the case, was discovered to be using his fee money to buy illegal firearms on his own. However, the agency obtained much needed budget-building publicity with pretrial articles about the magnitude of the supposed crimes.

In other cases persons charged with one crime were permitted to "walk" if they would produce convictions of other persons — including their friends — by attempting to buy or sell firearms under arrangements the friends thought were legal but the agents provacateur, and the federal agents, so arranged as to be illegal. (One federal court has held that even advice of counsel is no defense to certain federal firearms charges, so that entrapment was easily arranged once the intended defendant's ignorance of the law was known.)

As noted, an alternative to the hiring of informers is bounties to ordinary citizens who turn in their relatives, friends or neighbors. When Baltimore recently attempted to reduce handgun ownership, for example, city officials offered a reward of $100 "to any person who turns in someone illegally using or possessing a firearm."[54] Likewise, a report to the governor of Massachusetts, which strongly advocated a proposal to confiscate all handguns in the state, suggested offering bounties as the lynch-pin of the enforcement effort. The report went so far as to lay out guidelines: Informers might remain anonymous, giving code names or numbers. When a tip resulted in a confiscation, an appropriate notice would be given, and the person giving the code would be paid. But since a prospective informer's anonymity might reduce chances of obtaining a warrant (and therefore of confiscating the gun), those who attempted to make tips anonymously would be cautioned that this might reduce their chances of obtaining the payoff.[55] Boston's Sheriff Buckley, long a supporter of a national Sullivan Law, was recently asked if he did not find something frightening about paying children to turn in their parents, educating a generation to inform on their friends and neighbors for pay. He replied that he saw nothing wrong with it at all.[56]

The third alternative (or cumulative) enforcement mechanism is, of course, Inspector Domm's plan for setting up metal detectors in order to ferret out pedestrians carrying guns on the streets. Police would herd large numbers of citizens through the detector, detaining and searching those as to whom it gave a "positive" reading. It must be emphasized that the inconvenience and humiliation would not be limited to the part of the population that totes guns. A formerly free populace would suddenly be able to emerge from their residences to go to work, to the grocery, or to run other errands only at the risk of being forced into lengthy lineups such as they now encounter only when they voluntarily elect to travel by air.

Moreover, far more innocent citizens than gun-toters will be subjected to the further indignity of being detained and searched.

The experience with airport metal detectors is that about half of the millions of persons and packages that have gone through the machines have triggered a "positive" response, although only a few thousand have turned out to have guns when a physical inspection was made. Even when authorities searched only those who both triggered a metal detector and also fit a "highjacker profile," fourteen out of fifteen people indicated and searched were "false positives." Of course, even if Inspector Domm's system turns up comparatively few guns, it has other advantages which may make it worth the time and effort — at least as far as the police are concerned. For every time the machine registers "positive" it provides the police the convenient excuse to search and question, which may uncover not only firearms offenses, but a whole host of commodity-type violations and other criminal activity as well. Professor Andrews, after an extensive study of airport searches, noted that only 10-20 per cent of the resulting arrests were for weapons or hijacking charges. The remaining 80-90 per cent were for possession of innumerable other forbidden commodities, particularly drugs, as well as arrests of illegal aliens and AWOL soldiers discovered through ID checks.[57]

The authorities who enforce firearms laws are not graded or promoted by how much respect they have for individual privacy. Any large organization needs numerical quantifiers, and "guns confiscated" or "convictions obtained" serve just as did body counts in Vietnam. Entrapment thus furnishes an easy way to increase demonstrated achievement indexes and is extremely appealing to those enforcing this form of law. Likewise, invasions of privacy are essential: where contraband confiscated is easily quantified and forms an index of success, even the exclusionary rule may have little deterrent effect. Federal agents and their regional headquarters receive credit for the number of guns confiscated, even though those may not be useful in a later court hearing. Thus there may be even less protection against unreasonable intrusions and entrapment than there is against illegal police conduct generally. This certainly appears to be the case at present with the BATF, which enforces the federal laws. In one case, *Caplan* v. *BATF*, the court disclosed portions of a search manual used by the BATF, but withheld other parts. The Federal District Judge added the comment that:

Some withheld sections describe enforcement techniques that
are of dubious legality under the Fourth Amendment . . .
Although we do not decide whether any techniques described
are indeed unconstitutional, we do note our grave doubts
with respect to some of them. The agency might do well to
revise its enforcement guidelines with a heightened sensitivity
to developments in interpretation of the Fourth Amendment.

Now pending in the Fifth Circuit Federal Court of Appeals is a
class action by the National Association of Treasury Agents, the
employees of the federal agency involved. They have alleged that
they run the risk of termination should they refuse to utilize
illegal techniques:

. . . the denial of these rights leaves federal investigators who
refuse to utilize illegal methods of investigation with no
organization and less effective methods to defend themselves
from harassment by high governmental officials who had
subtly or otherwise decreed said illegal techniques. [Fifth
Circuit, Appeal No. 78-1258.]

Discriminatory Enforcement

A third area of concern from a civil liberties standpoint is the
risk of discriminatory enforcement of firearms laws. Here, again,
there appears a surprising tendency among some civil libertarians
to soft-pedal the objection.[58] But this has not been the reaction
of those who will be on the receiving end. Blacks and those
involved in the early civil rights efforts have often offered strong
opposition to gun laws. Too often firearms regulations become
dumping grounds for revenge against unpopular groups. The
present federal statute includes provisions making it a felony for
one dishonorably discharged, or having renounced American citizenship, to purchase a firearm. This was inserted, apparently, for
purely punitive purposes by the legislators. Massachusetts makes it
a crime for aliens to own guns, as well as those convicted of any
drug law violation, whether misdemeanor or felony. Even the
more rational statutes frequently incorporate provisions based
more on folklore than empirical evidence: prohibitions against
ownership by former mental patients are all but universal, despite
strong evidence that these persons have violence rates lower than
national rates (most committments are based on passivity rather

than aggression). Likewise, discretion is frequently given to the administrators: New Jersey provides that permits shall be issued to persons "of good character" and, in addition to specific prohibitions aimed at felons, former mental patients, aliens, etc., permits denial where issuance would not be in the public interest. Massachusetts permits issuance to a person not within a prohibited class "if it appears he is suitable. . . ."

If prejudice and uncontrolled discretion are frequent on the face of the statutes, enforcement practices are likely to be worse. Police unfavorable to gun ownership, or to the race, politics, or appearance of the particular applicant, frequently maximize the obstructions available; conversely, favored individuals and groups rarely experience much difficulty. It has been noted that in New York City:

> Most of the men and women who walk into gun shops looking for guns have almost no possibility of getting them — legally. The paperwork and delaying tactics employed by the New York City Police Department are usually enough to discourage even the most avid buyer. In fact, most gun store owners will advise middle-class citizens who are in search of guns that they will probably require the services of an attorney before they can buy a gun.[59]

As to practices in another permit-requiring city:

> Permits are automatically denied in St. Louis to wives who don't have their husband's permission, homosexuals, and nonvoters. . . . As one of my students recently learned, a "personal interview" is now required for every St. Louis application. After many delays, he finally got to see the sheriff — who looked at him only long enough to see that he wasn't black, yelled "He's all right" to the permit secretary, and left.[60]

Figures on actual enforcement of the laws likewise show strong racial tendencies. Although gun ownership is, if anything, lower among blacks than among whites,[61] enforcement in the strict anti-gun jurisdictions involves disproportionate arrest and conviction of blacks. Harvard's study of the new Massachusetts law providing for a year's imprisonment without probation for carrying a gun without permit found that only 33.3 per cent of defendants were white — 54.9 per cent were black, and 9.2 per cent Hispanic.[62] Chicago statistics showed 1,176 white and 7,636 black weapons arrests in a recent year.[62] This seven-to-one ratio was equalled only by the traditionally racially selective prostitution arrests. It doubled the three-to-one ratio of loitering and curfew violations.[63] In short, it appears that selective granting of permits and enforcement against owners of illegal weapons is likely to be a major problem. Under existing statutes, broad discretion is generally given and cheerfully abused. Even were criteria made totally objective — in which event little impact on crime could be expected[64] — enforcement efforts could still be expected to retain their present emphasis on unpopular racial and political groups.

Excessive Penalties

A final area where firearms regulation may call forth serious civil libertarian questions is that of the penalty provisions of recent statutes. In the face of predictable non-compliance, mandatory minimum sentencing requirements have become popular in the firearms regulation field, with penalties ranging from a few days up to several years without probation or parole. Likewise, strict punitive measures aimed at juveniles owning firearms have become increasingly popular. To the extent that even strong civil libertarians argue the need for firearms legislation in terms of lives lost and other considerations, they find themselves co-opted into acceptance of these measures. There can be little doubt that lax penalization has deprived present laws of deterrent impact,[65] and there is no reason to believe that future laws, similarly enforced, would have any greater success. Likewise, juveniles have a disproportionate involvement in gun law violations and violent crime. Civil libertarians have traditionally opposed harshly punitive laws on ethical and constitutional grounds. Yet it may be difficult to consistently combine such opposition with general support of strict firearm control. To the extent that one strongly believes that carnage and street crime are caused by the possession of guns in half the nations's households — and that, therefore, there is a pressing need for those households to provide police with their fingerprints and social history — one can hardly draw back from measures essential to enforcing actual compliance. To enact a criminal statute as an empty statement of commitment is hardly consistent with libertarian values; it further invites, as we have seen with criminalization of drug use and sexual conduct, selective enforcement and abuse.

Conclusion

The impact upon civil liberties of criminal legislation requiring licensing of firearms owners and users has generally been over-looked. Upon the rare occasions when the issue surfaces, its significance has generally been minimized by civil libertarians. Yet evidence indicates present widespread improprieties in the enforcement of existing statutes of this nature, taking the form of illegal searches, intrusions upon privacy, selective enforcement against racial and political minorities, and a trend toward increasingly harsh punitive legislation. At least to some extent, these defects appear inherent in the nature of the legislation. Measures aimed at conduct occurring mostly in the home, without a complaining party, necessarily require enforcement by informers or undercover solicitation, and numerous searches. Statutes aimed at gathering vague general information relevant to criminal tendencies necessarily must intrude upon privacy. Regulations that vest great discretion in the authorities must be recognized as inviting determinations consistent with those authorities' personal biases.

The consequences of such projected nationwide legislation are such, at the least, as ought to raise serious question among those who value civil liberties. The impact upon privacy of a national system of computerized and police-available information, containing fingerprints, photographs, and psychiatric and police-contact information on half the households in the nation, is an issue worthy of extensive consideration. The enforcement problems and tendency to increase present use of informers, electronic search and its abuses, and even rewards for turning in fellow citizens are likewise of grave concern.

The indirect impacts of such legislation upon the struggle to maintain privacy values against government intrusion must also be a subject of concern. Gun-owning citizens who have been required to furnish fingerprints, photographs, and personal information (perhaps to have the police interview their employers, friends, and neighbors) are unlikely to be outraged if, under other pretexts, similar intrusions are made upon the privacy of other citizens.

They may even applaud such things as the proposed National Identification Card system, or more extensive systems yet of government recordkeeping against individual citizens. Can those who are concerned with the ominous trend of government intrusion upon privacy afford to have the inhabitants of the half of our country's households that contain guns (or even just the 25 per cent that contain handguns) become inured to, and blasé about, such intrusions? Remember that the extent of the constitutional guarantee of privacy is unclear, and that much of the fight for it must necessarily be waged at the ballot box and in the legislatures.

The outrage of gun owners is likely to be focused upon the "civil libertarian" who ignores such intrusions (and the use of informers, rewards, and illegal searches) when these are necessary to social legislation he supports, but hypocritically condemns them in other contexts. Gun owners will find it difficult to respect protests against "massive inroads on [people's] privacy" perpetrated by "big brother in the form of an increasingly powerful government"[66] from a protester who blithely tosses off the remark that "[t]here is no reason why a state may not require a purchaser of a pistol to pass a psychiatric test."[67] Moreover, a civil libertarian who argues for more government control, more legislation and intrusions, in the gun area may be buying a bigger — or an entirely different — package than he bargained for. Polls have repeatedly shown the public much more favorable to such solutions to crime as drastic criminal penalties, stringently applied without consideration of rehabilitation (and for retrenchement on civil liberties), than for banning guns.[68] Accordingly, a civil libertarian who observes that "we are all familiar with the carnage caused by handguns"[69] should not be surprised when the argument returns from other quarters as an attack on the exclusionary rule:

> In the face of this carnage . . . scores of arrests each year are thrown out because of illegal search and seizure rulings.[70]

Casting aside the Second Amendment question, handgun confiscation poses an enormous hazard both to the continued health of the Fourth Amendment and to the development of its still fragile child, the constitutional right of privacy. Civil libertarians who embrace the confiscation cause risk being seen — and correctly so — as supporters of constitutional values only insofar as these inhibit legislation they care little about, but not their own pet proposals. If civil libertarians instead forthrightly oppose confiscation legislation because of its constitutional dangers, they not only help avert those, but seize a momentous opportunity as well. That is the opportunity to educate and sensitize our nation's fifty million handgun owners to civil liberties. There is evidence that gun owners may be ready to rally behind this type of leadership if civil libertarians are ready to give it. Harlon Carter, Executive Vice President of the National Rifle Association, was formerly head of the United States Border Patrol. In that position he, like most other police officials, opposed the exclusionary rule. Since joining the NRA, however, his position has altered 180 degrees. In fact, since federal handgun confiscation was first proposed in the early 1930s, the NRA has consistently pointed out the dangers it presents to Fourth Amendment rights. The NRA has also taken the lead in publicizing Fourth Amendment and other constitutional violations against gun owners by federal officers enforcing federal gun laws — violations as to which the ACLU has generally remained silent.

Illustrative of the "consciousness-raising" such publicization can produce among gun owners is their reaction to Inspector Domm's proposal for "reinterpretation" of the Fourth Amendment. Though no civil liberties publication seems to have mentioned it, the Domm proposal was fully reported in the monthly national magazine of the NRA. The response it received — from a police officer, no less — was a letter which no civil libertarian can fault either in its invocation of hallowed constitutional traditions or its dire conclusion:

> [Detroit police] Inspector John Domm was quoted in the March issue as urging a rewrite of the Fourth Amendment.
>
> Have we lost sight of why there are Amendments to our U.S. Constitution? The reasons are clear to me. They are to protect the citizens of our country from government. I am not talking about foreign government.
>
> Our founding fathers knew what it was like to live under a government which allowed anything for government and guaranteed nothing for the governed. They decided that when they finally won out over this tyranny it would not happen again, not in their country. So they wrote in

safeguards right from the beginning, and they wrote them clearly, strongly and very to the point.

I am also a police officer of ten years and more service. I know about the fear of police officers and the problems of weapons in the hands of criminals. I am also very much aware that as police officers we are extensions of the government. We enforce the rules of government, no matter what level. I will never ask for or hope for any law which will give me or any other police officer the right to search and seize with any greater freedom than is already at hand.

We should never ask for the elimination of a guaranteed right of the people.

There aren't too many left anymore.

BIOGRAPHIES OF CONTRIBUTORS

MARK K. BENENSON

Mark K. Benenson was born and raised in New York City and received his bachelor's degree from the City College of New York (1951) and his law degree from Columbia University (1956). Mr. Benenson was American chairman of the Amnesty International organization from 1968 to 1972 and remains its general counsel; in 1977 the organization was awarded the Nobel Peace Prize for its efforts on behalf of political prisoners around the world.

KENNETH L. CHOTINER

Kenneth Chotiner is a graduate of U.CL.A. (B.A., 1959) and Loyola University of Los Angeles (J.D., 1969). He has served as a Judge Pro Tem of the Los Angeles Municipal Court and on the Board of Directors of the National Rifle Association. Avocationally, he is currently Vice President of the American Civil Liberties Union of Southern California and Lecturer on Constitutional Law in the Los Angeles Police Academy. He is engaged in the general practice of law, particularly criminal, firearms, and constitutional cases.

COLIN GREENWOOD

See biographic information on pages 32-33.

DAVID T. HARDY

David T. Hardy practices in Tucson with the firm of Sharp, Sando and Hardy, specializing in consumer fraud and civil rights litigation. He received his undergraduate and law degrees from the University of Arizona in 1972 and 1975, with honors and *magna cum laude*, respectively. He has served as associate editor of the *Arizona Law Revtew* and as a fellow of the Institute for Humane Studies. He has written articles on search and seizure, informants, and other elements of constitutional criminal procedure and on firearms regulation for the Arizona, Chicago-Kent and William and Mary law reviews and the *Business and Society Review*. He is presently acting as project director of a national task force investigating civil liberties violations by federal agencies enforcing firearms statutes.

DON B. KATES, JR.

While still a student at Yale Law School, Don B. Kates, Jr. did civil rights work in the South, was a law clerk for William Kunstler and Arthur Kinoy, and drafted civil rights legislation for the House Judiciary Committee. From 1966 to 1975 he held various administrative positions with California Rural Legal Assistance and was deputy director and director of litigation for the San Mateo County Legal Aid Society, both OEO-funded programs providing free legal representation for the indigent. He specialized in major constitutional litigation before the United States Supreme Court and the lower federal and state courts, particularly police misconduct litigation. In 1970 he was denominated the nation's outstanding legal services lawyer by the National Legal Aid and Defender Association. He has also been a member of the California Advisory Committee to the United States Civil Rights Commission.

Professor Kates has acted as a police legal advisor to departments in California and Missouri and has been a consultant on firearms, firearms legislation, and civil rights legislation to police departments and state and federal legislative committees. His articles on firearms have appeared in police and firearms technical journals. His articles on firearms laws and "gun control" generally have appeared in *Harpers*, the *Christian Science Monitor*, the *Civil Liberties Review*, the *Criminal Law Bulletin*, the *Washington Post*, the *Los Angeles Times*, the *St. Louis Post Dispatch*, and various other periodicals. His articles on civil rights laws and litigation have appeared in the *California Law Review*, the *U.S.C. Law Review*, and the *Northwestern University Law Review*. Professor Kates currently teaches constitutional and criminal law and criminal procedure at St. Louis University and maintains a largely constitutional law practice in San Francisco.

JOSEPH MAGADDINO

See biographic information on page 56.

JOHN R. SALTER, JR.

Until recently, Professor Salter was Director of Human Development for the Archdiocese of Rochester, a position in which he represented minorities and the underprivileged and did community organizing around civil rights issues and in opposition to capital punishment. He has just taken a professorship at the Navajo Nation University in Tsaile, Arizona. Further biographical details are provided in his remarks.

CAROL RUTH SILVER

As an undergraduate at the University of Chicago, Carol Ruth Silver took part in the earliest of the Freedom Rides of the 1960s, sponsored by the Congress on Racial Equality (CORE) to integrate buses and bus stations throughout the South. She was imprisoned in Mississippi's infamous Parchman Penitentiary, where she lost almost a pound a day until thirty-five days later her conviction for violating segregation laws was overturned on appeal. After graduating from the Law School of the University of Chicago in 1964, she worked for Floyd McKissick, North Carolina civil rights leader and subsequently CORE National Chairman. From 1965 to 1967 she was a lawyer for Alameda County Legal Aid, providing free civil representation to indigents in the Oakland, California, ghetto, and then director of California Rural Legal Assistance's office near Delano, California. There she represented indigent Chicanos of Cezar Chavez's United Farm Workers' organization, including one of his principal aides, Dolores Huerta, in a brutality suit against the Delano police.

Thereafter, until 1972, Ms. Silver was director of an OEO-funded program providing free civil representation to indigents in the City of Berkeley. She left that position to teach at Golden Gate Law School and was also chief counsel for the San Francisco Sheriff's Department (1972-75). Her law practice is devoted primarily to civil rights and women's rights issues; she recently won the largest damage award ever given by a jury under the federal Housing Discrimination Act. She is also a member of the Board of Supervisors of the City and County of San Francisco, representing a Latino and Gay district. Ms. Silver holds a brown belt in Shotokan karate and has had instruction in both judo and police handgun combat shooting.

NOTES

Section I Notes and References

The comprehensive work on American firearms history is L. Kennett and J. Anderson, *The Gun in America* (Greenwood, 1975). Professors Kennett and Anderson devote much space to legal history, and I have relied heavily upon them for this and for general background. Much material on violence and firearms regulations in the Western states appears in P. Jordan, *Frontier Law and Order* (University of Nebraska Press, 1970), including reproductions of many of the early statutes and ordinances. See also F. Prassel, *The Western Peace Officer* (University of Oklahoma Press, 1972), p. 22. The history of firearms regulation in the United States also receives some attention in G. Newton and F. Zimring, *Firearms and Violence in American Life*, a staff report to the National Commission on the Causes and Prevention of Violence (Eisenhower Commission). Several cases concerning state laws affecting alien gun ownership are reviewed in the annotations that appear in Volumes 24 and 34 of American Law Reports, at pages 1119 and 63 respectively. Unfortunately, most of the early legislation dealt with in this article is not treated in any secondary source and can only be located by laboriously combing through the laws of the various states. Federal firearms ownership and sale restrictions and a compendium of state laws relevant thereto are gathered together in the Department of the Treasury publication *Firearms Regulation* (1978). But since many of the earlier state enactments, particularly those dealing with alien firearms possession, have long since been repealed, my primary legislative research resource has been the multi-volume sets of superseded state codes that are preserved in the law libraries of St. Louis University, the University of California at Berkeley, and Hastings College of the Law in San Francisco. David T. Hardy, Esq., of the Tucson Bar, was kind enough to provide me with the fruits of his research in Western and Southern firearms legislative history in a letter, an unpublished memorandum, and several lengthy phone calls.

The following were kind enough to review and criticize an early draft: Davis E. Keeler, Esq., Director of the Legal Project of the Institute for Humane Studies, Menlo Park, California; Professor Leonard Liggio, now a Fellow at the Cato Institute in San Francisco, William Marina, Professor of History, Florida Atlantic University; Dr. James J. Martin, Palmer Lake, Colorado; Professor Richard Metcalf of the History Department of Cornell

University; and Professor Roy Wortman of the History Department of Kenyon College. Though they did not have the opportunity to review the manuscript, Professors C. Vann Woodward of Yale and Kenneth Stampp of the University of California at Berkeley discussed its thesis and offered much aid and advice. Although I have benefited enormously from the criticism, help, and counsel of the foregoing persons, any errors of fact of interpretation in the article are entirely my own responsibility.

The various public opinion polls are available from (respectively) the American Institute of Public Opinion, Louis Harris and Associates, the Roper Public Opinion Research Center, Cambridge Reports, Inc., and Decision Making Information, Inc.

On nineteenth- and early twentieth-century attitudes toward the immigrants, see the following: R. Billington, *The Protestant Crusade* (Rinehart, 1952); J. Higham, *Strangers in the Land* (Atheneum, 1963); and B. Soloman, *Ancestors and Immigrants* (Harvard, 1956). See also Feldman, *The Philadelphia Riots of 1844*, and D. Kinzer, *An Episode of Anti-Catholicism* (University of Washington, 1964).

The judicial opinions cited and/or quoted from are: *Castro* v. *State of California*, 85 Cal. Rptr. 20 (1970), (English literacy requirement for voting unconstitutional as applied to Spanish literates); *State* v. *Rheaume*, 116 Atl. 758 (S.Ct. N.H. 1918), (upholding constitutionality of statute barring aliens from owning firearms); and *People* v. *Ramiriz*, 226 P. 914 (Ct.Ap. Cal 1924), (same). In two other cases, statutes barring alien arms-ownership were held to violate state constitutional provisions guaranteeing the right to keep and bear arms: *People* v. *Nakamura*, 62 P.2d 246 (S.Ct. Colo. 1936), and *People* v. *Zerillo*, 189 N.W. 927 (S.Ct. Mich. 1922).

Section II Notes and References

1. Green Paper, *The Control of Firearms in Great Britain*, Cmnd. 5297 (London: H.M.S.O., May, 1973).

2. Colin Greenwood, *Firearms Control* (London: Routledge & Kegan Paul, 1972).

3. *Report to the New York State Commission of Investigation Concerning the Availability, Illegal Possession and Use of Handguns in the State of New York*, 1974.

4. Office of Health Economics, Briefing No. 4, (London: January 1976).

5. Note omitted.

6. Figures extracted from *Criminal Statistics for England and Wales for 1975*, Cmnd. 6566 (London: H.M.S.O., 1976).

7. These figures are recorded in two places in the relevant issues of criminal statistics. Under firearms offenses are 51 and 46 as shown. Under homicide by shooting in each year, the figures are 46 and 43 respectively. The difference may be due to the fact that homicide figures are adjusted after recording in the manner described in the text, but the 'firearm figures' for those years would not have been so adjusted. It may also be that in some cases a firearm was used as a blunt instrument, in which case it would be included in the firearms offenses, but not in homicide by shooting.

8. Greenwood, *op. cit.*, p. 234.

9. A.D. Weatherhead and B.M. Robinson, *Firearms in Crime* (London: H.M.S.O., 1970).

10. *The Control of Firearms in Great Britain.*

11. Marvin Wolfgang, *Patterns in Criminal Homicide* (University of Pennsylvania, 1958), p. 82.

12. E.S. Tanner, *Homicide in Uganda, 1964* (Uppsala: Scandinavian Institute of African Studies, 1970).

13. Report in *The American Rifleman* (Washington, D.C.) September, 1976, p. 51.

14. *The Control of Firearms in Great Britain.*

15. For example, see F.H. McClintock and Evelyn Gibson *Robbery in London* (London: Macmillan, 1961).

16. Greenwood, *op. cit.*, Chapter 8.

17. See George D. Newton, Jr., and Frank E. Zimring, *Firearms and Violence in American Life* (Washington, D.C.), Chapter I and Appendix C.

18. Ramsey Clark, *Crime in America* (New York: 1970), p. 90.

19. Metropolitan Life Insurance Company, *Statistical Bulletin*, July, 1968, p. 5.

20. *Ibid.*

21. Albert P. Iskrant and Paul V. Joliet, *Accidents and Homicide* (Cambridge: Harvard University Press, 1968), pp. 93-97.

22. *Ibid.*, p. 94.

23. National Rifle Association, *Uniform Hunter Casualty Report* (Washington, D.C.).

24. Newton and Zimring, *op. cit.*, p. 33.

25. *Ibid.*, p. 36.

Section III Notes and References

1. New York City Police Department, Press Release No. 25 (March 14, 1967).

2. M. Wolfgang, *Patterns in Criminal Homicide* (Science Edition, 1966), p. 332.

3. In 1958, when *Patterns in Criminal Homicide* was originally published, Pennsylvania required a 48-hour waiting period on pistol sales, to permit an interim police investigation of the prospective purchaser (Pa. Stat. Ann. tit. 18, § 4628 [Purdon, 1958]).

4. *Supra.* note 2, pp. 81-83.

5. Wolfgang, "Violence, U.S.A.," *Crime and Delinquency* 14 (Oct., 1968), pp. 289, 294.

6. R. Narloch, *Criminal Homicide in California* (1958), p. 55. (Prepared by the California Department of Justice, Bureau of Criminal Statistics.)

7. 1967 FBI Uniform Crime Reports, p. 97.

8. Newsletter of J. Edgar Hoover to all law enforcement officials, June 1, 1963, reprinted from *FBI Law Enforcement Bull.* (June, 1963).

9. FBI, *Uniform Crime Reports* (1966), pp. 66 *et seq.* (Table 4 — Index of Crime by State).

10. *Ibid.*, pp. 60-65 (Table 3 — Index of Crime by Region).

11. *Supra*, note 1.

12. "The Regulation of the Firearms by the States," Wisconsin Legislative Reference Library Report, *Research Bull. 130* (1960), p. 33.

13. Hearing on S.1 before the Subcommittee Investigating Juvenile Delinquency of the Senate Committee on the Judiciary, 90 Cong., 1st Sess. 379 (Statement of Wayne County, Michigan Prosecuting Attorney William Cahalan), p. 695.

14. *Ibid.*, pp. 727-33.

15. *Hearings on S. 3691, 3604, 3634, 3637 before the Subcomm. to Investigate Juvenile Delinquency of the Senate Comm. on the Judiciary*, 90th Cong., 2d Sess. (1968), pp. 734-36.

16. *Supra*, note 2, p. 84.

17. S. Marshall, *Men Against Fire* (1947), Ch. 5.

18. Importation of such pistols, which were manufactured primarily in West Germany and Spain, is now banned by the Gun Control Act of 1968, 18 U.S.C. R 921 (Cum. Supp. 1969). For a description of such arms, and illustrations, see Statement of William L. Cahalen, *supra*, note 13.

19. *Supra*, note 8.

20. A. Krug, *Does Firearms Registration Work?* (1968), pp. 5, 14.

21. Harwood, "The Public Besieges the Gun Lobby," *Washington Post*, June 23, 1968.

22. Louis Harris poll, New York, N.Y., Sept. 16, 1967: 33 per cent of the Easterners queried said they owned a gun, as opposed to 54 per cent of those queried nationally.

23. *Trenton Evening Times*, May 9, 1968.

24. The *Times Union*, March 16, 1968, p. 14, col. 1, piled an even greater misinterpretation upon the FBI's original press release error; the paper reported in an editorial that the use of firearms in robberies "showed a leap of 58 per cent."

25. Pittsburgh data obtained from Pittsburgh Police Department; Philadelphia data obtained from FBI.

26. Starnes, "Philadelphia! Red Tape Nightmare," *Field & Stream*, May, 1966, p. 11; *"The Gun Law's Deadly Recoil,"* Greater Philadelphia, Aug., 1965.

27. Harris, "Annals of Legislation," *New Yorker*, April 20, 1968, p. 56.

28. *Hearings on Firearms Legislation before the Subcomm. on Crime of the House Comm. on the Judiciary*, 94th Cong., 1st. Sess., pt. 7, p. 2394 (testimony of N. Knox).

29. Crime Control Research Project (1601-114th St. SE, Suite 155, Bellevue, Washington: 1977).

30. Boston Police Department, *Handgun Control: A Survey of the Leading Law Enforcement Officials in the Country* (1976), p. 2.

31. Comptroller General of the United States, *Handgun Control: Effectiveness and Costs* (Feb. 6, 1978), p. 85. (Hereinafter "Comptroller's report.") Comments by U.S. Department of Justice.

32. See "The Relationship Between Firearms Licensing Laws and Crime Rates: A Statistical Analysis," *Cong. Rec.*, Vol. 113, pt. 15, p. 20060 (July 25, 1967); "The Relationship Between Firearms Ownership and Crime Rates: A Statistical Analysis," *ibid.*, Vol. 114, pt. 2, p. 1496 (Jan. 30, 1968); "The Misuses of Firearms in Crime," *ibid.*, Vol. 114, pt. 7, p. 8585 (Apr. 2, 1968).

33. Murray, "Handguns, Guns Control Laws and Firearm Violence," *Social Problems*, 23 (1975), p. 81.

34. See Gastill, "Homicide and a Regional Culture of Violence," *Am. Sociological Rev.*, 36 (1971), pp. 412, 417; D. Lunde, *Murder and Madness* (1976), pp. 20-21 (Southern rates ten times the Northern, prior to Civil War).

35. See Wright and Marston, "The Ownership of the Means of Destruction: Weapons in the United States," *Social Problems* 23 (1975), pp. 93, 96-108.

36. It has been noted that "homicides are concentrated among the poor and black" (*Hearings on Firearms Legislation*, pt. 2, p. 518; testimony of R. Bloch). The homicide rate for black Americans is approximately eight times that of the rest of the populace (Seitz, "Firearms, Homicides and Gun Control Effectiveness," *Law and Soc. Rev.*, (1972), pp. 595, 599-600.

37. Comptroller's report, p. 63.

38. *Hearings on Firearms Legislation*, pt. 7, p. 2306 (testimony of J. Gekas).

39. U.S. National Commission on the Causes and Prevention of Violence, *Commission Statement on Firearms and Violence* (1969); Research Associates Inc., *A Preliminary Cost Analysis of Firearms Control Programs* (Washington, D.C.: 1968).

40. *Hearings Pursuant to S. Res. 72 before the Subcomm. to Investigate Juvenile Delinquency of the Senate Judiciary Comm.*, 94th Cong., 1st Sess., Vol. 1 (1975), pp. 242-43 (statement of BATF director).

41. *Hearings on Firearms Legislation*, pt. 7, p. 2350 (testimony of Judge Fox).

42. See L. Kennett and J. Anderson, *The Gun in America* (1975), pp. 254-55; Hearings Pursuant to S. Res. 72, pp. 635-36, note 29 (report of Department of Justice staff).

43. *Hearings on Firearms Legislation*, pt. 7, p. 2428 (exhibit: "Handgun Control in Massachusetts: A Report to the Governor").

Section IV Notes and References

1. *The Regulation of Firearms by the States*, Wisconsin Legislative Reference Library Report, *Research Bull. 130*, (1960); Krug, "The Relationship Between Firearms Licensing Laws and Crime Rates: A Statistical Analysis," *Cong. Rec.*, Vol. 113, pt. 15, p. 20060 (July 25, 1967); Magaddino, "An Economic Analysis of State Gun Control Laws: A Statistical Study of 1970 Data" (doctoral thesis, Virginia Polytechnic Institute, 1972); Dyer, "Guns, Crime, and the Law" (unpublished manuscript, 1975); Murray, "Handguns, Gun Control Laws, and Firearm Violence," *Social Problems*, 23 (1975), p. 81; Professor Kates' analysis of 1974 figures is still in draft form. See also Krug, "The Relationship Between Firearms Ownership and Crime Rate: A Statistical Analysis," *Cong. Rec.*, Vol. 114, pt. 2, p. 1496 (January 30, 1968) and "The Misuses of Firearms in Crime," *Cong. Rec.*, Vol. 114, pt. 7, p. 8585 (April 2, 1968); Snyder, "Crime Rises Under Rigid Gun Control," *American Rifleman*, 117 (1969), p. 54; and "Statistical Analysis Shows Handgun Control Laws Don't Stop Homicide," *Point Blank* (July, 1975).

2. Murray, *supra*, note 1

3. See selection by British police Superintendent Greenwood, *supra.*

4. C. Greenwood, *Firearms Control: A Study of Armed Crime and Firearms Control in England and Wales* (London: Routledge and Kegan Paul, 1972), pp. 240 ff. Coming to essentially the same conclusion is V. Azeraj, *An Analysis of the Role of Firearms Control Laws in South African Society* (master's thesis, University of Capetown, 1973). It may, however, be argued that the failure of South African laws to control violent crime rates is a less relevant consideration, since the primary purpose of the enactment and enforcement of these laws appears to be the exercise of political controls over the native African population.

5. E.g., Zimring, "Fun and Games with Guns and Statistics," 1968 *Wis. L. Rev.* 1113.

6. Kennedy, "The Need for Gun Control Legislation," *Current History*, July/Aug., 1976, p. 27.

7. Knap, "Home Defense in Canada," in G. James, *Guns and Ammo Guide to Guns for Home Defense* (Petersen, 1974), p. 77.

8. L. Kennett and J. Anderson, *The Gun in America* (Greenwood, 1975), pp. 203-4.

9. *American Rifleman*, Feb., 1969, p. 22.

10. D. Lunde, *Murder and Madness* (S.F. Book Co., 1976), p. 1.

11. See discussion in selection from David T. Hardy, *supra.*

12. See, e.g., New York City Police Department, *Homicide Analysis* (1977); Seversey and Enloe, *Homicide in Harlem* (New York: Rand Institute, 1975) pp. 17 ff.; Chicago Police Department, *Murder Analysis* (volumes for years 1966, 1967, 1968, 1969, 1970, 1971, 1972, 1973, 1974, 1975, and 1976); *Hearings on S. 3691, etc., before the Subcomm. to Investigate Juvenile Delinquency of the Senate Comm. on the Judiciary,*

(1968): exhibit No. 7, pp. 75-76 (D.C. study). Similar national statistics are quoted in Lunde, *Murder and Madness*, p. 10.

13. J. MacDonald, *Armed Robbery: Offenders and Their Victims* (C.C. Thomas, 1975), pp. 427-28.

14. *Patterns in Criminal Homicide* (Science Edition, 1966), p. 332.

15. Zimring, "Is Gun Control Likely to Reduce Violent Killings?" 35 *U. Chi. L. Rev.* 721 (1968).

16. Correspondence from David T. Hardy to Professor Kates describing preliminary results of a study of homicide in Tucson, Arizona.

17. Zimring, *supra*, note 15. The handgun mortality figure cannot be precisely determined, since Professor Zimring is not always exact in distinguishing homicides and aggravated assaults committed with long guns from those committed with handguns. Further confirmatory information appears in yet another study by Zimring of Chicago homicide data, published as "The Medium is the Message: Firearms Caliber as a Determinant of Death from Assault," 1 *Journal of Legal Studies* 97 (1970).

18. Wilson and Sherman, "Civilian Penetrating Wounds of the Abdomen," *Annals of Surgery*, 153, pp. 639, 642; Ryzkoff *et al.*, "Selective Conservatism in Penetrating Abdominal Trauma" 59, pp. 650, 652-53 (1966); and see also general discussion in Benenson, "A Controlled Look at Gun Control," 14 *N.Y. Law Forum* 718 (1968).

19. J. Given, *Society and Homicide in 13th Century England* (Stanford Univ. Press, 1977).

20. See, generally, discussions in Kates' "Some Remarks on the Prohibition of Handguns," 23 *St. L.U. L.J.* 12 (1978) and "Reflections on the Relevancy of Gun Control," 13 *Crim. L. Bull.* 119 (1977).

21. If 70 per cent of the present 130,000 handgun assaults were instead carried out with knives, and 30 per cent with long guns, the increase in knife attacks would amount to 91,000 per year, while that in long gun attacks would be 39,000 per year. With 40 per cent of the latter resulting in death, the gun homicide rate would rise by 7,420 deaths from the present rate with handguns.

22. We do not mean to suggest that all, or any one, of these four objections represents the official position of any particular organized group that is working for handgun prohibition. These are simply the objections that have been made by the representatives of such organizations with whom we have appeared on television and on radio, and by those representatives and others supporting handgun prohibition in private conversations we have had with them.

23. See discussion in Professor Magaddino's article, *supra*.

24. Matt Brown, consultant to *Gun Week* on "crime and self-defense," in his May 26, 1978, column entitled "Ultimate Tranquilizer: Stubby Scattergun." See generally the advice given by such experts as Elmer Keith, Jeff Cooker, Bert Miller, and George Nonte in G. James, *Guns and Ammo Guide to Guns for Home Defense* (1975), pp. 40 ff., in a section entitled "Best Home Defense Gun."

25. See sources cited *supra*, note 16.

26. See sources cited *supra*, note 15.

27. See, e.g., J. Huizinga, *The Waning of the Middle Ages* (London: 1937), p. 18; A. Luchaire, *Social France at the time of Philip Augustus* (New York: 1912), p. 8; M. Bloch, *Feudal Society* (Chicago: 1962), p. 411.

28. Unpublished manuscript presented at the 1977 annual meeting of the American Society of Criminology.

29. "Strategic Choice Analysis" has been published by the Office of Policy and Planning of the Department of Justice. Professor Cook's other study is an unpublished manuscript which he was kind enough to supply us in second-draft form.

30. U.S. Department of Justice news release, Oct. 15, 1978, p. 3; Hindelang, *Criminal Victimization in Eight American Cities* (Ballinger, 1974), p. 263; Skogan, *Sample Surveys of the Victims of Crime* (Ballinger, 1976), p. 15; Greenwood, *Firearms Controls*, pp. 252-53. See generally MacDonald, *Armed Robbery: Offenders and Their Victims* (Thomas, 1975), pp. 138-39.

31. Unlike the serious-injury data (which come from victim surveys sponsored by the Law Enforcement Assistance Administration) the robbery-homicide data come from FBI figures. These do not distinguish armed robbery from unarmed robbery except for robberies in which the offender has a gun. When Professor Kates wrote for a breakdown of deaths caused by clubs, knives, hands/feet, etc., Professor Cook replied that his figures did not provide this information.

32. "Is Gun Control Likely to Reduce Violent Killings?" 35 *U. Chi. L. Rev.* 721 (1968).

33. *Supra*, note 18.

34. The Florida figures are contained in correspondence from James Barrett, executive assistant to the Florida attorney general, to Bill Garrison, dated June 28, 1977. The Massachusetts figures are contained in Beha (Harvard Gun Law Project), *And Nobody Can Get You Out* (Harvard Law School Center on Criminal Justice, 1976, p. 148.

35. See generally the extended discussion and notes in Kates-Benenson, *supra* at note 20.

36. L. Kennett & J. Anderson, *The Gun in America* (Greenwood, 1976), 202-3.

37. MacDonald, *supra*, note 30, pp. 124-43.

38. D. Grennell, *Law Enforcement Handgun Digest* (DBI, 1976), 104.

39. This four to one comparison is a very conservative one because it assumes that robbers would switch to shotguns and rifles in approximately equal numbers. If the switch were primarily to shotguns, lethality would be perhaps as much as ten times greater than with handguns, for shotguns are about three times as deadly as rifles, which are three times deadlier than handguns. See, e.g., Taylor, "Gunshot Wounds of the Abdomen," *Annals of Surgery* 177 (1973), pp. 174-75 ("Shotgun injuries have not been compared with other bullet wounds of the abdomen as they are a thing apart. . . . At close range they are as deadly as a cannon.");

DeMuth, "The Mechanism of Shotgun Wounds," *Journal of Trauma*, 11 (1971), p. 219.

40. This assumes, of course, that the handgun-prohibiting enactment does not make provision for compensating owners at approximately par value when they turn in their weapons. Although various proponents of handgun prohibition have from time to time proposed compensation as part of the scheme, most prohibition laws make no provision for this. In any case, both the general proposals and the handgun prohibition legislation that does envision compensation contemplate a maximum price (normally $50.00) for every gun that barely equals the value of the cheapest used guns now in circulation. Fifty dollars represents but a fraction of the cost of any presently available gun from any of the better American domestic manufacturers like Colt, Smith & Wesson, Ruger, High Standard, Charter Arms, etc.

41. Homemade firearms — ranging from the most primitive single-shot "zip gun" to very sophisticated revolvers or semiautomatic weapons — have occasioned a substantial literature. The most complete is a three-volume work by J. David Truby and John Minnery, *Improvised and Modified Firearms* (Paladin, 1975 and 1977). See also Koffler, "Zip Guns and Crude Conversions — Identifying Characteristics and Problems" (pts. 1-2), 60 *J Crim. L.C.P.S.* 520 (1969) and 61 *(ibid.)* 115 (1970); Smith, "Zip Guns," *Police Magazine*, Jan.-Feb., 1963, p. 10; DiMaio and Spitz, "Variations in Wounding Due to Unusual Firearms and Recently Available Ammunition," 17 *J. For Schi.* 377 (1972); and Hardy and Stompoly, "Of Arms and The Law," 51 *Chi.-Kent L. Rev.* 62 (99) (1975).

42. *Hearings on S. 2507 before the Subcomm. to Investigate Juvenile Delinquency of the Senate Comm. on the Judiciary*, 92d. Cong., 1st Sess., (1971), p. 190.

43. See, e.g., "Two Million Illegal Pistols Believed Within the City," *New York Times*, March 2, 1975, citing opinions of both federal and state law enforcement officials; and "Two Million Illegal Guns in the City," *New York Post*, Oct. 7, 1975, citing the opinion of the Manhattan District Attorney.

44. See generally Field Institute, *Tabulations of the Findings of a Survey of Handgun Ownership and Access Among a Cross Section of the California Adult Public* (1976), responses to Question No. 1. These would indicate a California rate of handgun possession of slightly greater than twenty to every one hundred people. Nationally the rate of handgun possession was eighteen to one hundred, according to responses to the American Institute of Public Opinion poll taken in March, 1975. In contrast, the estimated illegal rate of handgun possession in New York City was twenty five to one hundred.

45. Greenwood, *supra*, note 4, pp. 242-3.

46. See extended discussion in the Kates-Benenson article on homicidal attack, *supra*.

47. For over twenty years the magazine of the National Rifle Association has been printing eight to sixteen instances per month of successful civilian armed self-defense. (See discussion in article on women's armed self-

defense, *infra.*) Review of these columns and of data Professor Kates is collecting on self-defense (see same discussion, *infra*) finds many instances of robbers tipping off their intentions in this fashion. Rape victims also report that nervous or other suspicious behavior forewarned them before the attack that the rapist was contemplating it. (L. Copeland, *Rape: Prevention and Resistance* [Queen's Bench Foundation, 1976] pp. 15-16.) See also *Terry* v. *Ohio*, 392 U.S. 1 (1965), where the suspicious activities of a pair of would-be robbers were held sufficient to justify an observing officer in patting them down for weapons.

48. See the women's armed self-defense article, *infra*, describing Professor Kates' data, which show armed defenders succeeding in killing, wounding, arresting, or driving off attackers in 84 per cent of all cases, while being injured themselves in 11.3 per cent and killed in 6 per cent.

49. Typical statements (in these cases by Congressmen who have sponsored handgun prohibition legislation) are Conyers, "It's Time to End Our Romance with Guns," *Boston Sunday Globe*, July 23, 1978; Drinan, "Gun Control: The Good Outweighs the Evil," *Civil Liberties Review*, Aug.-Sept., 1976. See generally Yeager, *How Well Does The Handgun Protect You and Your Family?* (U.S. Conference of Mayors, 1976), a pamphlet prepared by the "Handgun Control Staff" of the U.S. Conference of Mayors, an organization which lobbies constantly for handgun prohibition. The pamphlet is devoted to proving that handguns are worthless for self-defense — Professor Cook to the contrary notwithstanding.

50. See discussion in Benenson, "A Controlled Look at Gun Controls," 14 N.Y. Law Forum 718, 730 (1968).

Section V Notes and References

1. From "The Best Home Defense Gun," a written symposium in G. James (editor), *Guns and Ammo Guide to Guns for Home Defense* (Petersen, 1975), p. 40.

2. "Firearms and Self-Defense," G. Newton and F. Zimring, *Firearms and Violence in American Life* (staff report to the National Commission on the Causes and Prevention of Violence).

3. Detailed comparisons of handgun, rifle, and shotgun lethality are contained in the articles "Handgun Prohibition and Homicide" and "Handgun Availability and the Social Harms of Robbery," *supra.*

4. These administrative policies date from at least as early as 1937, when a distinguished civil libertarian commented that it was impossible to get a permit in New York City "unless you know a local judge or a ward politician." (Morris Ernest, *The Ultimate Power* [Doubleday, 1937] p. 198.) Forty years later a review by *New York* magazine found the same situation in existence, despite the entry against the police of a series of individual and class action injunctions. (Susan Hall, "Nice People Who Carry Guns," *New York*, Dec. 12, 1977: The police "actively attempt to keep the number of pistol-packing New Yorkers at a minimum by refusing to give permits to keep a gun in the home"; the number of permits issued is "so low that even the police are embarrassed at having

to pretend that they believe the rationality of their own statistics. . . . The paper work and delaying tactics employed by the New York City Police Department are usually enough to discourage even the most avid. . . .") See generally Kates, "Some Remarks on the Prohibition of Handguns," 23 St. L.U.L.J. 12 (1978).

5. N. Morris and G. Hawkins, *The Honest Politician's Guide to Crime Control* (1970), pp. 60-61; FBI (Kelley), *Uniform Crime Reports* (1975), pp. 22-23; FBI *Uniform Crime Report* news release of Dec. 15, 1977, describing figures for Jan.-Sept., 1977.

6. Center for Constitutional Rights, *Docket Report* 1977-78, p. 8.

7. S. Baker, "Aggravated Assaults — Police Records for the City of St. Louis, Compilation of Six Months Data" (unpublished ms., 1978).

8. L. Schneider, *et al.*, "Representation of Women Who Defend Themselves in Response to Physical or Sexual Assault" (Center for Constitutional Rights, 1978), p. 10.

9. *Riss v. City of New York*, 240 N.E. 2d 860, 22 N.Y. 2d 579.

10. California Gov. C., Sections 821, 845, 846.

11. P. Cook, *The Effect of Gun Availability on Robbery and Robbery-Murder: A Cross-Section-Study of 50 Cities* (Center for Study of Justice Policy, 1978), pp. 18-19.

12. Van den Haag, "Banning Handguns: Helping the Criminal Hurt You," *New Woman*, Nov.-Dec., 1975, p. 80; Firman, "In Prison Gun Survey the Pros are the Cons," *American Rifleman*, Nov., 1975, p. 13.

13. F. Zimring and G. Hawkins, *Deterrence* (1975), pp. 158 ff.

14. Hirsh, *et al.*, "Accidental Firearm Fatalities in a Metropolitan County," *American Journal of Epidemiology*, 100 (1975), p. 504. The study itself does not mention that its authors are employing this unusual method of classifying suicide. Upon learning of the matter through another source, Professor Kates wrote the authors for an explanation. Although over a year has gone by since the letter was sent, there has been no response.

15. M. Yeager, *How Well Does the Handgun Protect You and Your Family?* (U.S. Conference of Mayors, 1976), p. 5.

16. See sources cited *supra*, note 4.

17. Massad Ayoob, a distinguished authority on firearms who is himself a police officer, has commented with some asperity that the average officer would be more interested in acquiring a good fountain pen than in having a good side arm. The latest available figures indicate that 27 per cent of all police departments do not test their officers in firearms use, and that almost 20 per cent don't even have a range where an officer who wishes to test or improve his skills can do so. A. Bristow, *The Search for an Effective Police Handgun* (Thomas, 1973) p. 47. See also Milton, *et al.*, *Police Use of Deadly Force* (Police Foundation, 1977), pp. 105-15.

18. Justifiable homicide figures for the period 1965-75 were supplied to me by the Chicago police, through the courtesy of Professor Fred Inbau of Northwestern University School of Law.

19. "Killings by Chicago Police, 1969-70: An Empirical Study," 46 U.S.C. L.

Rev. 284 (1973).

20. Milton, *supra*, note 17, pp. 65 ff.

21. *Supra*, note 3.

22. An observation confirmed by Professor Kates' colleague Professor Michael Wolff, who was a reporter for the *Minneapolis Star* for three years.

23. The Field Institute, *Tabulations of the Findings of a Survey of Handgun Ownership and Access among a Cross-Section of the California Public* (1976).

24. Copeland, *Rape Victimization Study: Preliminary Research Findings and Recommendations* (Queen's Bench Foundation, 1975); *Rape Victimization Study: Final Report* (Queen's Bench Foundation, 1975); *Rape: Prevention and Resistance* (Queen's Bench Foundation, 1976). (Hereinafter Copeland I, II, and III respectively.)

25. *Copeland III, supra*, note 24, pp. 65 ff.

26. An unpublished study described by Yeager, *supra*, note 15, p. 33.

27. M. Amir, *Patterns in Forcible Rape* (University of Chicago, 1971), pp. 141-42, 145.

28. B. Glueck, *New York Final Report on Deviated Sex Offenders* (New York Department of Mental Hygiene, 1956), p. 46. See generally Yeager, *supra*, note 15, pp. 32-33; Copeland, *supra*, note 24; and Amir, *supra*, note 27.

29. Compare Yeager, *supra*, note 15, p. 32, to Copeland I, 13 and III, pp. 22, 68. See also Amir, *supra*, note 27, p. 153.

30. See discussion in Hardy-Kates article on robbery, *supra*.

31. Yeager, *supra*, note 15, p. 33: " . . . according to a 1967 survey of police reported rapes in 17 American cities, only 1.4 per cent of rape cases cleared by arrests and only 0.5 per cent of uncleared cases resulted in the victim being seriously injured with a firearm. On the other hand, 17.7 per cent of cleared cases and 18.9 per cent of uncleared cases resulted in serious injury being inflicted through bodily means."

32. Hicks, "Point Gun, Pull Trigger," *Police Chief*, May, 1975.

33. See discussion in Hardy-Kates article on robbery, *supra*.

34. See generally S. Brownmiller, *Against our Will: Men, Women and Rape* (Simon and Schuster, 1975), pp. 197-206.

35. Copeland III, *supra*, note 24, p. 15.

36. James, *supra*, note 1, pp. 108-9

Section VI Notes and References

1. See e.g., Levin, "The Right to Bear Arms: The Development of the American Experience," 48 *Chi.-Kent L. Rev.* 148 (1971); Note, "The Right to Bar Arms," *19 S.C. L. Rev.* 402 (1967); G. Newton and F. Zimring, *Firearms and Violence in American Life* (staff report to the National Commission of the Causes and Prevention of Violence, 1969),

p. 113 (hereinafter Newton and Zimring); *1968 Hearings*, p. 32 (testimony of J. Tydings).

2. See Hays, "The Right to Bear Arms, A Study in Judicial Misinterpretation," 2 *Wm. and Mary L. Rev.* 381 (1960); Levine and Saxe, "The Second Amendment: The Right to Bear Arms," 7 *Houston L. Rev.* 1 (1969); and Caplan, "Restoring the Balance: The Second Amendment Revisited," 5 *Fordham Urban Law Journal* 31 (1976).

3. *United States* v. *Miller*, 307 U.S. 174, 179 (1939), militia defined as "all males physically capable of acting in concert for the common defense"; *Presser* v. *Illinois*, 116 U.S. 252, 265 (1886), "all citizens capable of bearing arms." See Ariz. Const. Art. 16, §1 (The militia of the State of Arizona shall consist of all able-bodied citizens of the State between the ages of eighteen and forty-five years. . . ."). See also J. Elliot, *Debates on the Adoption of the Federal Constitution* (2d. ed; 1888), Vol. 4, pp. 244-45 (hereinafter Elliot, *Debates).*

4. See Comment, "Constitutional Limitations on Firearms Regulation," 1969 *Duke L. J.* 773, 769-97. But see Levine and Saxe, *supra*, note 1, p. 18.

5. Compare U.S. Const. Art. I §8 with U.S. Const. Amend. II. This conflict becomes more prominent if bearing arms is treated as a term of art connoting general military duties, rather than the act of carrying a firearm. The guarantee of the right to bear arms would, if so construed, prohibit all federal regulation of militia activities, not merely the regulation of armament.

    One commentator has argued that the assertion of control over the organized militia by the federal government has extinguished any Second Amendment rights possessed by the states. See Note, "The Right to Bar Arms," *supra*, note 1, 402, 409-10. The rationale for applying the principles of adverse possession to constitutional guarantees is unclear. It is clear, however, that courts should attempt to reconcile constitutional amendments with the text of the original constitution, and that, where there is unavoidable conflict, the amendment will control. *Badger* v. *Hoidale*, 88 F.2d 208 (8th Cir. 1937).

6. A denial of access to public employment was found a sufficient infringement in *Gilmore* v. *James*, 274 Supp. 74 (N.D. Tex. 1967), aff'd 389 U.S. 572 (1968). Disclosure of membership lists was held an invalid infringement in *Gibson* v. *Florida Legislative Investigation Comm.*, 372 U.S. 538 (1963) and in *NAACP* v. *Alabama*, 357 U.S. 449 (1958). *Whelton* v. *Tucker*, 364 U.S. 479 (1960), invalidated a requirement that teachers reveal organizations to which they had previously belonged. The Court in *Elfbrandt* v. *Russel.* 384 U.S. 11 (1966) held unconstitutional on assembly and expression grounds a requirement that state employees take an overly broad loyalty oath.

7. See *Thomas* v. *Collins*, 323 U.S. 516, 531-32 (1945).

8. See *NLRB* v. *American Pearl Button Co.*, 149 F.2d 311, 318 (8th Cir. 1945).

9. See *Aptheker* v. *Secretary of State*, 378 U.S. 500 (1964); *Wallace* v. *Brewer*, 315 F. Supp. 431, 443 (M.D. Ala. 1970). In those cases where the Court has upheld limitations on active membership in subversive

groups, it has done so on the basis of a balancing of First Amendment interests against societal interests, and not on the ground that the failure of the organization in question to petition the government for a redress of grievances left it beyond the protection of the First Amendment. See *Communist Party of the U.S.A.* v. *Subversive Activities Control Board*, 367 U.S. 1, 97 (1961). Compare *Konigsberg* v. *State Bar*, 353 U.S. 252 (1957), with *Konigsberg* v. *State Bar*, 366 U.S. 36 (1961).

10. *Byars* v. *United States*, 273 U.S. 28, 32 (1927); *Fairbank* v. *United States*, 181 U.S. 283 (1901); cf. *Kansas* v. *Colorado*, 206 U.S. 46 (1907).

11. Mass. Const. Art. xvii (1780); see F. Thorpe, *The Federal and State Constitutions* (1909), Vol. 3, p. 1892.

12. Pa. Const. Declaration of Rights §13 (1776); see Thorpe, *supra*, note 11, Vol. 5, p. 3083. See also Pa. Const. Art. I, §21 (1969).

13. R.I. Const. Art. I, §22 (1776); see Thorpe, *supra*, note 11, Vol. 4, p. 3224.

14. N.C. Const. Declaration of Rights §17 (1776); see Thorpe, *supra*, note 11, Vol. 5, p. 2788. Right to bear arms provisions were also adopted in the constitutions of several states admitted to the union soon after the adoption of the Bill of Rights. See Ark. Const. Art. II, §21 (1836); Ala. Const. Art. I, §23 (1819); Thorpe, *supra*, note 11, Vol. 1, pp. 98, 270.

15. See Elliot, *Debates*, Vol. 1, pp. 371-72 (Luther Martin); Elliot, *Debates*, Vol. 4, p. 203 (Lenior). See generally Hays, "The Right to Bear Arms," *supra*, note 2, pp. 381, 392-94.

16. See *The Federalist*, No. 46 (J. Madison).

17. See J. Story, *Commentaries on the Constitution* (1858), Vol. 2, pp. 677-78.

18. The necessity of an armed rebellion, should the fears of the anti-federalists prove correct, was often cited in state conventions and in other contemporary sources as a rationale for the maintenance of an armed citizenry. See Elliot, *Debates*, Vol. 4, p. 203 (Lenior); J. Story, *Commentaries on the Constitution* (1858), Vol. 2, p. 678. Cf. Elliot, *Debates*, Vol. 1, p. 382 (Luther Martin). Virginia and North Carolina had proposed as a constitutional amendment that "the doctrine of non-resistance against arbitrary power and oppression is absurd, slavish, and destructive of the good and happiness of mankind." *(Debates in the Federal Convention of 1787, as Reported by James Madison*, Hunt and Scott ed. (1920), pp. 660, 676.) The framers apparently recognized as an ultimate political reality that all power grows out of the barrel of a gun, and proceeded on the principle that democracies should keep the sources of power in the hands of individual citizens. It should be remembered that the framers had just completed one of the most successful armed rebellions in modern history. The prospect of an overthrow of the government did not worry them so much as the possibility that the government they were creating might prove tyrannical.

19. *The Federalist*, No. 24 (A. Hamilton), J. Cooke ed. (1961), pp. 153-54 (emphasis in original).

20. See notes 10-13, *supra*.

21. *Debates in the Federal Convention, supra,* note 18, p. 658.

22. E. Dumbault, *The Bill of Rights and What It Means Today* (1957), p. 11.

23. *Ibid.,* p. 12. That the right proposed was seen as individual in nature is further supported by the inclusion of a proposal for a constitutional right to hunt game. *Ibid.,* p. 13.

24. E.g., the Pennsylvania proposal that "standing armies shall not be kept up in time of peace, and the military shall be subordinate to the civil power," or the New Hampshire suggestion that "no standing Army shall be Kept up in time of Peace unless with the consent of three fourths of the Members of each branch of Congress. . . ." Dumbauld, *supra,* note 22, p. 12; *Debates in the Federal Convention, supra,* note 18, p. 658.

25. Fairman, "Does the 14th Amendment Incorporate the Bill of Rights," 2 *Stan. L. Rev.* 3, 44-45; Frank and Munro, "The Original Understanding of 'Equal Protection of the Laws'," *50 Col. L. Rev.* 131, 141. See, e.g., the statement of Rep. Thaddeus Stevens in introducing the 14th Amendment in the House, *Cong. Globe,* 39th Cong., 1st Sess., p. 2449.

26. Reprinted in H. Hyman, *The Radical Republicans and Reconstruction* (Bobbs-Merrill), 1967), p. 217. [Editor's note: The denial of arms to blacks under slavery, in the post-emancipation Black Codes, and during the after Reconstruction is reviewed in Section I of this book.]

27. See, e.g., Rep. Wilson, *Cong. Globe, supra,* note 93, pp. 117, 118. Sen. Trumbull, *ibid.,* p. 1755; Rep. Raymond, *ibid.,* p. 1266; Sen. Howard, *ibid.,* p. 2765; Rep. Dawes, 42nd Cong., 1st Sess., p. 317; Rep. Clarke, *ibid.,* pp. 1838-9.

28. *Cong. Rec.,* Vol. 121, No. 189, pt. 2, p. 5 (Daily ed., Dec. 19, 1975); Decision Making Information poll of October, 1975.

29. In 1976 police made no less than 121,722 arrests for illegal carrying or possession of weapons. FBI (Kelley), *Uniform Crime Reports* (1976), p. 181.

30. Note, "Some Observations on the Disposition of C.C.W. cases in Detroit," 74 *Mich. L. Rev.* 614, 620-21 (1976).

31. Critique, "On the Limitations of Empirical Evaluation of the Exclusionary Rule," 69 *Nw. U.L. Rev.* 740, 750 (1974).

32. *Hearings on Firearms Legislation Before the Subcomm. on Crime of the House Judiciary Comm.* 94th Cong., 1st Sess., pt. 4, p. 1589.

33. *Ibid.,* pt. 2, p. 508 (testimony of Judge D. Shields).

34. Kates, "Handgun Control: Prohibition Revisited," *Inquiry,* Dec. 5, 1977, p. 23.

35. Drinan, "Gun Control: The Good Outweighs the Evil," *Civil Liberties Review,* Aug.-Sept. 1976, p. 44.

36. Lunde, *Murder and Madness* (S.F. Book Co., 1976), pp. 28-29.

37. *Wall Street Journal,* Oct. 7, 1977, p. 14.

38. *Detroit Free Press,* Jan. 26, 1977, p. 4.

39. S. Brill, *Firearms Abuse* (Police Foundation, 1977), pp. 134 ff.

40. "LEAA Nominee Quizzed Sharply On Past Views," *Washington Post*, Sept. 29, 1978, p. A-13; "Morris Tells Senators He Didn't Really Mean It," *Gun Week*, Oct. 20, 1978, p. 3.

41. U.S. BATF, *Operation Cue* (1977), p. 91.

42. *New York Times*, March 2, 1975, p. 1 (estimate by BATF); *New York Post*, October 7, 1975 (estimate by Manhattan District Attorney).

43. *Ibid.*; Cong. Rec., Vol. 121, No. 189, pt. 2, p. 1 (Senate, Dec. 19, 1975).

44. *Supra*, note 34, p. 20 (note 1).

45. See generally note 43 and the discussion of public opinion polls in Section I of this book, *supra*. A number of pertinent polls are reprinted in U.S. Department 4. of Justice, *Sourcebook of Criminal Justice Statistics — 1976*, pp. 345 ff.

46. See discussion and sources cited in Hardy-Kates article on robbery, *supra*.

47. *Adams* v. *Williams*, 407 U.S. 143, 150 (Douglas, J. dissenting).

48. C. Bakal, *The Right to Bear Arms* (1966), p. 156.

49. *Hearings, supra*, note 32, pt. 7, p. 2199 (describing New York law).

50. *Ibid.*, pp. 2200-2201 (describing New Jersey law).

51. *Ibid.*, p. 2204.

52. *Hearings Pursuant to S. Res. 240, before Subcomm. to Investigate Juvenile Delinquency of the Senate Comm. on the Judiciary*, 90 th Cong., 1st Sess., p. 70 (1968); statement of Ramsey Clark.

53. See note 39 *supra*.

54. *Hearings, infra*, note 65, p. 48.

55. *Hearings, supra*, note 32, pt. 7, p. 2428.

56. *Hearings, supra*, note 32, pt. 7, p. 2338.

57. Sturdivant, "Parcel Inspection System," in *Proceedings of the 1973 Carnahan Conference on Electronic Crime Countermeasures*, p. 74; *United States* v. *Lopez*, 328 F. Supp. 1077, 1084 (E.D.N.Y. 1971), citing studies on results of screening and searches; Andrews, *Screening Travellers at the Airport to Prevent Hijacking*, 16 *Ariz. L. Rev.* 657, 726-27 (1975).

58. Drinan, *supra*, note 35, p. 47.

59. Hall, "Nice People Who Carry Guns," *New York*, Dec. 12, 1977, p. 39.

60. Kates, "On Reducing Violence or Liberty," *Civil Liberties Review*, Aug.-Sept., 1976, p. 56.

61. One of the most extensive surveys done to date on firearms ownership, conducted by the National Opinion Research Center in 1973, found that approximately 49 per cent of whites owned firearms, compared to 38 per cent of non-whites; when the survey was limited to handguns, non-whites still owned slightly fewer firearms than whites. (Wright and Marston, "The Ownership of the Means of Destruction: Weapons in the United States," *Social Problems*, 23 [1975], pp. 93, 96.)

62. Harvard Center for Criminal Justice, *supra*, note 12-40, p. A-31.

63. Chicago Police Department, *Statistical Summary 1973*, Table 13.

64. *Ibid.* It has been noted that the traditional objective indicators — felony convictions, psychiatric commitment, and psychiatric testing — are not in fact useful to predict future violent activities, and that individuals singled out by these methods were unlikely to be composed predominantly of the more violent portions of the population. See Hardy and Stompoly, 52 Chi.-Kent L. R. 61 at 95.

65. It has been noted, concerning prosecutions under New York City's Sullivan Law, that only 29 of the 182 convicted in 1973 were incarcerated. (*Hearings Pursuant to S. Res. 72 before Subcom. to Investigate Juvenile Delinquency of Senate Judiciary Comm.*, Vol. II, p. 274.) Under the Philadelphia ordinance, in 1971, approximately 140 convicted defendants received incarceration, while approximately 770 received probation, suspended sentence, or fines only. (*Ibid.*, p. 30.) An Ohio survey showed that only 13 per cent of convicted weapons offenders were incarcerated. *Supra*, note 32, pt. IV, p. 1591 [exhibit].)

66. W. Douglas, *Points of Rebellion* (1970), pp. 26-29. Justice Douglas also noted that, if personality testing is utilized at all, "[T]he data collected should never enter the personnel file. The reason is plain. Someone's label 'schizophrenic,' 'neurotic,' etc., may give a person a life-time brand, ruinous to his career, although the label may have been improperly attached to begin with."

67. *Adams* v. *Williams*, 407 U.S. 143, 150 (Douglas, J., dissenting).

68. See Cong. Rec., *supra*, note 43.

69. *Supra*, note 35, p. 46.

70. *Hearings Pursuant to S. Res. 72, supra*, note 65, pt. II, p. 2274.